*the twisted
sisterhood*

the twisted sisterhood

Unraveling the Dark Legacy
of Female Friendships

KELLY VALEN

BALLANTINE BOOKS   NEW YORK

Published in the United States by Ballantine Books,
an imprint of The Random House Publishing Group,
a division of Random House, Inc., New York.

BALLANTINE and colophon are registered trademarks of Random House, Inc.

Library of Congress Cataloging-in-Publication Data
Valen, Kelly.
The twisted sisterhood : unraveling the dark legacy of female friendships /
Kelly Valen.
p.   cm.
Includes bibliographical references.
ISBN 978-0-345-52051-7 (hbk. : alk. paper) —
ISBN 978-0-345-52053-1 (ebook)
1. Female friendship. 2. Interpersonal conflict.
3. Women—Psychology. I. Title.
BF575.F66V35 2010
302.3'4082—dc22   2010033478

Printed in the United States of America on acid-free paper.

www.ballantinebooks.com

2 4 6 8 9 7 5 3 1

First Edition

Book design by Liz Cosgrove

For Tiggy, Daphne, and Sloane. Of course.
(And for Jack, who graciously sat this one out.)

You're an angel
You're a demon
You're just human

—James, *Lullaby*

contents

Part III: NEXT STOP, PARADISE? 119

introduction

While men can hurt my body, women can scour my soul.
—Rebecca, Feministe blog

Remember when you were a little kid, and you started out sort of naturally trusting everybody in the world—especially the women, who seemed so automatically *safe*? If your childhood was anything like mine, you pretty much felt this from birth. It was the ladies who baked us, birthed us, and cooed at us first, after all. Most of our teachers and babysitters were female. If we ever got lost, our adults taught us, all we had to do was find a cop or a "nice lady" to help us out. And when we stumbled and needed a little comfort or steadying, well, there was always the knowing bosom of Mom or Grandma or Judy Blume to lean into. We came to expect a lot from our women, when you think about it—probably even took them for granted. Because for boys and girls alike, women tended to be the rocks, the trestles around which we grew, the ones doing the day-to-day heavy lifting. They were the ones setting aside their own interests and applying the Band-Aids and keeping us on course by making us eat, sleep, study, and condition our hair; the ones who packed lunches and secured our prom dresses and gave us happy birthdays. In a world of uncertainties, it was the women who were usually home base. Anyone could see that.

Once girlfriends came along, of course, the glow of female fellowship only intensified. For a lot of us, our girlfriends became the marrow of our very beings, bonded to us in perpetuity over swapped secrets, shrieks, and dreams. Things could get complicated, sure, but, in the beginning, females were the unequivocal good guys—the ones who had our backs and made us feel wanted and worthy, like we actually mattered. Dad might have been our hero, but the greater male species seemed sort of exotic, at least to me. The Bogeyman was a man, the rapists and kidnappers lurking in the shrubbery were guys, and ubercreeps like Charles Manson and my personal tormentor, Rip Van Winkle, were definitely male. Boys? They were a pain, a mere sideshow. They'd break your heart, though, if you gave them a chance.

This is how it all started for me, anyway.

But you know how these things can go. One minute I was hosting all-girl slumber parties, giggling and ba-bumping en masse to Steve Miller's "Swingtown" over Twinkies and Sprite. The next thing I knew, a tsunami of mean-girling descended, and I found myself feeling awkward and wary around women for more than a decade. Expectations ran high, the letdown cut deep, and the fall from that innocent, sisterly grace proved very, very steep. Growing up, I'd heard all those grim, cautionary tales about men, so, legitimately or not, I've been a bit less surprised when they've disappointed me or behaved like Neanderthal schmucks. But my fellow females? That's a whole different kettle of fish. I didn't see it coming from them.

Not that you would have guessed any of this by looking at me all those years. I wasn't exactly broadcasting my discomfort with women—I was ashamed. Up until the end of 2007, in fact, I kept it all inside, convinced that I was the only woman on the planet nursing such a peculiar anxiety. I told myself it didn't really matter, constructed an otherwise fulfilling existence, and adapted on the female front by hiding at the margins, holding women at arm's length, and generally opting out of the so-called sisterhood. I can only imagine that along the way I broadcast a vague sense of inapproachability, too, warning other women to *Stand Clear!* or proceed with delicate caution.

I certainly never planned to write a book about all this. After practicing law for more than a decade and enduring one child care disaster too many, I settled into a relatively placid life as a stay-at-home mom of four in a sweet, leafy town just outside San Francisco. During some rare moments of downtime, I pecked away at my keyboard and dabbled in bits of "creative" writing, prose I'll never deign to impose on this world. Life was basically good.

THE *TIMES* ARTICLE

Then came one of those gloomy, gray, fog-laden mornings in the Bay Area, the kind that can catapult you toward inexplicable melancholy. I sat at our kitchen table, put pen to faded yellow legal pad, and wrote of the secret shame I'd managed for so long. I wrote about getting raped at a fraternity house after drinking too much one night back in college and how, as awful as that was, the worst part came afterward—with women. I wrote how the guy was kicked out of his fraternity, apologized to me, and left school shortly thereafter, and how my sorority sisters not only failed to support me but also blamed me for the whole thing. I wrote how they gossiped and distanced themselves, harassed me about everything and nothing, deemed me unworthy of their association, and, eventually, kicked me to the curb, biblical style. I wrote of my years of discomfort with women in the wake of that debacle and my relief over at last forging intimate connections with a gaggle of wonderful girlfriends. Perhaps most important, I wrote of my concerns as a mother of three daughters, about the gratuitous negativity and other nonsense I was seeing far too often among girls and women. None of this was about blame or bitterness, mind you. It was an attempt to come to terms with my gender-based issues in the most cathartic way I knew: by writing it out. Unlike my prior literary efforts, though, this one quite literally belched forth, projectile, filling the pages of that pad in under three hours.

When the *New York Times* ran the piece in December 2007, I didn't for a moment presume that my story would resonate with other women or cast "fresh" light on uncomfortable truths. Nor did I think my personal experience might offend anyone as heretical or disloyal to the gender. As it turned out, "My Sorority Pledge? I Swore Off Sisterhood" did both. The article struck a nerve, I'm told, by thrusting a new piece of the mean girls/warring women puzzle into the public consciousness—a glimpse at the aftermath and what we're really *doing* to one another. The notion that intrafemale incivility could sear a girl's essence with an enduring imprint, leaving her anxious within the gender and worse, prompted many to stop in their tracks and reflect. My observation that women are at once friends and foe and at times seem to swim in shark-infested waters of our own design sparked heated debate in forums like the website Jezebel, the blog Feministe, the *Washington Post*, academia, book clubs, the greater blogosphere, online religious-based groups like Feminist Mormon Housewives, and, apparently, the dinner table.

Some dealt vicious blows. How dare I air the ladies' dirty laundry! Get over it! Get therapy! Shut up! What a simpleton I was to attribute female infighting to females instead of the true culprits of the world: men. I was a "femalesogynist" to one blogger, an obviously bad mother and "asshat" to another—whatever that means. A few showered me with F-bombs, presuming wrongly that I was some "rich bitch" whiner stuck in trauma victim mode. The Jezebel writer said she plain "hated" me, and, in the online spectacle that followed, women began bickering back and forth. Most of the commentators defended my observations, pointing out that the knee-jerk judgments and personal attacks on me simply reinforced the whole point—that the women of the United States hardly present as a safe, supportive, or collaborative society of females. Then a kind but critical academic laid into me, floating a theory that neocons at the *Times* had used me to promote a patriarchal agenda. Why, she queried, was I writing about women instead of volunteering in a rape clinic? And anyway, she said, how could she possibly understand the dynamics relating to someone who had joined a sorority?

As it turns out, my skin isn't all that thick—even for a litigator. I wanted nothing but to crawl back to my cave of hausfrau anonymity and forget the whole thing. For months, I operated on dazed autopilot even as friends, family, and *Times* readers nodded along, their sobering refrains echoing loud and clear:

This put into words the things I've been feeling for decades.

I never knew there were others out there like me.

Girl-on-girl crime is the worst—you never forget that brand of ugliness.

I'm forty-six and still licking wounds from junior high.

I want to trust women but can't—been burned too many times.

I'm always cautious. Except for my closest friends, I keep women at arm's length.

Wake up, women! The enemy is within. We can't keep blaming men.

Intentionally or not, I'd found myself scratching the surface of something significant. The notion that women of all ages and backgrounds were writing to me not so much about date rape or the Greek system but to share their own hidden hurts and discomfort with other females really floored me. I mean, who knew?

Questions flooded my brain. Why does something as life sustaining and lovely as female camaraderie seem so threatening to many of us even as adults? Why do female-inflicted wounds sting so acutely and take such stubborn residence in our memory banks? I know some of these hurts are inevitable, but what about the harm that flows from all the gratuitous toxicity? How much overall confidence, productivity, and quality of life are we losing to that? If we considered the actual toll it's taking on women—the real consequences of our inhumanity—would we start thinking twice and cut it out? Hadn't the very concept of sisterhood become downright *twisted*?

THE SURVEY

I certainly wasn't up for another round of cyber beatings or censuring from anyone, but the interest people were showing piqued my curiosity. After all, if my sentiments resonated so deeply with women who happened upon a single newspaper article, surely there were others out there waiting to be coaxed from the woodwork. I scoured girls' and women's relationships books and saw that while a few hinted at the consequences of our interior aggressions, they typically left that final chapter—the *And then what happened?* or *What's it all mean?* analysis—hanging. With the help of my friend Maria Carson Breber, a former strategy consultant with the Monitor company and a master of qualitative and quantitative research design, I worked up a comprehensive questionnaire for women. The six-part, fifty-question survey addresses a host of issues falling under the general umbrella of "women's relationships," including past and present friendships; views on mothers, daughters, men, the media, sexism, and other cultural influences; the hurts, struggles, and coping strategies relating to intrafemale conflict; and the greater "sisterhood" in general. Most of the questions included optional, open-ended commentary boxes for women to elaborate on whatever they wished—and, boy, did they.

I launched the survey online through family and friends around the country in August 2008. The grapevine worked its magic, and, by week two, I'd heard from 1,000 women. Hoping to obtain a balanced pool reflecting all ages, socioeconomic levels, and viewpoints, I placed ads on Feministe and Craigslist, left copies at retirement homes, cafés, and libraries, and mailed off some to women who lacked computer access. On a cross-country move from San Francisco to Washington, D.C., I papered Dairy Queens, Subways, and Burger Kings. I even found the chutzpah, somehow, to reach out and talk with waitresses, baristas, and hotel personnel—anyone who seemed open to a chat.

I closed the survey at about 3,020 women, just to keep things manageable. The pool consists of females ages 15 to 86, of all backgrounds and perspectives, from rural towns in Washington and New Mexico, to Florida leisure communities, to Manhattan's Upper West Side. It's incredibly humbling to imagine each of these women taking ten to fifty minutes of her day to share private and detailed thoughts about her female connections. The survey is lengthy, somewhat tedious, intentionally broad in parts, and, according to many, emotionally rigorous. Thanks to that handy cloak of anonymity, though, most completed the survey and wrote paragraphs to pages of commentary, creating mounds of material on which to draw. Many called the exercise a "relief," an exhausting but important wake-up call about the ways we females are impacting one another behind the scenes. More than half listed phone numbers or emails—they wanted to keep talking. And while some felt comfortable revealing their identity, many, for obvious reasons, did not want to be named publicly. To that end, the names, professions, ages, residences, and other identifying characteristics of all survey respondents I refer to in this book, while genuine, have been shuffled, swapped, and otherwise anonymized.

We'll be hearing a great deal from these women about the contemporary female experience in this country, but, for now, consider these nuggets: Most of them emphasize the great importance of women in their lives—all but about 10 percent, in fact, say that they're enjoying at least one healthy and rewarding girlfriendship. That's fantastic news. At the same time, however, an incredible 84 percent say they've suffered *palpable* emotional wounding at the hands of other females. They've taken major hits to self-esteem and dealt quietly with a range of short-term and long-term fallout. Many feel they've moved on, but few have forgotten. A distressing number of them say that although they aren't exactly stuck in the past, or maybe haven't experienced all-out trauma, their prior experiences with other females have weighed them down, slowed them down, and *still* tend to color their attitudes, relationships, self-esteem, and general approach to women. To varying degrees, they harbor lingering insecurities and an eroded faith in the emotional safety of females. Many emphasize that the all-too-common bits of negativity, competition, narcissism, and superficiality they encounter only compound their ambivalence. And while each of these women offered a vastly divergent history and point of view, their collective voices made one thing eminently clear to me: I am not alone in feeling conflicted about the state of female relationships—or in wanting something better for us.

Then came the proverbial straw that prompted an even more urgent need to do something with all these stories and data I'd collected: I was standing in the lobby of an Oakland post office one day when I got word that a friend's niece had hung herself in the midst of Facebook harassment by her high school "girlfriends" and related teen pressures. While the root causes of such tragedies are never clear cut, it's a scenario I'm convinced might have played out differently had the girls involved operated from a more naturally empathetic place and appreciated the wretched propensities of their bullying—behavior they undoubtedly figured was just innocuous, garden-variety teen nastiness.

And here we are.

AN INVITATION

So much has been written about the joys and benefits of female friendship. And rightly so. As we'll see, making and maintaining positive female connections is demonstrably vital to our mental, emotional, and even physical health. At the same time, much has been written about the equally intense, sinister underbelly of our relationships: the letdowns and quiet but insidious girl, mommy, office, and social "wars" that continue to simmer and rage within the gender. Rarely, though, do you hear about the more nuanced negativity going on or the repercussions of it all—you know, like how this stuff affects us as individuals and as a putative sisterhood of souls who happen to comprise more than half of our society.

Why? It seems we've conditioned ourselves to deny, discount, and just plain swallow our intrafemale hurts as something we shouldn't indulge or whine about. As one psychotherapist told me, women think they should take their disappointments and mean-girling in stride, move on, and "get over it." Few of us are eager to acknowledge that we've been burned by our "sisters." Fewer yet wish to admit that we feel unsafe with certain women or that the primary threat to our emotional security radiates not from the usual suspects, like men, but from fellow females. Colette, an Ann Arbor, Michigan, grad student, offers up a sentiment I've now heard from too many others: Anxieties like these make us feel odd or "defective" as females. It seems vaguely antiwoman, too. Pointing fingers inward is uncouth—we have far more epic battles to fight *out there*, right? We smooth things over, then, in the interest of keeping the peace, fitting in, or getting on with life's more pressing matters. Most of us draw from an arsenal of surprisingly common coping strategies and return to the dance floor seemingly no worse for the wear, smile on face, tail between legs, inwardly tentative—confirming *Odd Girl Out* author Rachel Simmons's theory that beneath the "facade of female intimacy . . . lies a terrain traveled in secret, marked with anguish and nourished by silence."

I'm seeing a resigned complacency when it comes to the status quo as well: a sort of *Yeah, that's the way it is out there. But I have a nice little cluster of girlfriends, so I'm fine* complacency. This is, of course, complicated, multifaceted stuff—you can't generalize, stereotype, or paint women with too broad a brush. But get this: A staggering 88 percent of those I polled think that a distinct undercurrent of meanness and negativity plagues our gender, in many cases the very same women singing the praises of Girl Power, feminism, and female friendship in their lives. So I can't help but wonder: Is this really our endgame? Have we become so collectively busy, distracted, cynical, disconnected, or laissez-faire that we'll just accept entrenched negativity, quiet suffering, and the deterioration of basic civility and support as our lot, our *It is what it is*, the necessary cost of doing business as a female in this country? Isn't it time to revisit the fundamental tenets of sisterhood and humanity and try to quell the subterranean unease that percolates beneath these frozen smiles?

This book is an invitation to every girl and woman to pay more attention to what's going on within the gender, to reflect, and, ultimately, to behave. Our mileage varies, so its contents will surely speak differently to each of you. But make no mistake: We're not talking about just a few intimacy-challenged sisters with mean-girl episodes on the brain. I'm seeing a widespread, corrosive brand of ambivalence among all types of women and a whole lot of hidden, unresolved anxiety, frustration, annoyance, and residual hurt that hasn't found a voice. We all have a different story. Maybe you've racked up scads of girlfriends but on reflection realize that it's a qualified sort of intimacy—you're not really sure who you'd call with your 3:00 a.m. emergency. Maybe you've enjoyed predominantly trouble-free liaisons and managed to remain oblivious or above the fray but are now on heightened alert with your daughter, whose peers are excluding her. Maybe you had a diabolical female boss or high school experience straight out of *Carrie* and instinctively avoid groups or certain types of women. Maybe you turn to men for companionship because, all things considered, you find it lower maintenance. Maybe you've been a bully, gossip, excluder, traitor, or bystander—or simply insensitive—and never much considered the influence you have on other females. Or the hurt you've left in your wake.

Maybe you're among the legions of women I heard from who were traumatized or marginalized in school, in girls' summer camp, sororities, at work, or in the cotton-pickin' sandbox because you were fat, Jewish, poor, acne prone, dressed like a dork, boasted a confidence, brain, or beauty that threatened others, or did something that managed to trigger an estrogen-laced, *Lord of the Flies*–like wrath. Maybe you pulled yourself from a cesspool of shame but have never had a solid girlfriend to turn to, and long for one. Maybe you haven't quite dusted yourself off from a betrayal and are struggling with a crippled self-image, inability to trust, or loneliness. Maybe that's your mother, sister, or aunt. Maybe you're demoralized by what you see as a lack of authenticity in your circles or an inordinate focus on looks, status, and the material—artificial currencies that only fuel our insecurities and competitions. Maybe, if you're bluntly honest with yourself, you're making a crummy role model for your daughter.

Maybe, like me, you get viscerally jumpy in the company of women who tend toward exhausting dances of gossip, judgment, or status jockeying, and who invite you to join in through subtle, dangling remarks. Maybe, also like me, you're conscience stricken when you hear yourself playing along because it's so damned easy to do and has essentially become a habit, reflex, or bonding ritual among women you want to like and accept you. Maybe, when you think about it, the buzz lasts but a few minutes and leaves you feeling empty and disappointed in yourself. Maybe you think we need to clean our own house, stop blaming men, the media, and Mom, and start taking greater responsibility for our own naughty choices. Or maybe you just care deeply about humanity and the broader connectivity of women. Whoever you are, I'm hoping you'll agree: It's time, once again, to bring the dialogue to a higher plane than, say, *Real Housewives*, the 24/7 Angelina versus Jen patrol, and other cultural offerings that cheapen, exploit, and otherwise hijack the interior female experience by reinforcing the nasty, vacuous, and superficial as our reality. As if there's no alternative.

Some of you will scoff at the notion that conditions are in the vicinity of grim. You don't buy into silly rhetoric about a sisterhood, you're content with your chums and "don't need any more" in your busy, already full life, you feel sufficiently insulated from the ugliness down below. I get that—I've heard it all. But try for a moment to consider the larger picture. From what I'm hearing, our greater society of women is idling in an unhealthy, disconnected, and discombobulated state as we subtly turn away from one another, limit ourselves, and, in some cases, close down for business altogether. Several women admit that while they adore their immediate clutch of pals, that's as far as they feel they need to go these days. Besides, they're not so sure about the rest of us—you know, those Other Women out there like you and me. They've been burned before and are standing guard against future threats.

My investigation isn't the only troubling indicator that our incivility and aggressions, in all their disguises, continue to swirl about and wreak havoc throughout the broader landscape of our gender. Parents, teachers, psychologists, pediatricians, bullying specialists, lawmakers, and girls and women all around you are sounding the alarm, particularly in the wake of the highly publicized suicides of Phoebe Prince and Megan Meier. Even Michelle Obama has expressed concern about the "unhealthy" culture of mean. Lamenting that she fears for her daughters and the next generation of females, the First Lady says she works "so hard to teach them not to be mean girls." Authorities and educators in other countries, meanwhile, are way ahead of us. Consider England, where they've been doling out restraining orders, community service, the equivalent of juvie time, and even jail sentences for things like girl-on-girl Internet harassment. Why? Because, as one savvy judge there warned, we need to clue in and realize: The "evil, odious effects" of these hurts stay with us *for life*.

I do think we're well past the point of diagnosing the problem. Most of us know, or should know, what's going on with us. We can ignore it as Other People's problems, put blinders on, think happy thoughts, and hope something gives. We can keep talking and theorizing and writing and reading books about the behaviors themselves. But let's face it: It's sounding like business as usual out there. I'm convinced that we need to view our aggressions and negativity through an entirely different prism—by exposing the actual, enduring harm we're visiting upon one another. We need to recognize that our nudges and slights and overt cruelties aren't static events that happen in a vacuum. They're leaving lasting marks on girls and women everywhere.

I can't promise emotional deliverance or lend neat and tidy Hallmark solutions for engineering social change. I don't profess to be a sociologist, psychologist, gender scholar, or genius. I can't even hold myself out as a paragon of virtue who hovers above it all—I've been plenty nasty and inconsiderate myself. I don't mean to discount the subject of date rape by not writing about it here, as some have complained. And I'm not suggesting that competition, hostility, and negativity are exclusively female traits, ones that don't afflict boys and men, women in other cultures, or humanity as a whole. But those are different books. Within these four corners, I want to focus on us. We aren't letting anyone off the hook by pausing to look in the mirror. Nobody's saying we're in a done-deal, postfeminist society. But it's 2010. Women are rational, freethinking, capable beings. There should be nothing objectionable about examining the consequences of our internal discord, advocating some personal responsibility, and pushing for détente and kindness among ourselves.

We all know times are tough. Spooky geopolitical storms continue to brew in our post-9/11 world, many of us are chasing tails to pay mortgages and put dinner on the table, and girls and women around the globe are facing conditions I can't even begin to wrap my brain around. Issues like female infighting in America might seem low on the hierarchy of weighty concerns. And yet 96 percent of the women I've polled and interviewed say it's "important" to *"imperative"* that we advance the dialogue, empower ourselves through a more mindful and compassionate civility, and improve the state of relations among females here, too. As one anonymous blogger put it, "I think I'm beginning to want what Valen seems to want: a truce. For the sake of all women, for the sake of our daughters." I hope that you will agree.

PART I

A GARDEN OF
GOOD AND EVIL

CHAPTER 1

WE ARE *SO* WORTH IT

There is a kind of quilt called a friendship quilt, but I imag-
ine all of mine, no matter what their pattern, are emblems
of female friendship, that essential thread that has so
often kept the pieces of my own life together, and from
time to time kept me from falling apart.
—Anna Quindlen

Before we sully ourselves with the darker aspects of our relationships,
I want to make sure we're keeping our eye on the prize by underscor-
ing a fundamental but critical point: Most of us appear to value and
adore our women like nothing else.

And that would include me. By far, the most unsettling bits of criticism hurled my way have stemmed from accusations that I must hate
women or hate myself, probably suffered an intimacy-starved childhood, or never experienced females at their best. None of that is true.
The joys of female intimacy swaddled me straight out of the gate, actually, and have always remained apparent. Amazing men have
touched my life, and I often have an easier initial rapport with guys,
but my most compelling ties, notwithstanding the struggles, have
been with women.

Take my grandmothers, two of whom lived in the house next door
to me throughout my entire Minnesota childhood. For a developing
girl to have enjoyed such supportive, generous, and low-drama role
models—well, we should all be so lucky. These were women of

strength, authenticity, and grace, the real McCoys. Part of their gift to me growing up was about blood ties, sure, but much of it was plain old gender. They lifted, pushed, and pulled all the girls and women in their orbit up, maybe because it's just what women did back then. Through years of nothing more extraordinary than random chitchat, heated games of gin rummy and hide the thimble, intense baking and jam-making sessions, and quiet reading side by side, they drew me in and showed me that, ultimately, we could count on our women. They were my safety zone, my go-to counsel, my Giving Trees, always available with a patient ear and unilateral *no questions asked, no strings attached, no guilt involved* brand of support—the kind a lot of developing girls out there could use. I had loving parents, four siblings, an attention-starved dog on a chain, a true saint for a grandpa, and plenty of kids in the neighborhood to draw on, but as anyone from that era can attest, you could usually find me next door with the ladies.

It wasn't just my grandmothers, though. Looking back, I couldn't possibly have remained sane through the travails of dating, schooling, marriage, child rearing, hard-core lawyering, pulling up stakes at forty-three for a nomadic life abroad, or hormonal madness without my mother, sisters, long-suffering pal Teri, and, eventually, other girlfriends to turn to. It's that simple. What a relief to have finally found a few gals with whom I can be my unfettered self, to feel safe again, and to swap banter on everything from work and politics to food and hair to books, kids, and stain remover. How lucky to have stumbled upon my Diane Keaton–esque friend, Mary Kay, so consistently *good* and wise and accessible to me despite everything she balances in her own life. I still have my issues, as the women close to me know. But having lacked a baseline trust with female peers for so long, I am acutely aware of how much lighter life can feel with a posse of supportive women at my back.

Most of you know all this for yourselves. And, indeed, when all is said and done, the most heartening thing about this project has been this: Even as it's focused chiefly on the fallout from our shadowy tendencies, women haven't been at all bashful about sharing a bounty of heartfelt reverence for the women in their lives. As Julie, an actress from Los Angeles who wrote to me two years ago, emphasized,

"There's nothing on this planet like a bright, warm, open, loving woman. Believe it."

The fundamental findings of my survey, in fact, echo that very sentiment. Of the 90 percent who say they're enjoying at least one satisfying and fulfilling girlfriendship, nearly three-quarters call those relationships *authentic*, *intimate*, and *reliable*; 77 percent of them call those bonds very to extremely important, with the words *sacred*, *essential*, and *life-sustaining* popping up over and over. Hundreds gush that they can't imagine life without their girlfriends, and don't want to. These women appreciate that their healthy female connections keep them grounded and nourish their minds, bodies, and spirits. They know they're garnering strength and support from one another and living richer lives as a result. They recognize that, often enough, their friends are the very safety nets and security blankets critical to their well-being. As Anna Quindlen so elegantly put it:

> In our constantly shifting lives, our female friends may be the greatest constant and the touchstone not only of who we are but who we once were, the people who, taken together, know us whole, from girlfriend to wife and mother and even to widow. Children grow and go; even beloved men sometimes seem to be beaming their perceptions and responses in from a different planet. But our female friends are forever.

Or, as Jennifer Aniston said succinctly: "Girlfriends—Nothin' like 'em, man."

SOMETIMES IT'S THE SMALL THINGS

It isn't always about the grand gestures, though, like the "rocks" who drop everything to feed your family, walk your dog, and hold your hand when the cancer goblin comes knocking or the affair is exposed. It isn't just the old-time pals who are familiar with your every little secret and know instinctively whether to ask the hard questions or just be still and make casseroles. We find the everyday modest and mundane movements crucial as well—the colleagues, neighbors, and lunch pals who check in from time to time or suggest a run or a cocktail at the precise nanosecond of need, the ones who patiently indulge our love, work, and ethical quandaries de jour, or gift us with tiny windows of release through seemingly "nothing" coffee breaks, strolls, or two-minute phone chats.

I think of my sister Stacy in this light. Some of us poke fun at poor Stace because she literally calls our mother, me, and her legions of friends around the country up to two or three times a day while carpooling in her minivan. (My other sister, Tricia, escapes this attention by pretty much avoiding the phone altogether.) I really don't know how Stacy does it. Oftentimes, I'm sure I can't take the few minutes in my busyness, so I cut her off with a *Maybe later.* Other times I scold her for chitchatting on her cell while driving or ordering coffee. *It's dangerous! It's rude! Your politics are crazy!* And sometimes, yes, I ignore the call because I know I can take her for granted; she'll still be there for me. But you know what? Those calls—actually, the mere fact that she even thinks of me—really do leaven the day with a blast of comfort and familiarity that each of us on the receiving end would be devastated to lose. In the final analysis, women in our lives so often grant us the validation we crave by simply reaching out and showing up. I can't put it less tritely or more lyrically than that. Women like Stacy are our winking, blinking, beckoning lighthouses, ready and waiting for us in the shit storms and the calm.

Of course, nothing worthwhile, as they say, comes easy. A number of women in my survey emphasized how even the best of their friendships have proven high maintenance and weathered (or not weathered) some appreciable ups and downs; we're human, after all. Take my old friend Teri and me. We couldn't be more different. We've definitely ridden out the roller coasters (like, say, ditching each other in New York on our way to see Madonna in '88 over something trivial that neither of us can now recall). We've moved around so many times it's nothing short of a miracle that we remain tight. Yet, we can live thousands of miles apart, go for weeks or months without talking, and still finish each other's sentences or be struck by the same obscure cultural absurdity, confident that there's only one other person out there who'd truly get it. The woman knows all my quirks and secrets and hasn't bailed on me yet, not even when I've held out on her emotionally (which is most of the past twenty-five years), not even when I nearly killed her in a hideous motor scooter accident, not even when

I've proven a lame godmother. At this point, we've become such a *Beaches* cliche, it's ridiculous. And I take none of it for granted.

Some women insist that while all of this lady love is nice, gender really isn't the point; it's about respecting and making meaningful connections with *any* person, regardless of sex. We aren't bound to one another beneath the umbrella of sisterhood, the arguments go. We don't owe anything to one another because of our shared female status. We can enjoy superintimate friendships with men too, yada yada. And while I appreciate the intellectual appeal of those sentiments, I also think *Come on.* Men step up to the plate too, but most of us agree it's a different brand of camaraderie. We don't even have to get into testosterone and estrogen or Mars and Venus—I think it's disingenuous to deny the variances in complexity, depth, and tone that seem to characterize *most* female relationships.

How do I know? My own experience tells me so, for one thing. I have some really wonderful friendships with men, but it's just different. For another, all of this research I've done underscores, loudly and clearly, both the critical importance *and* the distinct nature of female camaraderie. If my more than three thousand survey respondents are at all representative of the contemporary American Everywoman— and I believe they are—the good, the bad, and the ugly of our girlfriendships absolutely merit special attention. As Judith Eve Lipton, a psychiatrist who works with breast cancer patients in Seattle, has explained, "The heart-to-heart stuff is female. We women talk to each other, confide, whine, wail, plan, and just plain kibbitz." This style of relating draws us uncommonly close and can literally become a life-sustaining support source. Like so many others, Lipton believes that women are key to de-stressing one another because we're so skilled at making the other feel heard and understood. Of course, there are exceptions. But, really, what's the point in denying that which makes us unique and desirable?

FEMALE CONNECTIONS:
OUR CHEAPEST, MOST EFFECTIVE MEDICINE

For years now, psychologists, neuroscientists, and other specialists have been confirming the important biological role that female friendship can play in a woman's life. The research in this area is nothing short of remarkable. I won't labor too much over the hard data here but, amazingly, experts have conclusively linked our positive female connections with an array of physical and emotional health benefits, perks they say don't necessarily extend to male-female or male-male relationships. Some insist it's all about evolution, that the patterns our female ancestors set a zillion years ago still drive the show. Ours is a socially nurturing brain, they say. We evolved as emotional and physical caregivers and come biologically preprogrammed to cooperate, coordinate, and talk, talk, talk, which, as linguistics professor and author Deborah Tannen points out, is the very glue that holds us together. In other words, girls and women have needed each other for pretty much always. Experts like psychologist Shelley Taylor, author of *The Tending Instinct: Women, Men, and the Biology of Our Relationships*, and Pepperdine University psychology professor Louis Cozolino seem to be taking it a step further, in fact, suggesting that when it comes to females, we need to tweak Darwin's survival theory to reflect that those who are tended to and nurtured best survive best.

To wit: The fascinating research Dr. Taylor conducted with Laura Cousino Klein while at UCLA found that female friendship not only makes us happier by lending a sense of acceptance, security, and validation, it can actually lower stress, blood pressure, heart rate, cholesterol, and overall risk for disease too. In lay terms even I can understand, the theory goes something like this: Women become more social in times of stress. Typically, we'll resort to the more protective, nurturing, "tend and befriend" types of behaviors—unlike men, whose coping mechanisms are more "fight or flight." We pick up the phone and call each other. We confide, commiserate, laugh, and bare our souls. We lean on and draw support from one another and, in doing so, create multiple sources of intimacy for ourselves.

No matter how you look at it, tending and befriending is a downright sound investment in one's health. When we turn *toward* one another and interact in these positive, nurturing, and empathic ways, we make one another feel safe, allowing our bodies to release increased levels of the "cuddle hormone," oxytocin. Oxytocin, as you may already appreciate, is basically a gift of sunshine, one that lends a sense of contentment, peace, and calm. It also helps flip on our internal social switch, leaving us motivated to reach out, make connections, and tend and befriend all the more. The latest research suggests, in fact, that oxytocin may help inhibit social phobia and is key to our ability to feel empathy or trust after a betrayal—precisely what we're going for in this book. For, as some experts in the field argue, when trust is absent we, in essence, "dehumanize" ourselves.

The bottom line? Women are good for one another. We're proven natural sources of oxytocin, we have a unique ability to make each other feel great, and we can actually help each other live longer and qualitatively better lives simply by making and maintaining positive connections. As Karen A. Roberto, director of both the Center for Gerontology and the Institute for Society, Culture, and Environment at Virginia Polytech Institute and State University, contends, "Friendship is an undervalued resource. The consistent message of these studies is that friends make your life better." Dr. Taylor agrees that we can't really overstate the importance of human connection to our health:

> When we erode our social and emotional ties, we pay for it long into the future. When we invest in them instead, we reap the benefits for generations to come.

Even the Mayo Clinic has weighed in. Its publication entitled "Power of Connection" explains that supportive friendships with a strong emotional intimacy component are vital to a person's well-being and a "major indicator of happiness." Noting that such connections tend to buffer stressors that can otherwise erode health, the clinic urged people to literally put themselves out there and invest in friendship. And here's something unexpected: It looks like the actual number of friends in your corral might make a difference. In a six-year study of subjects fifty and older, Harvard University researchers concluded that actively engaging in and promoting social connections could help boost brain function and hedge against memory loss. Those who had what was defined as "the most" social ties suffered memory decline at *less than half* the rate of those with "the fewest." No matter how you challenge their methodology or define the terms, that's a pretty significant ratio. A similar study involving nurses with breast cancer revealed that those who were more socially isolated or lacked girlfriends proved a full *four times* more likely to die from the disease than those who had ten or more girlfriends. It didn't matter if the friends lived near or far, and, interestingly, having a spouse didn't correlate in a similar way. Food for thought for those of us who've always stressed quality over quantity or insisted that our lives are too busy and friend filled to welcome any more. In fact, only a third of the women who took my survey said they had more than one to three "authentic, intimate, and reliable" friendships. This suggests that a lot of us might benefit from at least considering the thought of opening up, reaching out, and adding a few more beds at the inn.

But, of course, all of this good news applies when things are running smoothly and positively among girls and women, when we're behaving ourselves and practicing *good* tending, not bad. The opposite is, naturally, also true. Like other researchers, Robin Moremen, an associate professor of sociology at Northern Illinois University, has found compelling links between friendship and health among women. She and others have also, however, documented the punishing toll on women's health when things aren't going so well. Fear and stress and conflict, after all, lower those precious oxytocin levels and can affirmatively hamper well-being. As psychotherapists (and best friends) Luise Eichenbaum and Susie Orbach noted years ago, "Behind the curtain of sisterhood lies a myriad of emotional tangles that can wreak havoc" on the overall health and quality of our lives. We should also recall that our inclination to tend and befriend happens to sit right alongside that other basic instinct: to survive. When those values collide or the objects of our tending and befriending start presenting as some sort of emotional threat, we're bound to have some problems. In other words, we're certainly justified in celebrating the benefits of female friendship. At the same time, however, given the confirmed nexus between these relationships and our very health and well-being, we'd also do well to confront the hidden feelings, stressors, and struggles that threaten to undermine those benefits.

CHAPTER 2

BREAKING THROUGH
THE CONE OF SILENCE

I love women, but let's face it: We can be our own worst enemy.

—Nancy, sixty-three, retired, Tucson

We now come to that dark and rusty undercoat of female loveliness, or what Phyllis Chesler, in her groundbreaking work *Woman's Inhumanity to Woman*, calls our "shadow side." In thinking about this shadow side, it strikes me that many of us are living out an illogical syllogism of sorts. We value our friends and the idea of forging authentic and intimate liaisons with other women. We appreciate that such bonds are, as Shelley Taylor puts it, "the cheapest medicine we have" for leading healthy, happy lives. And yet, so often, we limit and stifle the very connections that could nourish us by turning away, perpetuating insults upon one another, and stirring up self-sabotaging currents that beat us back. I realize this isn't an airtight deductive setup, but these tendencies confound me. I'm really wondering what all this "bad tending" might portend. If, as presumably nurturing and socially evolved creatures, we're neglecting or backing away from demonstrably key sources of comfort and health in life because the sources themselves feel stressful, untrustworthy, or unsafe, aren't we losing something major? Aren't we actively shooting ourselves in the foot?

Since launching this project, I've often considered how much cleaner and more laudable it might be to quit while I'm ahead, expand the more uplifting subject matter of chapter 1, and call it a wrap. We all know it feels better to immerse oneself in life's positives than in its negatives. Like most of you out there, I prize the women in my life and can easily see the virtue in penning a book that celebrates the joy of friendship won through my struggles. Such an effort would come from the heart, after all, and reflect sentiments to which most women relate. Plus, the emotional dividends could be considerable—instead of being pummeled in the blogosphere, women might like me, really *like* me. Yes, a breezier book of that nature, though only half the story, would certainly feel rewarding, if in a soft-jazz or light-rock kind of way.

But, alas, the proverbial horse is out of the barn for me. Like it or not, my personal experience and research have brought to light some unpopular truths about women's impressions of their sisterhood. Even as many respondents wanted to downplay the incivility they see around them, their thoughtful commentary suggested they were seeing it all too often. No one is saying we're obliged to embrace every female who crosses our path simply because of our shared chromosomal makeup. But a shocking number of women admit that they regard others not from a stance of openness, acceptance, or benefit of the doubt, but from armored platforms of wariness, suspicion, and distrust. Perfectly happy, social, reasonable, and well-adjusted women use terms like *cautious, careful, audition, size up,* and *risk assessment* to describe delicate social interactions in what they feel is an increasingly inhospitable and inauthentic culture of women. To many, it appears, we're no longer kindly disposed, supportive comrades in arms—we're suspect until proven otherwise.

Rightly or wrongly, some women also harbor a rabid (if honest) resistance to the notion that females behave badly at all, much less of their own accord. Ask Dr. Chesler, who was nearly tarred and feathered for writing *Woman's Inhumanity* almost a decade ago. And with a single newspaper article, I, too, managed to earn a first-class ticket to Dante's Ninth Circle for speaking up. I get the sense it doesn't even matter what my personal experiences have been or how valid and widespread my concerns happen to be. Any suggestion that women are co-architects of their unhappiness or failure to prosper shall be deemed tantamount to misogyny, horizontal hostility, and internal sexism. We're to ignore, deny, shift blame, and sweep all evidence of internal thrashing under a rug of complacency. Play along, or you're antiwoman. Or just a dingbat.

But judging from what a sea of women are telling me, our greater society of women isn't all right—not by a long shot. And this shroud of secrecy is starting to remind me of that ill-conceived "cone of silence" from the 1960s TV show *Get Smart*, where those within the cone remain hopelessly mired in their antics and think no one's the wiser, while those on the outside see it all for what it is and find the predicament and players silly and endlessly amusing. Personally, I think we're fooling no one. Who can honestly or convincingly deny that inordinately rough conditions exist within our gender? As Dan Aykroyd might say in his best Bob Dole, "You know it, I know it, and the American people know it." Shushing one another, bunkering down in carefully chosen, exclusive clusters, and refusing to accept a slice of responsibility for the inhospitable culture we're fostering only perpetuates the vibe. If I've learned nothing else through talking with women and conducting all this research, it's that no rational being could consider the misdeeds and prevailing negativity acceptable or healthy, not once he or she appreciates what it's doing to us.

Still, nothing's black-and-white. I surely don't think that conditions are peachy keen, but I also don't think we're "at war" with one another, as some insist. I see things as far more nuanced, especially among adult women. We're fascinating, multidimensional creatures, after all. Most of us move in shades of gray, perfectly capable of being authentic and altruistic angels in one context; judgmental, petty, insecure biddies in others—and everything in between. We can deny or discount what goes on down under or insist it's just what Other Women are doing. We can discuss our hurtful interactions in a general or sassy manner, as we often do, without following through or inconveniencing ourselves with any behavioral modification. Trouble is, though, our shadow side is undermining our welfare in ways we haven't been appreciating. As we'll see in part II, girls and women are experiencing real, palpable fallout. They simply aren't talking about it.

ACKNOWLEDGING THOSE INCONVENIENT TRUTHS

It isn't just me and the women I've heard from. Issues like harassment, hazing, and bullying continue to gain all sorts of attention—if at times for tragic reasons. Conflict among women in the workplace is out of control and has become an area of intensified research and concern. Cyber bullying and stunts of desperation among girls and women increasingly make headlines. We're seeing mothers in denial and behaving even worse than their offspring. Researchers and mental health providers are finally seizing upon the lasting, soul-destroying effects of these nasties, and even Congress is starting to pay attention. Author Rosalind Wiseman, meanwhile, says that women haunted by their junior high school memories constantly ask her to "do something" to stop the ugliness. She and others link the fraught relations of girls directly to that troubling springboard of low self-esteem, which, as we know, can lead to all sorts of poor outcomes down the road.

Doctors have had enough, too. Concerned about the tenacious, enduring effects of bullying and relational aggression, the American Medical Association and the American Academy of Pediatrics have become more vigilant and outspoken. In June 2009, the AAP issued a new policy statement urging its pediatricians to team up with parents and schools and advocate more actively for kids in the prevention and treatment of bullying—by asking young patients about their relationships, starting a dialogue with parents, and reinforcing the notion that bullying is *not* a normal rite of passage. The statement specifically highlights the effects of girl-on-girl cruelty, noting that girls often experience greater emotional distress than boys in the relational aggression contexts. Even the venerable all-girls Miss Porter's School in Farmingham, Connecticut, found itself embroiled in litigation over these issues, a matter involving claims of systematic fem abuse and a student's nervous breakdown. I can't comment meaningfully on the environment at MPS, the propriety of its long-held traditions, or the merit of the lawsuit's salacious allegations out of context. I will say it sounds a little creepy that the heart of that mess involves a well-entrenched, exclusive, girls-within-girls society originally named for a Russian torture squad (the Oprichniki—since renamed, or disbanded, apparently).

In addition to Michelle Obama, we've been hearing other public figures and celebrities speak out on the sisterhood's downside, as well—often to their detriment. Over the course of a few months, I heard Taylor Swift sing of unlikely exclusion and loneliness in junior high, Gwyneth Paltrow anguish about schadenfreude and frenemies on her lifestyle website, GOOP, *Twilight* actress Kristen Stewart say she was relieved to leave school thanks to the nonsense, Jennifer Garner bemoan mom-judging, and the seemingly has-it-all actress Sienna Miller tell *InStyle* magazine, "I've been at war, without a doubt. I have really experienced the judgment of women. There's no sisterhood." How ironic that laments like these are often met not with empathy or considered reflection, but with instant snark and sarcastic jabs from unsympathetic women, many of whom weigh in not on substance but simply to be mean. I'm not an active celebrity defender—I won't insist that you all quit harshing on Paris Hilton or Lindsay Lohan for their latest gaffe or stunt. And, yes, I appreciate the duplicitous PR manipulations at play at most every turn in these people's lives. But still. The cultural implications of our immediate damnation of fellow women in virtually every context are *so* dispiriting.

Meanwhile, you know we're talking zeitgeist when Madonna has already penned books about a pack of menacing girls and American Girl launches an antibullying doll: Chrissa, the fourth-grade Iowan, standing tall, ready to slay those stylish "Mean Bees" at her new Minnesota school. Chrissa's accompanying movie and books are so au courant that they battle cyber bullies and seemingly clueless, enabling mothers. The books even include discussion points for kids and parents. Cynics, say what you will about Madonna's allegedly turgid or "vengeful" writing style and Mattel's convenient, simultaneous marketing of that doll's must-have clothing and accessories. I view these offerings as grains of progress and applaud anyone who wades into these waters to raise compassion and awareness in young girls—the precise point at which those seeds of inhumanity begin to germinate, after all.

But we all know social change doesn't happen overnight. I realize that the very women who most need a pep talk are the least likely to pick up a book entitled *The Twisted Sisterhood*. I hope I'm wrong about that, but let me illustrate the sort of denial or obliviousness that seems to prevent some otherwise smart, kind, and interested women from appreciating their role in all this. Months back, I was sitting at a basketball game when a woman (let's call her Sally) approached me, mentioned my writing, and began to rather indelicately challenge me on what she presumed were my views about female friendship. I appreciated that she was talking to me in real time, face-to-face. Still, it was awkward, to say the least. One could see her confusion, the quizzical sort of *Just what planet are you from?* expression. She told me she'd had an amazing sorority experience, "loved" women, and enjoyed a network of girlfriends she couldn't live without. It seemed heartfelt, if a little defensive, but she wasn't saying anything I disagreed with—I'm happy for anyone who's had better luck with women than I have.

So far so good, I thought. Except then she insisted she'd never seen pettiness, backbiting, or anything like that in her circles. Never. To Sally, "all those mean-girl and catfighty books" were just dramatizing and sensationalizing reality for profit. Now, intellectually, I should have recognized this spurious claim as (1) denial in the extreme, (2) social tone deafness, or (3) a *doth-protest-too-much* platitude. But, unfortunately, that's not how my social brain works. Call me neurotic, but I went home that night and yet again began doubting this project.

In a strange twist of fate a few weeks later, I was heading to a friend's house for what I thought was a quick glass of wine, one-on-one. I nearly U-turned for home when I spied a swarm of cars out front—I'm still not so comfortable in groups. I'm proud to report that, ultimately, I parked, checked my anxieties at the door, and went in, only to find Sally and a denful of women drinking, noshing, and chatting. It was unexpected, I was awkward as usual, but it was *fun*. Over the course of about an hour, I got to know Sally better, found her charming, laughed hard, and came to really like her. And yet stitched into her banter were no fewer than a baker's dozen of dangling critiques, veiled judgments, eye rollings, and unnecessary status-related jabs about women right there in that room and beyond—the very same women I'd seen her chumming around with on a regular basis for the past five years! These are the kinds of dynamics I've noticed fairly often with women over the years. It drives me bonkers.

And kind of remarkable, I thought, that Sally wasn't even bothering to suppress the negativity before her friendly neighborhood Grand Inquisitor. (She was aware, after all, that I was writing a book about this very thing.) Was it because she didn't think she was doing anything unusual or inhumane? Has mindless, gratuitous gossip and dissing on each other, even one's friends, become such an accepted bonding mechanism, such conventional protocol, that we no longer see it for what it is? Has it become a deeply ingrained cornerstone of the female experience, one we should all just expect? Are we really this desensitized? As someone on the Web magazine *DoubleX* put it recently, "Dishing dirt invites others to do the same—and anyone willing to gossip *with* you will also gossip *about* you." No doubt. After seeing this in action, could you really blame me or anyone else for having a hard time trusting Sally as a true intimate, despite our new-found "friendship"? It was another one of those internal lightbulb moments confirming the viability of my worries: *This is what school-girls mean when they call each other two-faced! See, Kelly, you're not nuts.*

The takeaway here is that some of us, I'm sorry to say—no matter how sweet, fun loving, and otherwise altruistic—appear to be soaking in thickened, saccharine-infused custards of denial about our true so-cial selves and frolics on the dark side. Some would call it hypocrisy, but I'd like to think of it as a colossal lack of self-awareness, one this book might help address. As Shoshanna, a Virginia psychology stu-dent, told me, "We deny it goes on or say we hate those who are like that, and yet most of us are doing it ourselves. We need to wake up."

A DIFFERENT TAKE ON STEPFORD

So why do we insist on causing each other such trouble? Biological, anthropological, social, political, simple lack of respect—pick your poison. Our aggressions may well lurk in our genetic past, but most studies do seem to pinpoint our insecurities over the perceived supe-riority of another female as the basis of our competitions and negativ-ity. It's hard to settle on just one thing. Most of the theories I've heard sound compelling and reasonable, even as they negate or contradict others that are equally compelling and reasonable. For a while, in fact, I started to lose myself in all the evolutionary, sociological, and psy-chological possibilities, desperately seeking that silver-bullet explana-tion that I could pass along to you all here.

Ultimately, though, I'm happy to leave it to the experts to figure out what breeds our aggressions. Because, at the end of the day, it's all very interesting to intellectualize and theorize and psychoanalyze the historical "whys" behind what we do. But has that actually gotten us anywhere? We've been working from that angle for some time now. We can talk about the "reasons" ad nauseam, use them as crutches to excuse or explain away our inaction and complacency, and even feel sorry for ourselves. But at some point, we really do have to look within ourselves, examine our role in it, and just "do" or *stop* doing certain things. We may not be able to control which emotions envelop us, but we can certainly manipulate, suppress, and otherwise control how it all manifests in terms of our outward behaviors and the effect we have on others. Right?

It's not just *why* we're doing it, by the way. A lot of us are also wondering why our intrafemale wounds sting so acutely and tend to have such an enduring quality. Jeannine, a personal trainer, thinks it's more painful between females because the types of aggressions we usually use against each other are so personal and affect us on a much deeper level. Males can perpetrate incomprehensible harm upon us too, of course—I certainly don't mean to imply otherwise. But as Rebecca said at the very start of this book, there's something about our falls from sisterly grace that hurt us uniquely and profoundly, to the point where they "scour our souls" in the ways that the monstrosities of men sometimes do not. In their detailed responses to my questionnaire, women noted this distinction again and again, offering all sorts of comments along the lines of "My last best friend broke my heart harder than any guy ever has" and "With women, it's a whole different world of hurt."

Psychologists and writers have long attempted to tease out the epic conundrum that while female intimacy can bestow the best of life's dividends, when things go awry, it can wreak havoc on minds, spirit, and health with an equal force. Like Henry Wadsworth Longfellow or that Little Girl With a Curl poem explain, when we're good, we are very, very good—and when we're bad, we can be pretty darned horrid. Or, as renowned psychology professor and author Marion Underwood tells us, females have great capacity for an in-depth, highly intimate style of relating, which makes us excellent friends but terrible enemies. Think about it: As I explained up front, most of us were socialized to trust and rely on females almost automatically. We share a lot about ourselves and expect a lot from one another in return. It's the old tyranny of expectations and shattered illusions model of suffering. Our heightened expectations and deep connections raise the stakes, leave us emotionally exposed, and, quite simply, put us at greater risk for hurt.

Consider the friendships of girls, where the stakes can be particularly high. "Girls very much value intimacy," Underwood explains. "They share so much information when they are friends that they never run out of ammunition if they turn on one another." Phyllis Chesler agrees, noting that "girls are social beings who need to belong." Because they have a "greater need for dyadic and expressive interpersonal intimacy than boys do, and are more adept, sooner, at engaging in it," most girls crave a best friend and form small, "exclusive, intense core groups consisting of two or three members." They need to feel included and remain quite terrified of being rejected, excluded, or otherwise cut off. In other words, Chesler explains, they can begin to "need each other too much"—a recipe for heartache, as many of us know too well. Guard down, intimately exposed, emotionally vulnerable, we set ourselves up neatly for profound disappointment and uniquely harsh wounding when things go awry. It's a familiar pattern that women confirmed over and over in their responses to me. And when it happens, it not only tends to hurt badly. As we'll see, many women are left unwilling or unable to so readily put themselves out there again. It's far easier to back off or turn away from a potentially good thing than to risk another round of disappointment and hurt.

I've long held an alternative view of Stepford, actually, one in which contemporary women aren't mindless, spineless, impotent creatures functioning at the Man's behest, but mighty, independent, free-choosing beings who in many ways subtly control one another. After reading thousands of pages of commentary from other women, I'm convinced of this. So often—more often than I think we'd like to acknowledge—it is our fellow females who pull our strings, yank our chains, get our goat, influence our decisions, and, yes, also hold us back. On the one hand, we cherish one another and so very much want approval and acceptance; on the other, we're hoping to avoid the land mines of negative judgment, exclusion, rejection, inferiority, irrelevance, and heartache. It's a delicate dance.

Take appearance. There's actually research confirming the theory that women care more about other women's opinions of attractiveness—like, say, being thin—than they do men's. Many of us know this already through personal experience. Sure, most of us probably know a woman or two who seem to choreograph their every move for men. And certainly some women feel comfortable being themselves only in the company of women. But I've observed this type of must-impress-the-gals rush over and over, as have dozens of women who shared similar stories. Laurel, a twenty-two-year-old designer's assistant, thinks "women dress up for other women because though the men appreciate a woman who looks terrific, it is the other women in the room who will rip you to shreds if your shoes aren't 'right.'" Shoshanna, the psychology major, says much the same:

> My boyfriend swears that girls get dressed up to impress other girls way more than other guys. I think he's right. Sometimes it's weird to think that way, but I feel like it's definitely true. You would think with a male-dominant society, girls' outfits and makeup choices would be 100 percent intended for guys.

Angela, a confident, no-nonsense lobbyist, says that she never worries if her husband finds her attractive. "I know he does. But I do worry if other women find me worthy or are noticing all my faults and blemishes." Kelly, a journalist in her thirties, agrees:

> Look at Hollywood, ads, the Internet. Much of it is about how we can be more beautiful, or who is most beautiful. Get this surgery or go on that diet; you'll be a better person and be more popular. I've made the choice to withdraw from several groups that I used to attend because the talk is so superficial. It's all so judgmental and negative too. How can we judge what's beautiful or not? We are all beautiful in many different ways. But women get trapped in the cycle of pleasing other women and competing with them. The men I know aren't as caught up in the whole world of appearances like their wives are.

During my brief and regrettable sorority tenure back in the eighties, I can remember watching the curious spectacle of my roommate's frantic preparations for our Monday evening chapter meetings. Each

week, she'd labor over finding just the right look, just the right accessories, just the right aura that might elevate her status and, perhaps,
trigger admiration among our "sisters." She was transparent about
her insecurities in those moments only—and only in front of me. The
woman had a boyfriend, yet I'd never once seen her fret this way or
ask me repeatedly, "Does this look okay?" before their dates. Given
that climate, it's really no wonder that our executive board once cen-
sured me for wearing sweatpants.

Of course, it might just be the circles I run in, but, other than my
childhood friend Anthony, who has never minced words with me, I
can't think of any man who outwardly seemed to care whether I was
thinner, better dressed, better accessorized, or could outstyle someone's girlfriend, sister, or wife. Sure, men want us to look scrumptious
and all—we know it's mostly about the visual with them. And, certainly, some women are slicing and injecting, sculpting and dieting,
and enduring all sorts of high-maintenance preening for a guy's benefit because they find their value that way. But a lot of us suspect the
more frequent motivator for these gestures is to gain a favorable opinion from other women—the same people to whom we also quite often
hand over the keys to our self-worth.

Apparently, more than a few ad executives think this way too.
They're convinced that we live to tick off other women by being more
fabulous in some way. Take the ads Lord & Taylor floated recently,
the ones screeching dreck like "This Dress Will Make Your Friends
Insanely Jealous . . . Which, You Have to Admit, Is Pretty Much the
Goal." Or how about the old Pantene shampoo commercial with
Kelly LeBrock bleating, "Don't hate me because I'm beautiful"? Or
those truly awful Reebok EasyTone ads, the ones that objectify us
right as they're targeting us: Wear our shoes, they say, and we'll de-
liver a better butt, the attention of men, and the jealousy of other
women! As ridiculous and demeaning as these types of ads are, they
do contain that tiny grain of truth—we can, to some extent, be
counted on to do the required surveillance, to notice, evaluate, and
one-up each other, to compete, compete, compete, and, in the
process, permit other women to influence and even dictate our movements. Or, at the very least, drive our purchasing decisions.

On a similar note, several respondents acknowledged that while
their brains might say "Can't we all just get along?" their subcon-

scious may be saying something more along the lines of "Sure, right after I get that promotion and you don't," or "Not until I get pregnant like you did." Hardships and setbacks absolutely seem to bring out the intuitive nurturing instincts and sisterly spirit in us—females can be downright champions this way. And yet, women are asking, why is it so often easier to root for a woman who is fragile or down on her luck than for a woman of ironclad confidence or happiness or good fortune? Maybe John Irving was spot on when he wrote in *A Prayer for Owen Meany* that a "truly happy woman drives some men and almost every other woman absolutely crazy."

In response to my *Times* article, the writer Rebecca Woolf offered up her own candid views about the great chasm between what we'd ideally like to believe about ourselves and what is, all too often, the less pleasant reality:

> Women are manipulative. We hold one another down in ways that are debilitating to ourselves, often gesturing toward men and misogyny as a what's-what to blame. And none of us are innocent. It is far more difficult to congratulate a friend on exciting news than it is to console a friend in times of need (jealousy is the antithesis of pity). A strange paradox during a time when women are congratulating themselves for being so modern . . . Women aren't evolving as much as we say we are. We're just talking more shit behind each other's backs. And what is perhaps most upsetting is that, as I criticize this inexcusable behavior, I am more likely than not, just the same, a judgmental and often catty creature unable to see such character flaws in myself.

This is a pretty depressing thing to feel about other women, much less about oneself. But Rebecca was far from alone in calling out women for this kind of duplicity. It's this kind of lurking unease that makes women like forty-two-year-old Maddie say in all seriousness, "If you have good news, tell a man. If you have bad news, tell a woman." Whether you agree with Maddie's advice or not, I think Rebecca was quite brave to publicly out herself on her blog and acknowledge her own hypocrisy and failings on the female front. If you're anything like the 96 percent of women in my survey pool who say they want something better for girls and women, after all, you'd probably agree that the first step toward that goal is getting more of us to come clean like Rebecca and really own up to our personal shenanigans and negativity—at work, at home, online, and wherever else we find ourselves indulging our dark side.

CHAPTER 3

INCIVILITY: HERE, THERE, SEEMINGLY EVERYWHERE

Ugh, this survey is truth by torture. No, I haven't had such a great run with women.
—Katie, twenty-four, Houston

Before we can meaningfully consider the effects and consequences of our unpleasantries, I think it's useful to survey the scene, check our collective pulse through the voices of the women I've heard from, and illustrate some of the ugly patterns and trends we're seeing out there among girls and women.

Suffice it to say, the prevailing attitude appears to be, at best, one of complex ambivalence. On the one hand, you'll recall that very few women I've heard from *don't* have at least one girlfriend to turn to. Wonderful news. But dig a little deeper, and an unsettling, dissonant truth emerges: 84 percent of them say they've suffered terribly at the hands of their "sisters" at one time or another. A whopping 88 percent report that, despite their friendships, they nonetheless feel currents of meanness and negativity emanating from other females, not to mention insincerity and other unfavorable attributes. These women reflect a range of hurts and resiliency, of course. Yet how sad that only a handful—fewer than 16 percent of all the women I've heard from—feel that they fly in rarefied airs above it all and *haven't* endured serious, life-altering knocks in the female garden. All the rest—rural and urban; stay-at-home, student, professional; gay, bisexual, straight; women of all ethnicities, religions, and educational backgrounds— acknowledged, usually reluctantly at first, that they've suffered some form of unnecessary, palpable wounding.

Oh, the things we do to one another. These women cite the usual parade of horribles, and, as much as we hear about these things, I still found myself stunned to hear women actually confirming them. For example, 76 percent of those responding to my survey said they've been hurt by episodes of jealousy and competition, while 74 percent have been stung by other women's criticisms and judgments and 72 percent have been the targets of gossip, rumors, and behind-the-back duplicity. Exclusion, rejection, and shunning came next (64 percent), followed by group or clique cruelty (57 percent), betrayal or disloyalty (50 percent), lying or deceitfulness (49 percent), and manipulation or shifting alliances (47 percent). A disturbing number—almost 20 percent of all respondents—say they've been on the receiving end of mean, manipulative, or cruel behavior so many times "they couldn't possibly count" them. As we'll see, many of these women have dealt quietly with a variety of aftershocks, everything from the mild and merely annoying to the tragic and debilitating. At the same time, well over half of those in my survey pool admit that they too have been nasty and indelicate with other females—though it's nice to hear most of them say they feel "bad, remorseful, or guilty" about it.

.THE SOCIAL CIRCUIT

But, again, you needn't take my word for it. Look at our everyday social encounters. I don't want to overstate anything; most of our interactions are undoubtedly pleasant, well intended, even sweet. At least on the surface. And yet roughly 60 percent of respondents say they still find themselves feeling *uncomfortable, anxious, wary, awkward, cautious, intimidated,* or even *distrustful* of other females as a result of past experience. Some say they don't know where they stand much of the time.

"You know the drill," I heard time and again. Pay attention and you're bound to see a curious, almost primitive ritual playing out whenever girls and women come together. Female checks out female, sizes her up, compares self. Hmmm, she may be thinking. Prettier? Smarter? Better pedigree? Better job? Better house? Better figure? More charming? More attractive-successful-attentive boyfriend, girl-friend, husband, kids? Better accessories? Better vacation? Better life? Find a flaw, and you can exhale—luxuriate in your superiority. Or maybe you feel you're just way above all this. Dismiss the gal on display as frivolous, unintelligent, or irrelevant, and move on. Phew! Recruit some reinforcements to buttress your thoughts, and you're really set. To Kim, a thirty-six-year-old editorial assistant, this is the reigning culture within the circus of our gender: one of raging insecurities, comparisons, competitiveness, haughty superiority, and quiet schadenfreude. As the writer Rebecca Woolf acknowledged, and Kim and many others insist, "We all do it to some degree. Some are just better at hiding it."

I have to admit that this raw assessment of female social dynamics struck me as unduly harsh (not to mention depressing) the first time someone described it. But so many women have now echoed that description. And, of course, I've witnessed bits and pieces myself. To be fair, I think (and hope) that much of this sizing up stems from an innocent curiosity and appreciation. My mother's like that. She loves checking out other women's clothes, hair, personalities, and manners—the whole package. Females fascinate her to no end, and I suspect it's a part of what makes her such an engaging and charming girlfriend. She somehow makes everyone in her orbit feel like her best friend because she's genuinely interested and always offering up heartfelt compliments. Me? I have an excuse for staring at you. Before I switched things up and went to law school, I started out as a design and textiles major, staging amateur fashion shows with Teri as my model, drooling over bias cuts at the Costume Institute, and poring over *Vogue*, *Harper's Bazaar*, and *Women's Wear Daily* with the intensity of an insurer studying actuarial tables. I might be sporting pilled J. Crew sweaters these days, but I so appreciate the beauty and adornment of women and think I've done a pretty decent job keeping the admiration in check. It's the one area within the gender, come to think of it, that I just might have mastered—though, on second thought, maybe the women I've been surveying all these years have understandably misinterpreted my interest.

It isn't just the physical aesthetics, though. From the sound of it, a distressing number of women are caught up in a desperate quest for status too. Some of the harshest, most unrestrained commentary I read and heard came from women who are fed up with competing and what they call "social fraud" and status obsession. This is where the claws came out. I could feel the annoyance, resentment, and, yes, disdain seeping through my computer screen. By the same token, women of all types also lamented what they see as a growing insincerity to our interactions, a more guarded and unwelcoming vibe, and a very real challenge to making genuine, reliable friendships. Several suggested that if you're someone who defies stereotypes, fails to conform to the local culture—or you have the audacity of being "okay" with not being part of it all or caught up in it—you'll be pegged a threat.

Ditto if you appear too confident, especially if you're attractive, successful, or wealthy. Many respondents underscored that what we really want to see are some flaws, failures, and vulnerabilities before we'll feel comfortable with you; we don't like our women *too* pretty, smart, or perfect. Some who described themselves as attractive or successful said they have routinely lowered their stature to put other women at ease and gain a quicker path to acceptance. Carla, a fifty-year-old real estate office manager, was one of the many who told me that the best strategy for gaining acceptance with other women these days almost always involves things like feigning modesty and insecurity, self-demotion, self-deprecation, and cobbling together some compliments even if they're somewhat insincere because "you don't want to be too perfect, that's for sure." Another (anonymous) woman was even more direct:

> I hate having to do it, but it sure as hell works. Women want things even-steven. I do think female relationships work fine when both parties are equal. The minute one friend loses weight, gets a boyfriend or husband, gets a promotion, a makeover, or in some way steps an inch above the other friend in any way, though, it's over.

I saw this "burdens of attractiveness" thing play out with my own mother, who always fell on the physically fetching side of the equation and, I guess, had that whole threatening package going on. She might not acknowledge it—that'd be a breach of Catholic modesty—but I will. It would have been impossible for us kids *not* to have noticed women eyeing her skeptically and backing away out of intimidation or whatnot through the years. It would have been even harder not to have heard the petty snickers and whispers. She seemed to ignore it or take it in stride on the outside, but it undoubtedly hurt and took its toll. We saw her cope by always—*always*—demoting and poking fun at herself to win over the wary and green-eyed in her midst. It seemed exhausting and not a little theatrical, really, but I get it now. I think it's great, on the one hand, that she knew better than to flaunt her gifts, that she made those additional, mindful efforts to reach out and put other women at ease by being extra (sometimes over-the-top) friendly and inclusive. On the other hand, I think it's sad that she couldn't just be herself, without all the fear-based flourish and self-conscious desperation to avoid the judgments of women who had time and again proven such tough critics. It seems such a uniquely female adaptation, this self-demotion, and, for some of us, I daresay not always an authentic one. I myself am no great beauty, but I certainly understand that sense of needing to conform, toe the line, or alter oneself slightly to fit in and gain acceptance with certain women in certain contexts. It really is a bit silly to realize that many of us will react to the same woman extremely differently depending on nothing more than, say, her outfit, accessories, and level of confidence as she walks into a room. Think about it.

And those who refuse to self-deprecate or tone things down, like the actress Megan Fox? Well, they don't seem to win too many girlfriends. Fox admits she can't be bothered. She's been criticized pretty brutally for acknowledging her gifts and issuing tough words about female competition, though, as usual, there are at least some bits of truth to this type of rant:

> Girls can be a nightmare . . . Women tear each other apart. Girls think I'm a slut, and I've been in the same relationship since I was eighteen. The problem is, if they think you're attractive, you're either stupid or a whore or a dumb whore. The instinct among girls is to attack the jugular.

A whole lot of other women out there, meanwhile, are linking their gender-based struggles—and admittedly soured attitudes—to the environments in which they've chosen to live and work. To lend just a flavor of the simmering unease that might be fermenting beneath the cheerful veneer of your very own neighbor or coworker, consider thirty-two-year-old Karen, who says she felt tension with women on a daily basis while living in Irving, Texas. For her, doing a "180-degree turn" and moving to Minneapolis proved a much better fit. Heather, forty-one, on the other hand, "can't stand" the Twin Cities. She cites rampant consumerism, status obsession, and what my Buddhist friends call "wanting minds" as unavoidable culprits that draw women in and pit them against one another in her upscale Minneapolis suburb. "Prior to moving, I didn't have this feeling about women," she explains. "But I've found a definite passive-aggressive veneer here. It's a superficial, money-obsessed culture that I wasn't expecting; one that turns otherwise nice women into fakes. I'm my real self only with my old girlfriends but, of course, none of them are here." Kate, a twenty-five-year-old from Denver making a new life in Boston, finds women in her new city equally unwelcoming:

> It's just harder here. The women at work and even my apart-ment building are clubby. They don't try to reach out or wel-come you in any way. I've never been asked to lunch or drinks even when they all head out together. They smile but quickly look away, though I've seen them giving me the once-over, like they're suspicious of me. I feel like I'm back in high school. I'm not sure how I'll make friends here; not even sure these are my kind of people. I've even considered buying new clothes and acting hip or snarky just to fit in! How pathetic!

Joyce, a forty-two-year-old stay-at-home mom living just north of San Francisco, says she was oblivious to the "frivolous" culture that invaded her sought-after community during the eleven years she spent working in the city. She admits that she's felt overwhelmed and unhappy with her transition to stay-at-home life and finds it tough to meet women with similar values and interests. A physician named Jessica says matter-of-factly that she continues to work grueling hours because her fear of living as a stay-at-home mom "in the sorority-style environment there is stronger than the appeal of staying home."

Ouch! Gretchen, likewise, says she's constantly wary and uncomfortable in the coveted town she and her husband "overmortgaged" themselves into. "I live right outside D.C., and everything's a competition. It's about who you know, who your family is, what you drive, what you wear. I can't relate." Mia, forty-seven, says the same about her suburban Chicago existence:

> It's very, very hard to find "real" women here, so I feel isolated. Sure, we could pick up and move, but we'd sell our house at a loss. The public schools are exceptional, and we can't swing private tuition. We're kind of trapped. Besides, would we just be running away? I'm starting to wonder if maybe it's like this everywhere—more a comment on women generally than this one town. I really don't know. But I know I'm not happy.

It isn't just the urban and suburban dwellers. I heard from women in smaller towns who sound equally disenchanted. Rachel, a fifty-three-year-old waitress at one of the Tennessee diner joints my family stopped in during our cross-country drive, assured me that it's not so much about status or the material on her side of the pond. Instead, she says, the women are just plain petty. "The girls around here are even worse. I see it every day. It's like they got nothing better to do, so they band together and find a target. Just about anything can get them going. And I feel terrible for the ones they're doing it to. You can just see it in their faces."

Obviously, choosing wisely factors into all of this—whether we're talking about who we pass time with, where we work, or where we live. Some places and some people are just better fits; birds of a feather and all that. You can call it whining, but remember: These women weren't out there just idly complaining. They were invited to anonymously share private thoughts in a survey and are silently looking for support, acceptance, validation, and a sense of community and connection with other women. For whatever reason, they aren't finding it. And, really, it shouldn't be such a tall order to find open, welcoming females, right? We can wonder why these women don't "quit complaining," pick up and move, or just relax and try a little harder to smoke out the gems that surely populate any office or neighborhood.

But I see what they're saying: It isn't always easy. Professional and personal circumstances don't often make it a simple matter of tweeting, "I'm outta here." And, besides, as Mia wondered, who's to say the same clouds won't be hovering over your next stop?

WORK

And still, as challenging as the female social maze can be for a lot of us, it sounds like conditions at work are often worse. It's curious, but nobody seems to agree why women spar so much at the office. Is it really just a fight for survival, about dominating rivals and slamming the gates on the competition? Is it simply part of the human condition and natural pecking order? Are women hardwired to openly and secretly tear down one another because our opportunities remain limited in a man's world? Do we, as one women insisted, "sometimes just have to make the other woman look bad so we can look good"? Are we trying too hard to be strong and dominant, as if it's the only means of proving we're capable and deserve to get ahead? Is it because the American workplace tends to reward aggression and self-promotion over caring and cooperation? Or are we just on autopilot?

Whatever the case, the ugliness appears rampant. Consider a recent study by the aptly named Workplace Bullying Institute, which reported that about 40 percent of office bullies are female. I suppose this isn't terribly surprising considering that we comprise more than half the workforce. But here's where it gets troubling: While male bullies torment male and female coworkers pretty equally, women much prefer to bully their own—more than 70 percent of the time they're at it. Some insist that's because women are afraid to bully men, but many people don't see it that way anymore. The writer Mickey Meece, who penned a controversial article on women's workplace bullying for the *New York Times*, really nailed the implications of this trend, asking us to consider whether women might, in fact, be more than a little responsible for their own failure to thrive and prosper in the jungle:

At least the male bullies take an egalitarian approach, mowing down men and women pretty much in equal measure . . . How can women break through the glass ceiling if they are ducking verbal blows from other women in cubicles, hallways, and conference rooms?

As with so many other aspects of female aggression, these incidents go largely unreported. Women, in general, hesitate to discuss it. They fear retaliation, want to be seen as competent, solid team players, and don't want to risk making matters worse by calling attention to what a male friend of mine calls our "silly girlfighting." Yet the gossip, competing, and sabotage appear rabid, oftentimes with other women standing by and even encouraging it. Grace, who posted a comment online in response to Meece's article, explained that it's been a daily "chore to stay above the fray" at work given the lurking wrath of female managers, all of whom she's convinced "revel in making others feel miserable." She said she dodges the female bullets only by carefully and quietly crossing her t's, dotting her i's, and smiling. Another fed-up online writer argued that "women are the new men" and thinks the term *bullying* isn't strong enough for what we're doing to each other:

Lots of these snakes are mothers, and that's deeply disturbing. I've seen a bunch of so-called religious women give a very competent and nice female coworker a hard time just because she was pretty. There's a lot of jealousy, insecurity, and downright childish behavior. And I think that if women, as a group, don't grow up, they don't deserve positions of power in high numbers. Personally, as a woman, I'm so disgusted by some of what I've seen in the workplace, that I would never report to a woman boss.

Unfortunately, I heard the same from my survey pool. Negative office gossip is out of control. "Ganging up" and shifting alliances are common. Cries of "Gimme a male boss any day!" are rampant. There's a lot of talk about our insecurities. Many women insist that there's just nothing more threatening to a woman who lacks self-esteem at the office (or anywhere else) than another who doesn't. Barbara Brock, a professor of education at Creighton University in Omaha, stumbled upon this dynamic by accident while researching a book about the teacher-principal relationship. In a lecture she gave at the 2008 Women in Educational Leadership Conference entitled "Sisters or Saboteurs? When Sisterly Support Turns to Sabotage Against Women Leaders," Brock explained that women target each other as threats out of insecurity, typically over another's "youth, attractiveness, competence, popularity, and friendships with men." Like others who have looked into these issues, Brock was struck by the depth and endurance of pain in her interview subjects even decades after the fact. Struck, too, by the deep reluctance of women to talk about it and the catharsis they found in finally opening up.

One surprising tidbit, at least for me: The world of nursing cropped up as one of the more acutely Darwinian professions, with more than a few nurses suggesting their environment had become "survival of the nastiest." But, apparently, I'm behind the curve. A July 2009 study from the United Kingdom documents the extreme prevalence of bullying among *midwives*—you know, those supernurturing women who take a holistic, female-focused approach to childbirth? More than half of the 164 subjects in this five-year study reported major hits to self-confidence and increased anxiety as a result of their superiors' excessive and sustained criticism, disparagement, and general oppression. In a four-article series addressing this bullying culture in the quarterly journal *Midwifery Today*, we learn that "many midwives leave the field early, students give up the path, and too many young midwives feel shut out and very lonely in their community." One of the articles tells the story of twenty-five-year-old Jodie Wright, who was so deeply disillusioned and frustrated with the constant judging and lack of support among her fellow midwives that she began doubting her value and abilities, fell into deep despair, and, ultimately, gassed herself in her car.

I appreciated the candidness of those articles, but something's off because the same publication's subscription page goes a little overboard in painting the profession's collegiality as the sisterhood of all sisterhoods, urging fellow midwives to subscribe so they can be part of an international community of supportive, encouraging, and interconnected birth practitioners:

> It's like sinking into a nice warm bath, or sharing birth stories with a best friend. You're at home here, you know the issues,

feel the excitement, understand the pain . . . Enjoy a warm hug,
a good laugh, support and encouragement.

Again, saying and wishing something is so doesn't make it so. It's
hard to know what to think. But, then, even the hallowed halls of academia are not immune. I don't doubt that some wonderfully supportive academic environments exist for women. All I know is that an
inordinate number of educators used my survey to vent anonymously
about a peculiar species of gender-based backbiting, particularly on
display, they say, during one's quest for tenure. Linda, a forty-one-
year-old humanities professor, assures me that while high school girls
can be cruel, "university professors are a pretty mean bunch too."
Others describe a quiet, stealthlike brand of "torture" among lady
colleagues that forces them to operate at a sustained level of alert.

Katherine, a tenured professor in her fifties, says that while she has
a group of friends with whom to attend dinners, readings, and the odd
movie, the duplicitous, behind-the-scenes aggression she's encountered for more than two decades has left her feeling distrustful of
most female faculty at her university—the very souls with whom she'd
hoped to form bonds given their shared predicament, interests, and
challenges. I find this beyond sad. Here's this woman with a mighty
cranium at the pinnacle of her profession at the institution of her
dreams. And yet she finds herself dealing with childish game playing
among her so-called sisters, nonsense that tampers with her day-to-
day business and has left, she says, a "deep impact" on her psyche.
Katherine and some of her colleagues, while stoic and resigned, also
sound deeply frustrated, like they're operating in a quiet, depressed
haze. To be honest, the imagery of female professors skulking about
the brick and ivy, dining at the trough of nasty, and purposefully
going out of their way to sabotage one another would seem to have an
almost comical, cinematic quality if it weren't so disturbing.

Much of this still shocks us and flies in the face of conventional
wisdom, of course. Some are so entrenched in thinking it's "the Man"
holding us back—which may or may not be a factor in your own personal work dynamic—that we fail, as Meece notes, to consider our
own role in the collusive dance of oppressing, demotivating, and
keeping the numbers of women in senior positions down. As social
critic and author Leora Tanenbaum explains in her book *Catfight:*

Women and Competition, it's as if "we cooperate in our own subordination." The veneer of harmony or surface cheers for other women to succeed ring nice and all, but scratch that surface, and a darker picture of backbiting, betrayal, and thwarted expectations often emerges. At least three dozen self-identified attorneys and corporate professionals in my survey, for example, shared tales of being thrown under the bus by female coworkers who went out of their way to torpedo or stall plum assignments, promotions, and partnerships. A recent American Bar Association survey and an *American Lawyer* magazine article entitled "The End of Sisterhood" confirm what they're saying: Most professional women prefer a male boss and are tired of dealing with the acrimonious and competitive tensions among female colleagues.

One thing we do know about conflict in the workplace is that those pesky expectations we have for our fellow women can again play a major role in the degree of harm when things go awry. A widely publicized study of U.S. workers from the University of Toronto confirmed this phenomenon. In comparing stress levels and health ailments among various pairings of employees and supervisors, the researchers had a single core hypothesis: The all-female pairings would promote harmony in the workplace.

You probably know where this is going. Of every possible combination, it was the female employees with female bosses who reported the highest levels of distress—bad stuff, such as depression, anxiety, headaches, trouble focusing, and sleep disorders. Researchers believe it was the employees' expectations of warmth, nurturing, and support from their superiors that teed things up for trouble. Not only were the lady bosses not giving it—they were demonstrably harder on their female underlings. That clash between expectations and reality, they concluded, left female workers at least doubly vulnerable to psychological and physical fallout and, presumably, far less productive.

In my thirteen or so years as a practicing lawyer, I really didn't experience women acting egregiously at the office. I enjoyed incredible mentoring, support, and friendship from the top down with the women at my old firm, one of those larger institutions that might have easily offered a rougher experience. Indeed, it was a culture that helped open me back up to women and female friendship—I've found some of my dearest friends there. How lucky to have landed in a place where both men and women offered understanding and support as I birthed four children, bailed early for bed rest each time, and negotiated an array of part-time schedules in the midst of delicate, demanding cases. Scratch that. I *know* I was among the lucky because the nightmare stories I've now heard, the 192 comments to Meece's article, and the ABA survey accompanying that *American Lawyer* piece have revealed an alternative universe—one I hope never to visit. For far too many women, it's a grim *Devil Wears Prada* reality—stripped of clever banter and delicious clothes, of course.

THE MOMMY FRONT

It's no picnic on the mothering front, either. I'm not the first to lament the senselessness of this ongoing struggle, and I surely won't be the last, but why, oh why, can't we simply respect one another's assorted mothering choices and leave it at that? We have so much more in common than we think. The phantom rivalries, snubs, and critical judgments among us mothers can really taint the whole experience and add those extra layers of unnecessary burden to an already challenging undertaking. It's stay-at-homes vs. working moms, breastfeeding vs. bottle moms, co-sleeping vs. Ferbering moms, private school vs. public school moms, society-crowd moms vs. cerebral moms, too-strict moms vs. too-permissive moms—moms vs. moms, period. Here we are, in the midst of some of the most joyful, challenging, and hormonally vulnerable moments in life. And while I think many of us lend each other great companionship and support, do bond over the experience, and are in fact being lovely and amazing most of the time, let's be honest: Some of us are judging each other every step of the way. It's like we can't restrain ourselves. It's this raw, primal need to find something—anything—to criticize in another mom's performance to reassure ourselves that we're doing okay. Or are the better, more competent one.

I've straddled both sides of the stay-at-home and work equation, and while I've known every kind of wonderful, generous, self-assured mother, I've witnessed the tensions and insecurities firsthand. In the five or so years since I've been home full-time, for instance, I've heard no fewer than a dozen times some form of the preposterous declaration that poorly behaved kids are usually the offspring of working mothers. I loathe that kind of thing. Clearly (if anyone is thinking clearly), we aren't better mothers by virtue of a stay-at-home moniker. I'd be lying if I didn't admit that, personally, I may have been a *more* present and attentive mother when I worked at least part-time outside the house. My kids got less face time during the workday, perhaps, but, exhausted or not, I usually walked through the door refreshed, excited to see them, and ready to give them my laser-beam focus. Being away from them for bits of time actually gave me a chance to *miss* them. Maybe I'm just waxing nostalgic here and romanticizing my past, but sometimes I fear I'm a shadow of my former mothering self. I've become something of an impatient hollerer of late and am undoubtedly one of Ayelet Waldman's so-called Bad Mothers. (Ask any of my kids. They'll tell you.) But, again, all of this is just my opinion tailored to *my* life. Whatever happens to suit you is really no business of mine—or the maternal peanut gallery's.

On the other hand, like a lot of stay-at-home moms I've heard from, I too have felt marginalized by the occasional rushed and haughty working mom who couldn't be bothered with little old me or the drudgery of day-to-day school and community issues. I encountered this especially as "lice lady" at my kids' school. There were moments when I was barked at like a servant—not as a hapless parent volunteer who did, actually, have other things to do beyond raking her hands through the greasy, nit-infested hair of another woman's child. You could just tell sometimes that it never occurred to a couple of these ladies that some of Us, in sweatpants and fleece (or kitten heels and cashmere; whatever your style), were once one of Them in a former life but had since chosen a different path. Or we weren't and didn't, and remained perfectly secure in our choices until we began feeling the disapproval of other moms. Whatever. I've done my share of eyebrow raising, cocking of the head, and deep contemplation about the choices of other mothers, but the truth is, unless a given woman is somehow raining on my brood's parade—and some do—I really have no legitimate standing to question her motives or family predicament. I have enough trouble paddling my own canoe.

It isn't just the reflexive judging among mothers. I heard a number of tales about moms going after young girls too. I've even seen it myself. Just last spring, I was minding my own business in a local park when a well-known mom began gossiping loudly on her cellphone at the sand pit's edge—oblivious to the surrounding children and parents. For upward of ten minutes (yes, I counted), she tore into a neighbor's fourteen-year-old daughter, picking apart the kid's clothes, personality, mother, and even her complexion. Then she flipped her phone shut and chatted merrily among us, as if that cyclone of quasi-craziness hadn't just blown through. Equally egregious was the mom drama my sister Stacy just shared with me. In this episode, a mother she knew had the presence of mind to launch an "anonymous," venom-filled letter-writing campaign against her daughter's *cheer team rivals*. We're talking gated community, churchgoing, presumably educated, and presumably evolved people in the enlightened twenty-first century. We've publicly excoriated women like this for years, punished them, avoided them, even rendered them caricatures in made-for-TV movies. And *still* they don't learn their lesson?

OUR GIRLS

I think a renewed call for engaged, mindful mothering makes a lot of sense given the extent to which our girls seem to be struggling. Mary Pipher, Marion Underwood, Lyn Mikel Brown, Rachel Simmons, and Rosalind Wiseman have all written brilliantly on this struggle, and I urge you to draw on their wisdom. For our purposes, it's worth recalling that experts believe these covert aggressions and maneuverings begin to brew by age four or five and possibly before. Research suggests that our little girls are quick studies—adept at figuring out how to manipulate their environment for better or worse, and savvy about securing standing in the social hierarchy through a sophisticated mix of both positive and negative behaviors. Some, of course, are more adept and savvy than others. Tim Fields, coauthor of the book *Bullycide: Death at Playtime*, puts it this way:

> Quite simply, girls have a superior social intelligence. Both genders bully, but girls are better at it; they are more switched on to the nuances of social interaction and use psychological forms that are harder to detect and easier to deny, and they can do it with a smile.

I've now consulted with more than a dozen elementary school teachers and counselors about this issue. Would you believe that even after years of overseeing hurt feelings from exclusionary games, possessiveness, and other aggressions among their girl students, most of these people still find themselves scratching and shaking their heads? There's no consensus about what causes it or what to do about it. Take my mother-in-law, Merna, one of those saints who taught elementary school for over forty years. She can't explain it. My sister Tricia, a devoted, award-winning, street-savvy second-grade teacher, says she's stumped. It certainly isn't about impressing boys at that age, to her mind. What do these educators and counselors agree on? It's worsening, it is exceptionally difficult behavior to control and change—particularly in the face of powerful cultural influences and parents who aren't paying close enough attention—and it's frustratingly difficult for educators to feel they're having any impact.

Their best guess about why girls do it? Our girls are driven by a desperate need to fit in and feel secure, just as the psychology professor and author Marion Underwood has suggested. Girls wield their power and aggressions to ensure belonging and inclusion, to harm peers who threaten their status or friendships, and to protect themselves from rejection. Unfortunately, since their methods often prove effective, they see little reason to abandon them or knock it off as they grow. Left unchecked, of course, the tactics tend to become even more refined and sophisticated. At the same time, most girls are sensitive and vulnerable to social wounding. The friendships they make, particularly in the preteen and teen years, are often all-consuming. If an adolescent girl's social group disses or excludes her, or things go otherwise south at that tender stage, experts say, it can compromise her ability to interact socially *for good*. As Wendy Troop-Gordon, an assistant professor of psychology at North Dakota State University who has researched these issues, explains, "Turning eighteen is not a magical age when you leave all of these experiences behind. People do seem to carry these experiences with them."

My three daughters, ages ten, ten, and fifteen, are still working their way through these stages, so I've seen a lot over the years—and I don't for a moment doubt what I'm hearing from other mothers. Little surprises me anymore. I've seen the beneath-the-radar game playing firsthand and heard the "She's so fat," "She sucks at basketball," and the "No offense, but, well, you aren't really pretty enough to play Belle." I looked on—from afar, thankfully, since my girls weren't involved and I learned of the situation weeks into it—as second-grade girls banded together and formed exclusive "clubs" that flew in the face of school policy but passed muster with parents, some who seemed to encourage it, purposely ignore it, or consider it "no big deal." Think second-graders don't know what they're doing? The teachers I've spoken with beg to differ. This particular situation erupted and caused all sorts of trouble and hurt feelings, pitting club girls against nonclub girls, enabling parents versus disgusted parents—and catching teachers, counselors, and even the principal in the middle. One savvy young teacher warned that if we all didn't start taking these matters seriously and nip the nonsense in the bud right then and there, she guaranteed that those same girls would graduate to greater mischief down the road.

An apparently prescient call, for it's two years later, and the same class still has its share of girl drama. I won't write about the latest out of respect for the privacy of those families involved. But I will say that while this group includes plenty of lovely, sweet, and stellar girls and families, one definitely detects an undercurrent of exclusivity and meanness coursing through the class too. Like that teacher warned, if something doesn't change and parents don't start taking things more seriously, I can only imagine the mayhem that'll be served up once these girls hit middle school.

It isn't easy being a developing adolescent in any decade, girl or boy, but things really do sound exponentially more complicated and hazardous today. As one middle school guidance counselor told me, these kids are getting pulled in all sorts of directions and dealing with social and academic pressures most of us never had to. One need only view the documentary film *Race to Nowhere* about today's achievement culture, or consider the success of books like psychologist Madeline Levine's *The Price of Privilege*, to get a sense about why so many kids are floundering (well, at least the middle- to upper-middle-class kids). And while there's important renewed concern about the needs of boys in this culture, it sounds like girls definitely aren't faring so well either. More often than not, we're talking about nice-enough girls who are stressed out, poorly socialized, questionably parented, disengaged, feeling empty and/or inferior, or any combination of the above. At the same time, they're bombarded with sophisticated, age-advanced media influences and getting caught in the midst of competing, confusing demands and interests—all while seeking a piece of the popularity pie to enhance self-worth. They're manipulative, hurtful, and cruel to each other and, all too often, turn it right back on themselves. Look no further than Meg, the downtrodden daughter on the animated TV series *Family Guy*, who in one episode can be seen lightheartedly—and yet so obviously not—pointing to the many cuttings on her wrist, each of which she says represents a different "mean girl" trauma from her life. As much as I love that show, I couldn't help but wince in realizing that mean-girling and its consequences had become so commonplace that we now joke about it and trivialize it in the mainstream.

And if headlines are any indication, trouble in Girl World might be worsening. Even with increased awareness and intervention, it sounds like today's girls are more insecure, manipulative, and quietly desperate than ever before. To wit, consider a 2008 incident in Florida in which six girls beat a female classmate—and videotaped it for YouTube glorification. The county sheriff called those girls "animalistic," among the worst things he'd seen in thirty-five years of law enforcement. Now, we can debate whether such physical aggression among girls is actually increasing, but this wasn't an anomaly. A similar scenario played out the very week I wrote this while living in northern Virginia for a few months. This time, a group of nearby Maryland girls beat a cheerleader for kicks during a high school football game—half-time entertainment, if you will. Their handiwork was posted online, went viral, and delighted the girl bullies to no end as other kids began LOL-ing, cracking jokes, and expressing approval online.

Even the little ones are at it. Farther north, ten-year-old Rikki Triana of Erie, Pennsylvania, made the mistake of asking two girls to stop splashing her sister with water at a local park. Their response? They stomped on her head and body, shattered her hip, and left her permanently handicapped. These beatings seem all the more shocking, I suppose, because most of us are accustomed to seeing girls engage in a more indirect, covert brand of aggression; it's been young boys, after all, who have been the perpetrators of school shootings and other violence in national headlines. Not to psychologists, though, some who say these episodes mark a creepy upward trend in our girls' eagerness to win peer acceptance and approval through increasingly outrageous behaviors.

Which I guess might explain the allure of having one's name on a "slut list." Years ago, I remember my ob-gyn mentioning some bizarre business of middle school girls giving "oral favors" during the school day, apparently in an effort to gain status and popularity—with girls as much as with boys. My daughters were tiny, so I'm sorry to say that I shrugged it off as some curious aberration among a few bored and privileged girls. It seemed so far-fetched. In my experience, after all, the ramifications of being labeled a slut or a whore are, as authors Peggy Orenstein and Leora Tanenbaum have detailed, wholly shameful and can last a lifetime. Girls have historically been so fiercely protective of their reputations, so keenly aware of that tart versus nice girl distinction. Indeed, negative gossip and rumor spreading about this very thing are often the weapons of choice for slandering another girl's rep—wielded in the hopes of preserving one's own. Studies confirm the phenomenon of girls distancing themselves or avoiding friendships with the purportedly promiscuous among them, all for fear of reputation by association.

I have to believe this remains the case in most quarters. So what is going on when we find very young girls doing a 180-degree turn and actively flaunting their sexual prowess as social currency? In some circles, we're seeing girls using sexually charged labels, rumors, and acts of promiscuity not as weaponry or insults to reputation, but as valuable street cred for admission and acceptance into the "popular" club. Gaining a coveted spot on a "slut list," these girls say, can lend a sense of power and instant (if transient) status. My eighth-grade son confirms this blatant promiscuity among girls his age and younger but, of course, claims to be oblivious about what's motivating it. When pressed, though, he says that while girls might do it in *part* to win guys over, he sees it mostly as a power thing among and about the girls themselves. Whatever the case, my wonderful doctor was right to worry.

THE INTERNET

In 2009, the National Crime Prevention Council estimated that cyber bullying touched the lives of at least half of all teenagers in this country. According to a 2007 Pew Research survey, one in three Internet-using teens has been targeted by menacing online activity. No matter how you define the terms, no matter how you parse through the methodology, that's troubling. But I can't say I'm surprised. In fact, having trolled my kids' social networking sites and seen the ugliness myself, I'm willing to bet that the true figure is much, much higher.

Don't get me wrong. I am all for the Internet and First Amendment protections. But there's palpable cause for concern here. Psychologists and bullying experts increasingly warn that the Internet's cheap, instant, and anonymous thrills are affording kids (and the rest of us) unprecedented opportunities to showcase aggression—in ways they never imagined and in ways they wrongly assume are safe, harmless, and private. It's a medium that seems especially alluring to girls, who, again, have historically favored the more indirect, behind-the-scenes, under-the-radar styles of bullying. It's awfully tempting, if that's what you're into: You can sound cool or clever with a few careless whispers on a Facebook wall or any other venue that welcomes comments. Or, in a mere couple of clicks, you can diss someone subtly through photo tags, postings, cuttings, pastings, forwarded matter, and pokes, scoring direct, amplified hits on rivals with dronelike precision, all without having to see or deal with actual, real-time, real-life consequences. Anonymously or not—your choice. To those lacking a solid moral compass, it's just one more gamelike option in the arsenal.

It's not just the tragedies between girls, like with my friend's niece or fifteen-year-old Phoebe Prince, the South Hadley, Massachusetts, girl who killed herself this year after being tormented online, via text, by phone, *and* in person. Consider Libbie Roney, a single mom in Hawaii who ran out to the market, leaving her nine-year-old son home alone. She returned to find him hanging by his karate belt in the bathroom. In her absence, he'd played the "choking game" and, instead of merely blacking out, died. The grieving mother made the mistake of reading her bad press on the Internet—the judging, blame, and other harassment for having left the boy by himself—and became so distraught and ashamed by these judgments that she killed herself. As Dr. Wendy Walsh of the online magazine *MomLogic* reminded her readers (some of whom had posted the very commentary Roney saw), all moms are overwhelmed, and "that's why the mom village is so vital as a support system, rather than as judge and jury. Cruel gossip doesn't help any of us." Walsh issued the same kind of battle cry I'm trying to here:

> I hereby make a motion for all of us everywhere to reinstate our vows today. "I vow to support mothers everywhere. To not judge but to offer compassion, understanding and help." Care to join me?

We're seeing online stalking, harassment, and fake advertising from hypercompetitive mothers too. Most of us probably remember Lori Drew, the Missouri mother who joined forces with her daughter, set up a fake MySpace account, and harassed the daughter's contemporary, thirteen-year-old Megan Meier, to her literal death back in 2006. Or Elizabeth Thrasher, the forty-year-old mother of two who posted a teenage girl's photo and personal details on Craigslist's Casual Encounters section in 2009, suggesting that she was looking for sex. Unlike most who get away with this stuff (including Lori Drew, who was ultimately acquitted for her harassment), Thrasher was arrested, stripped of computer access, and, last I heard, facing fines and up to four years in state prison under Missouri's aggressive new cyber bullying law, which was passed after Meier's suicide.

Indeed, in the wake of the Meier case, California representative Linda Sanchez and other members of Congress said enough's enough and put together the Megan Meier Cyberbullying Prevention Act. The bill, introduced in April 2009, hopes to impose fines or prison terms of up to two years on anyone engaging in certain acts of online hostility. Though, again, I wouldn't be surprised to learn that the true figures climb higher by the day, the bill notes that a whopping 60 percent of the mental health professionals consulted said they'd treated at least one kid for a problematic Internet experience:

> Cyberbullying can cause psychological harm, including depression; negatively impact academic performance, safety, and

the well-being of children in school; force children to change schools; and in some cases lead to extreme violent behavior, including murder and suicide.

As you might imagine, battles surrounding the potential impact on civil liberties began brewing at once in connection with this proposed legislation. At the time this book is going to print, the bill was resting in a House subcommittee, its fate unknown, though issues of criminal and civil liability in connection with the Phoebe Prince case have reinvigorated the debate.

At the same time, as I noted earlier, other countries have been quite vigilant in raising public awareness and holding even young girls accountable for their online aggressions. The UK organization Beat-bullying, for instance, has taken a leading role in demanding action from Internet organizations, schools, government, and parents, most recently asking social networking sites to make it simpler for kids and families to report offensive posts and, if necessary, to pull them within six hours. One English judge, meanwhile, minced no words in sentencing a teenage girl to a youth offender's facility after she topped off four years of physical and psychological abuse of a peer with Facebook death threats:

> Since [she] was 14, you have waged compelling threats and violent abuse towards her. Bullies are, by their nature, cowards—in school and society. The evil, odious effects of being bullied stay with you for life. On this day you did an act of gratuitous nastiness to satisfy your own twisted nature.

You have to appreciate the conviction—that judge really gets it. As a mother, I think we need something to curb these tendencies. We can't just sit idly by and continue to watch these things happen unabated until they hit our immediate neighborhood. Still, we have some murky constitutional and legal issues to wrangle with before we'll be seeing that kind of response here—and we really do have to ask ourselves whether and to what extent we want it. After all, how do you hold people accountable without trampling on sacred constitutional rights? What should constitute harassment and what shouldn't? Should it be punishable *by law* to publicly trash someone on, say,

Facebook or Twitter? By email? If you forward it on to others? The first time? The tenth? Where do you draw the line between teasing or cruelty we can live with and teasing or cruelty we can't? How much government involvement do we want? As a society, what legal consequence do we want to see? Jail time, fines, community service? For kids? How young? What about for adults? Would punishment be about deterring would-be cyber bullies or simply about giving them their just deserts? As much as I'm all for accountability, this is a complex, slippery slope that's going to require a great deal of forethought before we take any legal leaps. Suffice it to say, I see much legal and political wrangling in our future. In the meantime, I think we'd all do well to start asking these questions to help clarify for ourselves what is and isn't acceptable, and to discern which types of limits, if any, we'd be comfortable living with.

OTHER CRIMES AND MISDEMEANORS

Unfortunately, our darker tendencies aren't confined to Facebook walls, universities, hospitals, sandboxes, lunch tables, stroller-strewn parks, or cutthroat corporate hierarchies. We can't even restrain ourselves in church. Take this wedding I attended years back. While I personally found Father Malone's sermon riveting, a couple of other women apparently did not. They opted to liven things up by making audible, blatant fun of a groomsman's wife sitting alone in a nearby pew: snickering, nudging each other, calling her Little Orphan Annie—that kind of thing. Her chief offense? A tightly curled and apparently unfashionable hairdo.

Now, this is the kind of nonsense in which a lot of us partake. I've definitely been a player in the eminently amusing *If you can't say something nice, come sit by me* game. We think it's clever and "harmless joking." And sometimes it is. But you never know, do you? In this case, the target, barely thirty, was undergoing treatment for late-stage breast cancer. She'd weighed her options about flying across the country, decided to go for it, and bravely donned the wig—only to get kneecapped by the senseless, stone-cold cruelty of two bored and insensitive broads. I wish I were making this up; it still chills my heart. And I really don't mean to sound caustic here, but if there's a "special place in hell for women who don't help other women," as British prime minister Margaret Thatcher cautioned, I can only imagine the fire and brimstone on order for this kind of thing.

But lest I sound like the pharisaic pillar of morality, I'm sorry to say that I too am no angel. I'm as complicated as the next woman and can be terribly impulsive and formidably aggressive myself, especially where my kids are concerned. My past contains some pretty indefensible behavior for which I'm still ashamed. Take elementary school. Corpus Christi. Somewhere around sixth or seventh grade, I remember turning on a girl I'll call Siobhan. I didn't limit my harassment to mere playground taunting; no, I went for the jugular. I knew it was wrong, and, as I sit here today, I can't explain why, but I actually made fun of Siobhan because her dad drove an Old Dutch potato chips truck for a living.

What the bloody hell was wrong with me? To think that she internalized the hurt and kept her game face on as the tiny bits of shrapnel spread, penetrated, and took up residence within—well, what can I say at this point? The father had every right to call in a fury and rip me good. I can't begin to know the humiliation and hurt I caused them both. And I never did learn what became of Siobhan, but the fallout was obviously unpleasant. She transferred schools pretty soon thereafter, while all I got was a crummy day of grounding. As I've sat here reading the life-altering descriptions of episodes like these from grown-up women like Siobhan, I'm sickened by my behavior and can only wonder: *How did things turn out, Siobhan? Did my depravity cling to you? Did you come out of it okay?* If only I could take it back. . . .

Siobhan wasn't the only one. After muzzling myself responsibly for over a decade, I finally let loose and wrote some harsh and immature things to a woman a few years ago in a situation too complicated to flesh out here. In my defense, I'd put up with plenty and didn't particularly like or respect this gal—we aren't going to love every sister out there—but I definitely regret whatever hurt I caused. In the end, it just isn't worth it. High school was another story. My closest friend from those days, Kasia, is an Audrey Hepburn–esque mother of two who speaks an obscene number of languages with proficiency. She's lived around the world as part of the foreign service community, tutoring ESL kids by day and hobnobbing with Bollywood stars by night—all the while spreading her own brand of soft, charming diplomacy. A lovely woman. None of this mattered back in high school, though, when I decided she was a pain. The final nail in the coffin was the night she copied my trashy look de jour during our early-1980s Prince + Madonna phase. I'd felt quite clever, I'm sure, for swiping my dad's thick black belt and fastening it just so across my neon lace top. Kasia's mistake was having the audacity to copy me. Instead of viewing the gesture as a compliment, like an evolved person might, I summarily dumped her, Sicilian style. Over a belt. After years of distance and silence, we've now reconciled and even laughed about our dorky high school tendencies. And that, my friends, feels good.

Do we all have regret lists like these? Hard to say. I can only hope that I've properly atoned for dealing such unnecessary blows to these other human beings, even those dealt in my dunderheaded youth. Call it karma or something else, but Justin Timberlake is right: What goes around does indeed come all the way back around. It's an awful thing to realize that you had the capacity to flatten someone's spirit in one fell swoop and did so for no compelling reason. I think that's a big part of the trouble with us. Females are a pretty resilient species, all right, but, again, I think we're a lot more vulnerable to one another than we care to acknowledge. We might not always mean to cause the harm, but I'm convinced that, all too often, we're not thinking enough about the "later" in all this. Sure, there will always be those who take pleasure in humiliating and hurting others. That's what the renowned psychologist Paul Ekman calls pure "evil." But, seriously, how many of us really *want* to be cruel or negative or thoughtless? Very few, I have to believe.

Bleak? Yes. Does every woman feel this way about the world of women's relationships? Of course not. But the frequency with which these stories and sentiments have rolled in troubles me and implicates us all. Steeped in a brew of competition, wariness, and mutual mistrust, it's hardly surprising that instead of supporting and respecting one another, we can still be found blithely tripping the prom queen, fighting like cats, tearing each other down, acting fake, and scurrying about to out-Bee one another. It's a miserable cycle. But remember: As tiring and tedious as it is to discuss and acknowledge these behaviors, it's far more exhausting to partake in them, fall off the wall, and try to put ourselves back together again.

Bottom line: When you start to really pay attention to what's going on within the gender and read comment after comment laced with these struggles and ambivalence from women of all walks, from around the country—from women who say they enjoy and love their girlfriends, just like you, just like me, just like most of us—the patterns of consensus begin to hint at a hidden malady that's pretty tough to ignore. At some point, it becomes difficult not to feel an element of greater responsibility for what's happening out there, at least toward those with whom you interact. Never say never, but on a basic level of human decency, I don't think you'll find me wielding my lady power so fecklessly again. Regrets? Yes, I have plenty. In some ways, you could say, this book is as much an apology as it is a battle cry.

PART II

AFTER THE FALL

CHAPTER 4

THE POWER OF MEMORY AND OUR NOT-SO-SPOTLESS MINDS

The past is never dead. It's not even past.
—William Faulkner, *Requiem for a Nun*

When I first undertook this project, I thought I'd be focusing almost exclusively on women who had nursed some pretty severe battle wounds thanks to specific, readily identifiable episodes with other females: the sorority debacles, the Facebook bullying, the girls' camp traumas, the workplace sabotage, that sort of thing. And, indeed, there are plenty of us out there. Without question, we have been dealing each other some pretty potent, often cumulative, doses of hidden sadness, self-doubt, anxiety, humiliation, shame, and worse. Still, as I started hearing from women, I realized fairly quickly that it wasn't just the Walking Wounded who wanted to talk. Turns out you needn't have experienced a watershed, Queen Bee–like moment in your past to feel the kind of unhealthy wariness, distrust, and ambivalence we're talking about here. It appears these sentiments can grow from conditions that are far more subtle, though no less insidious, in terms of what they're doing to the fabric of our gender.

To be sure, even with the leitmotifs of joy and satisfaction running through the commentary, my survey results paint a disturbing picture. Again, 84 percent of these women say they've suffered some degree of short- or long-term emotional wounding from a fellow female's "mean, manipulative, or cruel" behavior. They're admitting—many for the first time—to spending inordinate amounts of time, energy, and precious emotional reserves on coping and moving forward. You might never know it by looking at them, but a full 60 percent of all respondents quietly acknowledged that they haven't necessarily gotten over their past emotional blows. Many admit to feeling "uncomfortable, anxious, wary, awkward, cautious, intimidated, and/or distrustful" with other women. Consciously or not, though, they've grown accustomed to suppressing all evidence of emotional wrangling.

It gets worse. Nearly half of those who acknowledged those earlier troubles with females believe that the fallout may well rise to the level of "lasting distress, pain, trauma, and/or emotional scarring." Almost a quarter of those women call their scars "deep and profound," while for an unfortunate 9 percent, it's as if a part of their psyche has broken—they haven't been able to trust women or forge any meaningful female connections. As Lisa, a fifty-eight-year-old legal secretary, explains, "What doesn't kill you might make you stronger, sure, but I suffered a huge depression" thanks to "some recent female aggression and, frankly, nearly didn't make it as a result. This stuff is serious."

It appears so. While each of us boasts different experiences and varying levels of sensitivity, resiliency, and suffering, the most affected voices weren't anomalies. Now, some women claim to be impervious to the negativity; they've scoffed at my concerns, told me to "grow a spine," or insisted that female competition and gamesmanship are "just part of life." The vast majority of my randomly polled women, however, beg to differ. To them, it's hard to imagine that their struggles with self-esteem, motivation and concentration, social vulnerability, sense of shame and worthlessness, depression, isolation and loneliness, psychotherapy visits, or eating disorders, substance abuse, and suicidal fantasies—trials they link directly to trouble with other females—were a necessary cost of doing business as a girl or woman in this country. Perhaps, as Richard Holloway, the writer and former Bishop of Edinburgh, explains in his book *On Forgiveness*, many of us remain skeptical because we fail to appreciate just how severely we really can hurt one another:

The tragedy of the many ways we trespass upon each other is that we can damage people so deeply that we rob them of the future by stopping the movement of their lives at the moment of the injury, which continues to send out shock-waves of pain that swamp their whole existence.

About half of the women who said they'd endured these memorable, difficult experiences told me they'd learned from them and, for the most part, no longer consciously feel wounded. As Brooke, a thirty-four-year-old dental hygienist, sums it up, "Yes, some memories are still painful, but I don't let it control who I am. If I'm scarred, it's so embedded that I'm not conscious of it. I have plenty of other things to focus on in my life now rather than dwell on the past." And, of course, many women are indeed "over it." What I found fascinating, though, was how Brooke and several dozen other women who say they don't "dwell on the past" went on to qualify their initial responses in subsequent questions, often confirming a quieter but subtly tenacious fallout from their past female-related troubles.

Much of this is my fault. A few respondents told me that my survey's wording on those questions—*pain, distress, trauma, scars*—seemed too strong, dramatic, intimidating, or clinical sounding for them to adopt. For example, in the section that discussed one's prior run-ins with women, I asked, "Do you feel that you have experienced any type of lasting distress, pain, trauma, or emotional scarring as a result of your prior negative experience(s) with females?" Darcy, an indie-film producer in her thirties, offered a reaction I got from at least fifty other women: "I wouldn't call it any of those. It's more like an awareness, a watchfulness, or a cautiousness." Some women who initially said they'd moved on later added qualifiers like: "but I don't really trust women or make friends easily now," "I still avoid groups," or even "thank God for therapy." A few others within this *I'm-over-it* group told me they hold on to the hurt only in the sense that it reminds them to be more empathetic and to avoid hurting other women the way they'd been hurt—obviously not a bad thing.

Shoshanna, the Virginia psychology student who offered up all sorts of insights, lends an illuminating sense of the vibe I've gotten from conflicted women who initially marked "no" to the *pain, distress, trauma,* and *scars* question. She clarified that it's possible she's still living out the effects of earlier aggressions, but she isn't particularly keen about acknowledging it—not exactly surprising considering that 43 percent of my survey pool admitted outright that they felt the need to "keep to [themselves], hide, or otherwise suppress [their] anxieties, fears, difficulties, struggles, and/or true feelings about other women." Still, what Shoshanna described doesn't sound at all benign to me:

> The fact that I still can remember where I was at the exact moment the middle school girls (whose names I still remember) teased me about having a "mustache" and remember how I had such poor body image shows the impact is stronger than most people give it credit for . . . I am a different girl now, but it's taken an emotional toll on me. I wouldn't say trauma or lasting pain, but it's all definitely in the back of my mind. I went to counseling for it at age sixteen, so I now understand that I don't have to open up to anyone I don't think is worthy.

Poor body image, "emotional toll," counseling? I'd call that a negative impact. One woman who taught high school for thirty-four years told me that during her career she formed brown-bag discussion groups with students to focus on issues of "female consciousness." She said that "at least seventy-five percent of these girls—all extremely intelligent and many of whom are now successful professionals and mothers—suffered emotionally at the hands of other girls." Hundreds of others offered similar thoughts or experiences, explaining that their past isn't a constant source of distress, but recognizing that the events nonetheless left their mark and still influence them in terms of how they view and approach other women:

> Regarding the experience with gossiping colleagues, I wouldn't say I'm scarred, but I'm less personable and open with all of my colleagues now.

> That [being scarred language] sounds dramatic, and I hate to say yes. I'd like to say I am over it. But, yeah, I do believe I have some emotional scars.

> Actually, now that you mention it, there were a couple of instances with girls that probably left me with lasting

pain and confusion. It's certainly left me feeling less able to trust people. Yeah, that's probably where it all started.

I wouldn't say I'm emotionally scarred, but it's difficult for me to develop the kind of relationship with women that I apparently want.

It never quite leaves my memory. Or it comes back if I'm in a similar situation.

It affects me just when I try and be sociable anywhere. I guess I just let them get into my head and believed what they said about me, so when I'm in a social situation, my mind races. I wonder if every person thinks that same way about me.

In other words, you might not be stuck in "pain, distress, or trauma" per se, but, as these women's commentary reveals, that doesn't mean the negativity or cruelty hasn't impacted your inner self-narrative, taken a toll on your confidence and self-esteem, or otherwise manifested in some less than healthy manner.

THE WOUNDS THAT JUST KEEP ON GIVING

The other half of these self-described "wounded" women seem far more certain that their prior negative experiences with females left their mark. The number of times the phrase "I can't trust women" came up floored me. Jasmine, another grad student from the Midwest, was among many who told me they wrestled with acknowledging residual wariness in my survey because it seemed so "wimpy." Still, says Jasmine, there is no question that she deals with lingering trust issues as a result of her past trouble with female colleagues. "I hate this, but I distrust people now, even if they are being good to me. I am always waiting for the betrayal shoe to drop." Much of it, of course, has to do with corroded self-esteem and the fear that we won't ever measure up or prove worthy. As Kiki, a dancer in her twenties, explains, "The feeling of loneliness I felt was really hard, and I think I still have trouble today because of it—it's that sense that I am still not good enough."

Elayne Savage, a Berkeley-based psychotherapist and author of *Don't Take It Personally! The Art of Dealing with Rejection* and other publications, finds these results unsurprising. She's seen a number of women who have dealt with enduring, gender-based scarring in her practice. The unfortunate truth, she explains, is that "early dings and dents take their toll, and many women don't emerge unscathed from female-inflicted wounds." They carry powerful impressions, memories, and emotional baggage that can "for years" dictate life choices, relationships, and attitudes toward other women. For many, Savage assures me, it's a "shameful or embarrassing" secret they've suppressed or tried to bury beneath busy, otherwise fulfilling lives.

Echoing the voices of hundreds of women I heard from, Dr. Savage reminded me that a lot of women, by their very nature, tend to dwell on these events and twirl them about in their minds. And, try as we might, some of us lack a resilience to convincingly move on. As a result, she says, the fears, scars, and vulnerability persist and "absolutely relate to subsequent relationships. You might very well grow up and not trust females for friends." Cheryl Dellasega, a Penn State professor and author of various books on female aggression, has also warned of the lasting and cumulative effects of female-on-female incivility, noting that it "can lead to profound changes in the way [a female] views and relates to others." These episodes can, she says, stunt our basic ability to trust others, prevent us from forming genuine relationships, and impose a "heightened sense of vigilance against future threats." In one of her videos on relational aggression, Dellasega says that the emotional scars from such traumas "go to the heart, and they can last a lifetime. I know because I hear from adult women who say 'I remember that moment.'" Leora Tanenbaum, author of *Catfight* and *Slut! Growing Up Female with a Bad Reputation*, agrees, writing, "Clearly, we never fully recover from the exclusivity games of our teenage and young-adulthood years."

Yet the memories are there, for the victims, aggressors, and bystanders alike. As Dr. Savage explained, "we never really forget the hurtful slurs and actions of other females." Most of the women I polled and interviewed—from the rarefied few who boast trouble-free liaisons to those with the gnarliest emotional scars—said they hadn't forgotten their past sisterly run-ins. Nearly 60 percent call the memories "vivid, detailed, and powerful." Some, like Sharon, a nurse-practitioner, literally have flashbacks or dreams about their teen years. For many, these memories can still evoke tangible feelings of sadness and shame. As Barbara, a forty-eight-year-old PR executive, puts it, "Getting hurt by a woman never goes away. It burns into your memory even if you've forgiven and moved on." Nan, a thirty-five-year-old occupational therapist, agrees. "Being treated like a 'less-than' for a couple of years will resonate for the rest of your life." And while the greatest percentage of women I heard from say those dreaded junior high years dealt the worst bits of torture, many summoned detailed accounts from as early as kindergarten, continuing through high school, and on into adulthood. Not exactly "safe" or healthy waters for swimming—even for those of us with girlfriends to cling to as buoys.

I often think of Edna, a woman in her eighties who wrote to me about a humiliating girls' camp experience that led to years of gender-based ambivalence. Edna went on to become an esteemed professor, mother of six accomplished children, and an award-winning, published author of stunningly beautiful poetry—a damned full life. Yet even now, she tells me, one of her most validating life endeavors involved reading "Mean Girls" at the Yale Bookstore, a poem memorializing that formative girls' camp moment. Marie, a thirty-seven-year-old mother of three, initially told me she didn't actively think about her past troubles, but, on further reflection, acknowledged that the memories of clique-related abuse in middle school have actually come back to haunt her at random times, especially when she crosses paths with women who remind her of that "type." Many, many others offered sentiments along these lines:

> I can remember just how it went down—like it was yesterday.

> It all comes rushing back so easily if the right trigger arises.

> It took me years to get over—they had a very real power over me.

I can forgive and move on, sure, but I'll never forget.

I'd like to say it's all in the past, but the memories are still just so vivid.

Even those who seem to bounce back with aplomb can carry their memories forward like a sack of bricks. The actress Kate Winslet, who in high school was taunted because she weighed nearly two hundred pounds, told *Harper's Bazaar* that she thought the great minds at Lancôme were joking when they asked her to be its new face. She's an incredible actress, but I absolutely believe she's being truthful to her core about this. Professional success or stardom, healthy kids, and general contentment in adulthood don't magically erase this kind of scar tissue. Winslet continued: "I think what you feel like as a teenager never really goes away. If you were teased for being fat or thin or having bad teeth, you're always a little insecure about that particular area of yourself." She was even more direct about it in *Vanity Fair*: "Once a fat kid, always a fat kid."

Writers have long spun engrossing tales about the powerful and lasting wounds of female relationships gone awry, often from the safe haven of fiction. Given my issues, I'm sorry to say that I came to Margaret Atwood late in life, right around the time I began writing this book. We hear a lot about Atwood's *Cat's Eye* in the so-called mean-girls genre. And for good reason. Her brilliant tale of the complex, emotion-laden power of girls, along with the hurts, scars, and enduring memories, grips you by the throat and doesn't let go. She's crawled right up there inside the crevices of my rattled psyche, that's for sure.

In *Cat's Eye*, we find Elaine Risley, the novel's narrator, who really could be any of us. Elaine, a painter, remains haunted by the cruelties and manipulations of a group of girls from her youth and, ultimately, by her own bad behavior. Like many of the women I've heard from, Elaine would play the scenarios of girlhood over and over in her mind for years, vacillating between that razor's edge of love and hate, wondering what she'd do if she bumped into Cordelia—the girls' ringleader—again, wondering if they'd act civilized toward each other or just continue playing their hurtful games:

Would she turn, give a theatrical shriek? Would she ignore me? Or would I ignore her, given the chance? Or would I go up to her wordlessly, throw my arms around her? Or take her by the shoulders, and shake and shake.

Author Laura Lippman has also written about the deep emotional attachments of females and the lasting memories and pain when things go south. Lippman, who says she still tears up over her own junior high memories, told the *New York Times* she's embarrassed by how well she remembers. "All that stuff is always very close to the surface," she says. "Maybe it's because I'm still immature. But maybe it's because the first person who breaks a girl's heart is usually another girl. Isn't that true for all of us?" The author-illustrator Marissa Moss, meanwhile, who has tackled mean-girl issues in her popular *Amelia* books, told me she gets "a lot of response from mothers about how they experienced it and were left deeply affected even years later."

It's clear, then, that for many, moving past one's sisterly troubles isn't a simple matter of saying *I'm over it*—whether victim, bystander, or aggressor. Our sullied pasts cling to us in apparent and not-so-apparent ways, driving and shaping our attitudes and behaviors, often without us even knowing. Hundreds of women reported detailed memories that, while not actively dwelled on, still held a curious, vague power over them. One woman says she gave up on "mean girls" after elementary school but still struggles within the gender and finds herself gravitating toward the more reserved and ambivalent types like herself:

> I've made a lot of effort over the years to have more female friends, but, honestly, I've never bonded with any enough to call them true friends. I like girl time to talk about things boys don't understand, but that's only a small part of friendships. And these relationships tend to be with other women who also have few female friends; it's like we're the exceptions that prove the rule for one another.

Others say their previously "forgotten" memories have come rushing back in the face of certain triggers—like, say, running into a former sorority sister. Dozens more offered variations on the sentiment "forgave but haven't forgotten." And some say they've carried around parcels of vague, inactive guilt for their own role in tearing down or failing to stand up for other girls and women.

Wherever you happen to be along this spectrum—fine, sort of fine, actively frustrated, or struggling—there can be little doubt that, like anything else in life, our past experiences with other females bear great relevance to our emotional present. But it isn't just the impact on an individual life that should concern us. More than 1,500 women from my survey say that their prior brushes with the dark side—the jealousy, the comparisons and competitions, the judgments, the exclusivity, the gossip, rumor spreading, and shifting alliances—have negatively impacted or colored the way they view and relate to other women in society. That means you and me.

When you have waves of women feeling more guarded, less open, cautious, suspicious, and slow to trust, it *is* going to have broader implications for the gender and, eventually, society as a whole. This type of climate, after all, is hardly conducive to cultivating those meaningful female connections we spoke of in chapter 1, the ones that lend those crucial, life-enhancing health benefits. It's hardly the legacy of sisterhood anyone envisioned, either. All of us, as friends, mothers, daughters, colleagues, and fellow humans, hold a stake and stand to benefit from understanding the enduring marks our actions and words can leave on others.

A GROWING POOL OF UGLY EVIDENCE

Even if you wanted to discount what I'm saying here, it would be pretty tough to ignore the growing body of research relating to that closely connected, overlapping area of adolescent bullying. The results are grim, beyond compelling, and, as you'll see, tend to mimic the precise fallout that the adult women in my survey have identified.

While researchers in other countries have for years been studying the long-term effects of bullying and related aggressions, attention to the effects of social cruelties in this country has been comparatively slow in coming. Until pretty recently, says Young Shin Kim, MD, an associate professor at the Yale School of Medicine's Child Study Center, many adults were likely to dismiss bullying with the old "Oh, that's what happens when kids are growing up." Finally, parents, educators, mental health practitioners, and pediatricians in the United States are beginning to appreciate that those common, everyday, seemingly innocuous insults and aggressions can make mincemeat of our kids' emotional selves, leaving them with indelible, lifelong souvenirs of woe for their trouble.

This increased attention certainly pleases Nicholas Carlisle, a psychotherapist and director of the San Francisco–based nonprofit organization No Bully. Carlisle has long viewed social aggression as a form of trauma that can impact individuals for life. Sticks and stones, physical abuse, rumors, gossip, excluding, hazing, harassment—all of it has the potential to cause significant long-term effects. He says he's seen an array of tragic manifestations among his adult clients:

> They almost universally link their childhood bullying to the difficulties they now have in relationships, particularly in making friendships, belonging to groups, dealing with authority figures, facing conflict, and in relating to their significant others. They also report long-term feelings of shame, entrenched beliefs that they are unlikable, anxiety (often most intensely in social situations), difficulties with anger, thoughts of revenge, and depression.

Carlisle's in good company. Study after study in this area yields roughly the same disturbing conclusions. In a groundbreaking project led by the London-based antibullying organization Kidscape in 1999, for instance, researchers examined a group of adults who'd been mentally or physically bullied as kids—70 percent of them female. Predictably enough, they found that the stresses attendant to being bullied tended to follow victims into adulthood, leaving "dramatic, negative, knock-on effects" on their overall quality of life, including tenacious, long-term feelings of anger, bitterness, low self-esteem, difficulty relating to people, depression, and even suicidal thoughts.

Cathy Street, coauthor of *Not a Problem? Girls and School Exclusion*, a study of girls ages thirteen to sixteen in the UK, describes the culture among girls as a hidden "constant drip-drip of torture." She cautions that it "can undermine the child's whole life and development" and, indeed, has found "notable numbers" of girls who admitted to dealing with their hidden difficulties by withdrawing, disengaging from learning, and finding a "sense of escape"—such as self-excluding, sitting at the back of the classroom, cutting out the world around them, and "simply not turning up." The exclusion study concludes with the grim warning that continued institutional failures to meaningfully tackle these manipulations and aggressions among girls will thwart their development and contributions on a variety of fronts and ultimately impact the broader society. Street is quite matter-of-fact about the gravity of harm, suggesting that girls who do cope through avoidance and withdrawal during their formative years are very likely to carry those unhealthy adaptations into adulthood:

> I spoke to thirteen-year-olds for whom this behavior had already become entrenched. These girls won't suddenly learn how to interact normally once they leave school. They could easily suffer marked emotional difficulties for life.

A 2005 physicians' panel for the National Association of School Psychologists echoed these findings, highlighting once again those trouble-causing expectations females have for one another. The panel concluded that bullying is especially devastating for females because we expect so much from each other and "sometimes feel that [we] are in part to blame and therefore deserve to be isolated," which in turn "makes [us] feel socially inept and unattractive, and thus more deserving of isolation"—ultimately leaving us stuck in a cycle of self-defeating anxiety and loneliness. The American Academy of Pediatrics policy statement I spoke of earlier likewise flags the serious psychosocial consequences that can manifest well into adulthood, including depression and suicidal ideation, problems that the academy specifically notes can be harder on girls and "more likely to result from the indirect, relational bullying behaviors that are more typically engaged in by young girls and that can be notoriously elusive to identify."

I could go on and on with the research. The bottom line, though, as noted in the *Journal of Pediatrics*, "is clear and consistent." Social aggression is a highly prevalent, multinational problem. There really is no question about the effects. As all of these formal studies, my own research, and the voices of thousands of women in this country collectively confirm, the bullied, harassed, and otherwise targeted frequently suffer from a range of short- and long-term problems that can extend well beyond the event itself. These folks deal with lowered self-esteem, anxiety and distrust, loneliness, depression, increased susceptibility to illness, and worse—most of it unnecessary and ultimately quite costly to society. Much of what needs to be done is so obvious, and yet, time and again, we stay on the same course until something terrible happens to shake us up—and then only momentarily. But, really, if this sobering data about the long-term effects of our gratuitous inhumanity and incivility aren't enough to make us think twice about how we treat one another, I'm not sure anything can.

HURT ON THE BRAIN

Maybe it isn't about you personally. Maybe you're like the more than 1,400 women from my survey pool who said that, beyond themselves, they know *other* women who "often seem uncomfortable, anxious, awkward, cautious, or distrustful around other women and seem to avoid social situations." Maybe it's a mother, sister, neighbor, or colleague. Many women told me they've detected a shyness, self-consciousness, apprehension, "lack of eye contact," or "solitary vibe" that a socially reserved woman gives off, "almost like they're trying to get outta there," and are curious about what's behind it all.

A handful of others, meanwhile, have dismissed the whole notion of relational fallout with a dose of cynicism and snark, dropping an assortment of labels like "weird," "insecure," and "loners stuck in trauma-victim narratives." They argue that the entrenched aggression and negativity among females isn't such a big deal—the eggshell complainers among our ranks just need to toughen up. A few told me they've never understood gals like me, lumping together Walking Wounded types as defensive, cold, distant, paranoid, "overly critical," or "annoyingly overaccommodating and pleasing." Others said they've always taken wariness, social excuses, and a reluctance to reach out as a personal slap, assuming the woman at issue was aloof, haughty, or just plain deviant. Sensing high-maintenance trouble or the prospect of intense, "dramatic" backstories, some admitted that they simply keep their distance. And a couple of women insisted it's all just a self-fulfilling prophecy—that because wary women anticipate the bad and look for it, that's precisely the evidence and type of response they find in other women, case closed:

> I think it's all about perception. People see things through their own filters of opinions, biases, and judgments. If you believe women are big meanies to each other, you'll see it everywhere you go. If you don't believe that, you won't see it.

Jenny, a twenty-seven-year-old litigator who responded to my survey, said she thinks women who retreat from other women are just using their past as a "convenient crutch or excuse" for socially "deviant" behavior:

> I have a hard time with people who blame their childhood for the way they are today. We all have things that happened when we were little. It doesn't mean we can use these experiences as an excuse for how we are today and how we live our lives.

Fair enough. But I think this black-and-white style of criticism misapprehends the experience of many and fails to appreciate the larger point. I want to underscore here that very few of these women seem to be crying "victim" or looking for sympathy; they responded honestly in a private, anonymous survey. They generally didn't *sound* bitter, whiny, or vindictive, either—although a solid 49 percent of my overall respondent pool say they do, in fact, "currently hold a 'grudge' or feelings of bitterness or anger" toward one or more females as a result of their prior run-ins. Nor do they fit the dysfunctional profile of, say, your insecure, reclusive aunt Lois, the one with all those cats. Although they certainly come across as emotionally vulnerable and socially cautious, it sounds like most of them have moved forward with other aspects of their lives in perfectly "normal" fashion. They've endured discernible patterns of emotional wrangling and drawn from an arsenal of common coping strategies but, like me, haven't necessarily been dwelling on their past or discussing their female troubles openly. Most aren't stuck in it or unable to prosper on other fronts. And, to me, none of them comes off as haughty—these are not women who sit around assuming that other people are clamoring to gain access to their cocoonlike, holy sacristies. Quite the opposite. After all, remember what Colette from Ann Arbor told us? These women are ashamed. Their anxieties make them feel "defective" and unworthy of your companionship.

The pages upon pages of commentary I have on this, in fact, suggest that none of these women has enjoyed the ride. They don't want to have these internal dialogues about other females. They aren't "choosing" to feel uncomfortable, awkward, judged, or on display. A lot of them seem fine on the outside and are simply dealing with these feelings of social inadequacy as best they can—alone and quietly. Nor do these women march about bitter or embalmed in self-pity, expecting that life be fair and the world of human relationships pain-free. While bits of defensive bravado do, from time to time, pepper their stories, most of them say they want to open up to other women, to free themselves from the tyranny of bad memories or social wariness, and to view women as safe, welcoming, and lovely. Their powerful reflexes and deep-seated fears, however, have something else in mind.

Certainly, some of these women are missing out on a great life pleasure; I did for years and, to some extent, still do. Some of them might be misjudging or miscalculating others' intentions. Some might even be engaging in self-fulfilling prophecies or making paranoid mistakes of generalization, as a few bloggers have charged. But it's not like they're engaged in criminal behavior and trying to make excuses for it. These women aren't normally hurting anyone with their wariness, after all, or looking to blame anyone to get away with "social deviance." No, from the sound of it, I'd say most of them would prefer to make easy connections in a more welcoming, supportive, and forgiving world of women.

Perhaps most important, though, these criticisms discount the power of memory and emotion and those all-too-common events that validate, reinforce, or exacerbate insecurities in a woman's daily life. As it turns out, there may also be some sophisticated psychological and biological mechanisms working to keep us in our social rut. You can tell someone like me to just get over it, and I may very much like to do that, but emotions and memories don't simply do what they're told—they have their own say in all this. The way the brain consolidates emotionally disturbing events and helps us process risk in the face of people or situations that have threatened us in the past might not excuse the wariness or "social deviance" that Jenny and others complain of. But the science behind it should certainly help explain what frequently lies beneath our social ambivalence—and hopefully render these sentiments more palatable or less "oddball."

The world of neuroscience has, in fact, become increasingly intrigued about the ways memory and our emotional unconscious drive social behavior. The way some tell it, the field of cognitive science long gave our emotional lives short shrift, preferring to view our minds as logic-driven computers stripped of emotion. But we aren't Vulcans. And, as it turns out, our brains don't so easily let the emotional happenings of our lives just slip away. As Dr. Louann Brizendine, a neuropsychiatrist at the University of California, San Francisco, explains in her book *The Female Brain*, women actually have stronger memories for detailed information than men do, including emotional events, thanks to our larger hippocampus, an area of the brain involved in memory function.

We should also understand that fear trumps logic. As the New York University neuroscientist Joseph E. LeDoux details in his fascinating book *The Emotional Brain: The Mysterious Underpinnings of Emotional Life*, emotions are biological functions of the nervous system. We can't will them to occur or not occur—they happen to us, riddled as they are with blood, sweat, and tears. Once a powerful emotion rears its head, in fact, we actually have limited control over it no matter how logical we tend to be. Ask anyone who's ever fallen in love. We can try to arrange external actions and events to manage them, tame them, and rein them in. But that's about it.

Emotions also don't merely influence memory—they drive it. In his book *Memory and Emotion: The Making of Lasting Memories*, neurobiologist James McGaugh from the University of California, Irvine, reminds us that all memories are not created equal. Different experiences create memories of different strengths. And, as any psychologist, evolutionist, or neuroscientist will assure you, our brains come predisposed to favor the exciting and arousing—the surprising, yes, but also, unfortunately, the distressing, arresting, traumatic, and hurtful. Emotional events cause our bodies to pump out stress hormones like epinephrine, which, in turn, influence how our brains encode, consolidate, store, and recall those events later on. Highly stressful and disturbing emotions, writes McGaugh, known for his work on memory and emotional stressors, tend to bump the more mundane experiences from our awareness, burning themselves "indelibly" into our brain's circuitry.

Much of this action takes place in and around the amygdala, the small, almond-shaped spot in our inner brain that creates memories and regulates emotional intensity, including our responses to fear. As any scientist in the field will tell you, the amygdala "is quick to learn and slow to forget." Alain Brunet, a psychology professor at McGill University, says, "It's amazing how a traumatic memory can remain very much alive. It doesn't behave like a regular memory. The memory doesn't decay." Like it or not, then, once an upsetting social memory takes up residence in the old noggin's hard drive, it can gain "tenacious hold" and literally stay etched in our minds until the day we die, quietly influencing our attitudes, anxieties, and social choices without our even realizing it. As psychology professor Louis Cozolino explains in another intriguing book, *The Neuroscience of Human Relationships: Attachment and the Developing Social Brain*, our "learned fears are tenacious and tend to return" when we find ourselves under a similar stress later on:

> These old fears take hold of us without our even knowing that it is happening. When we are in a situation that feels similar to painful experiences in the past, we may become gripped by fear or anxiety, without making any conscious connection to our original learned fear.

Sounds kind of depressing and sinister, no? Many women, in fact, told me they suspected they had a form of post-traumatic stress disorder (PTSD)—some in jest, many not. Others insisted *I* had it. I am many things but not a neuroscientist, and I don't know if I'd go that far; we aren't talking certified anxiety disorders here. Still, a few women did say that they'd try pretty much anything to wipe away their disturbing memories and allow themselves a clean slate so they could connect with and trust women again. That's how grim things can seem.

All in all, it's pretty clear that the words and actions of our fellow females—both the high crimes and the misdemeanors—can leave a demonstrably profound impact on our mind and well-being. No one is making excuses for behavior here, but the fact that our brains prefer to hold on to life's difficult or traumatic experiences helps explain why some of us feel disinclined to throw ourselves into new and risky social scenarios. For many of the excluded, rejected, or otherwise emotionally wounded in our midst, you see, coping isn't a matter of simply choosing to forgive, forget, and move on.

Thankfully, in addition to the bits of criticism I've received about women who feel wary of women, I've also seen a great deal of empathy, compassion, kindness, and curiosity. Tori, a graphic artist, says that one of her oldest friends is socially awkward. "Other girls in high school made fun of her, and I think it still affects her and how she interacts with others." She says she wants to understand the phenomenon better to put her friend and women like this at ease. She thinks, as I do, that a lot of other women misunderstand what's really going on. "I'd like to know more because I've been around plenty of women who are quick to assume the worst about anyone who seems more reserved or wary." Peyton, a secretary in her forties, also makes an interesting point worth considering: She says she wishes women like this would understand they're not the only ones feeling this way in social situations: "In fact, I think most people do most of the time, even if they're afraid to acknowledge it."

As appealing as it sounds to manipulate or dampen the emotional wallop of our difficult memories, the truth is: We aren't there yet. Unfortunately—or fortunately, depending on your perspective—the beta blocker propranolol (otherwise known as the *Eternal Sunshine of the Spotless Mind* substance) and other controversial treatments come with a battery of bioethical and related concerns, are still considered experimental at this stage, and are certainly not for everyone. *Eternal Sunshine* screenwriter Charlie Kaufman might be a genius, but for now, it looks like our emotional brains sort of have us by the tail. Beyond trying things like psychotherapy, hypnosis, acupuncture, meditation, tai-chi, yoga, chocolate, and, perhaps most important, feeding one's brain with positive female experiences, new memories, and quality associations to counter or "repair" the bad, it appears nothing is going to *synthetically* erase or blunt our painful memories and emotions. Once bitten, then, we're left with figuring out how to adapt, cope, and otherwise manage them.

CHAPTER 5

ONCE BITTEN, TWICE SHY

On some level, I'm just waiting to be hurt again, which makes it pretty hard to be open and authentic.
—Sasha, thirty-one, struggling artist

The adaptation patterns of women who feel awkward or wary with other women are undeniable: These reluctant ladies resort to a host of common coping strategies. Probably the most prevalent maneuver you'll see is avoidance—backing off, bowing out, begging off, and otherwise turning away. As psychotherapist Elayne Savage explains, a lot of women seem to be coping with past hurts "by quietly retreating from other women because they've simply paid too high a price for trusting them in the past." If the women from my survey are any indication, a whole lot of us are substituting the "tend and befriend" style of relating with an all-out "duck and cover." Some, of course, are simply frustrated with women in general—their avoidance isn't necessarily tied to any discernible event or person. A staggering 1,200 others, however, admit that they regularly employ avoidance to manage their discomfort, anxiety, and distrust of other females thanks to past issues.

Phyllis Chesler was certainly among the first to warn us that our careless whispers, mind games, and gratuitous aggressions weren't really so harmless—they could inflict wounds of a considerable, lasting, and cumulative nature that leave us smarting and feeling cautious and distrustful of one another. Oftentimes, she explained, our inhumanity leaves a woman feeling fragile, like she "simply hasn't the heart to begin anew, to open oneself up to pitiless exclusion" or other risks attendant to female intimacy. In her book *Girlfighting: Betrayal and Rejection Among Girls*, Lyn Mikel Brown similarly acknowledges the hidden scar tissue that remains for so many women:

> In recent years, when I have talked about girls' friendships and girlfighting at conferences and other public settings, women respond, filled with the ghosts of their girlhoods. They examine old scars from relational triangles and cliques, relive betrayals and losses in the most vivid terms, speak to the girls who hurt them as if they were in the room, email me with long and detailed stories of betrayal. These are successful, sometimes openly political women connecting with the wounds of the past that haunt their present lives and friendships . . . Old fears and confusions atrophy their present interactions and stymie the possibilities available to them.

Odd Girl Out author Rachel Simmons has also flagged the reluctance women can feel about putting themselves back out there, noting, "There is a sad number of women who, again, because of what they went through, feel they can never trust another friend again. They spend their whole lives trying to determine what it was that was wrong with them that caused them to be treated this way." Clearly, our wariness is a phenomenon that many have appreciated, but one that has somehow remained woefully underexplored.

THE WALKING WOUNDED

Again, not every woman has an epic mean-girl trauma tucked away. We've all experienced different gradations of gender-related annoyance, negativity, aggression, suffering, and resilience. If you've been supremely lucky, you're one of the few among that 16 percent who say they've managed to sidestep much of this. Whatever the case, you wouldn't want to be among the Walking Wounded—those who've been hit hardest by it all, still struggle to some extent, and have adapted by swearing off on most, if not all, forms of female intimacy—for years, sometimes decades. It turns out there are quite a few women out there building the functional equivalent of moats and walls around themselves to ease their discomfort, frustration, and wariness. Many of them, sadly, sound so incredibly resigned to it, issuing flat statements like "I'll never be able to trust women again," "I don't see myself having intimate friendships with women anytime in the foreseeable future," or "It's taken me years to even consider the notion of female relationships."

Consider Rose, who says she's still affected by a humiliating sorority experience three decades out. She says that the way they treated her and, apparently, viewed her as a person, "remains a significant part of my 'emotional baggage,' and forever changed the way I approach women." Evelyn, an eighty-one-year-old living in South Dakota, shared her story about the decades of shame she's felt around other women after a humiliating bout of class-based mockery and exclusion in college back in 1944. She says she still remains "stunned that any good qualities I might have had could be completely erased" by women at school simply because of her family's lower status and wonders why the go-for-the-jugular type of cruelty always seems to come from our fellow women rather than men.

Fearful of repeated emotional beatings, women like Rose and Evelyn have opted to avoid or hang back from other women as a defensive, self-protective, and preemptive strike—pushing away the very intimacy some of them admit they long for and know would be good for them. Many have turned inward, withdrawing into cocoons of carefully chosen friends—or, worse, withdrawing into themselves. Andrea, who is in her fifties, says the early harassment and the sense of irrelevance she felt with other girls, "compounded with all the negative-toned dealings" she's had with female peers in adulthood, has turned her away from most women:

I continue to seek validation, sure in my own skin that I was wronged, and not "wrong." But it's an uphill battle. I don't know what the answers are, but I'm familiar with the questions. I have no close female friends—anytime I've allowed myself to indulge in feminine camaraderie, it ends badly for me.

For a few others, it's plain that the old hurts have hardened into all-out distrust and withdrawal. They've pretty much given up on us entirely. Tara, the owner of a dog training business in California, is a pretty good example of the Walking Wounded. She says that after multiple "nasties and traumas," she stopped socializing for the most part and still "avoids all prospects of female friendship" beyond two college pals who don't live anywhere near her. She sounds a little wistful but also seems genuinely resigned to a life devoid of female friendship. Carmen, an accountant in her forties, says she never saw herself as a victim following the usual "nasty middle school stuff" and a crippling clash with a female boss. But she admits to avoiding women out of what she dubs an "almost Darwinian" instinct to preserve her emotional sanity:

It sounds so extreme, but I know I avoid women and social circumstances to protect myself. And I know I've probably missed out at times because I've been too cautious, shy, or nervous. Maybe I've misjudged women, thinking they would be mean to me, and it's easier to avoid or dislike them at first. It's lonely, I've got to admit. But I just can't get that trust back.

Judy, an accountant in her forties, says that after various assaults on her sense of worthiness over the years and assessing the social risks, she's pragmatically opted out of most types of female camaraderie. "If you don't invest so much emotional weight into hanging out and being friends with other women who may or may not enjoy your company, you can't be hurt. When you relate to others openly and honestly," she submits, "it leaves your belly exposed for potential abuse, and I think we're all too afraid to do that." Sue, meanwhile, a thirty-three-year-old nutritionist, sums it up this way:

I'm pretty closed down these days. After everything I've been through and all the leaps of faith, I've consciously decided not to get that involved or too close or invested in any women. I guess it's because I'm tired of getting hurt so often, but whatever. It's done.

I have to come clean here: Though I never consciously made a decision to write women off, I've certainly walked the Walking Wounded walk. And I've long utilized avoidance as my coping mechanism of choice. I don't have a lot of other tools in the shed, so it's worked for me. Sure, I present okay at first—I look like a duck, walk like a duck, put myself together in ducklike fashion. You'd never know that I find you all so incredibly intimidating. But still waters run deep. On closer inspection, it probably wouldn't take you long to notice that something's slightly askew. One friend told me that while I initially struck her as possessing that lethal hat trick of confidence, wit, and Minnesota Nice, she soon detected the awkwardness idling beneath the hood. Before you write me off as Sybil II, though, I should probably defend myself here. I've been lucky in life, to be sure—no poverty, no disease, no mom with serious hang-ups. It's true that I haven't quite licked the fallout from my 1980s fall from sisterly grace. But it's not like I'm some delicate flower who doesn't enjoy life, or who whines and cowers in the face of just anything. I've actually slain some pretty mighty dragons over the years.

Take airplanes. As a kid, I was nearly sucked from an old Piper Cherokee 180 when its defective cargo door burst open just a few feet from my clueless unbuckled body. Everything in the area flew out but me—it was absolutely life-threatening. Yet somehow I've never had a fear of flying. I've been flattened by both a car *and* a motorcycle while riding my bicycle but limped back into the saddle each time with my semibionic knee. As an entirely green twenty-five-year-old lawyer, I didn't come unhinged during my *Silence of the Lambs*–like visits with Fred, my ballpoint-brandishing client who was on San Quentin's death row for murder. I even have twenty-four weeks of bed rest under my belt, along with some pretty harrowing posterior, breach, and accidentally "natural" childbirth stories I won't bore you with. Oh, I can prove my mettle in countless ways. But you get the picture: I'm a pretty tough cookie.

And yet, put an old sorority sister before me, and I fall to pieces anew. Even a group of chatting mothers at my kids' soccer games can bring on that old, familiar anxiety. I smile, listen to myself making socially inept small talk, and wonder how all the other women seem so effortlessly competent and sociable. I *know* that my anxiety and self-flagellation are irrational wastes of time. But I can't lie: I usually feel awkward. I've crossed streets to avoid certain women and blown off so many phone calls, emails, and social invitations over the years I couldn't count them. Put me in a room with women I don't know well, and my body betrays me at once: You'll see a mottled red rash start at my chest, creep slowly up the neck, and relax upon my cheeks in two minutes flat. I'm no fan of the social white lie, but, as my husband can attest, I'll happily draw on any *legitimate* excuse to avoid parties, especially all-women affairs. I don't mean to objectify my children, but the truth is that while having kids forces one to put oneself out there sometimes, they've also gifted me with solid cover these past fifteen years, keeping me busy and affording just the cache of handy excuses necessary to lay low and keep myself off the radar. I'm not kidding around here. It wasn't long ago that I flew to L.A. for Teri's ladies-only fortieth birthday party and—despite everyone's loveliness—promptly stowed myself away in a bedroom till the coast was clear. Oh, the lengths some of us will go. But, of course, while it's easy to write about this from a cozy distance in a padded room all by myself, it isn't all that fun or funny in real life. I'm living proof and here to remind you—there's something uniquely monstrous about wounds of the female varietal.

AVOIDANCE: THE STRATEGY OF CHOICE FOR THE WARY

Of course, avoidance isn't *necessarily* an irrational response to situations that have proven toxic to one's emotional health in the past. Since prehistoric times, in fact, our ancestors have utilized avoidance quite successfully as a protective adaptation strategy in the face of potentially hostile threats. According to Harvard's Roger Pitman, a professor of psychiatry and leading PTSD researcher, the survival and adaptation instincts of modern humans are often profoundly underappreciated. Deeply ingrained in the human brain since Paleolithic times, Dr. Pitman told me, these instincts could well play a role in influencing a woman's emotional and social responses following a sisterly run-in—including her ability to mix comfortably with women down the road.

It's only logical. If you don't like what you saw at the buffet, or outright got salmonella last time around, you're probably not going to rush back for seconds. Or, as NYU neuroscientist Joseph E. LeDoux is fond of saying, "If you find out that going to a certain water hole is likely to put you face-to-face with a bloodthirsty predator, then the best thing to do is to avoid going there," right? After all, says Dr. LeDoux, our brain circuitry comes preprogrammed to detect the kinds of dangers our ancestors confronted (evolution's "gift" to us) and the dangers we've confronted personally in our own past experience. Pepperdine's Louis Cozolino suggests that those who've paid close attention to others and best predicted their intentions and actions have historically *maximized* life's advantages in terms of safety and competition. So, again, avoiding women isn't necessarily unreasonable—but it is unfortunate.

It sounds like scientists have really only put a dent in deciphering the neurological workings of memory and social anxiety. What we do know appears to center on the old amygdala and, possibly, what's called the bed nucleus of the stria terminalis, or BNST. The wondrously mysterious amygdala is actually quite in vogue these days. Research appears to be on the rise, the media has latched on, and we're seeing otherwise composed scientists writing and performing songs about it. For good reason. When functioning properly, the amygdala is like your own personal watchdog—it's got your back. It functions like a set of "social brakes" against potential emotional threats, discriminates the familiar from the new and strange, and is always on the lookout for danger. As Dr. Cozolino explains, its prime directive is "to protect us at all costs." The BNST, meanwhile, is a bit more chill, says Cozolino, "activating a sense of concern over a longer period of time."

Face-to-face with a perceived "predator" or other recognized threat, then, our brains do us the favor of switching to autopilot, producing automatic, involuntary emotional responses tailored to the situation at hand. Our amygdala lets us know that we'd best respond, whether that means proceeding with caution, hitting the brakes, staying home, or hitting the road. Once all these emotions occur, says Dr. LeDoux, "they become powerful motivators for future behaviors." In other words, we avoiders might seem ridiculous to some, but from a survival perspective, LeDoux would tell you that, in the face of a stick we mistook for a snake, we're still better off to have "treated a stick as a snake than not to have responded to a possible snake."

In short, we're clever creatures. We get burned, we tend to learn from it, and we adapt by avoiding what burned us. Not unlike lab mice who realize it's best to stay away from that spectacular light show at the rear of the cage, the socially ambivalent sense that they've been there, done that, and will protect their emotional health by hiding from or otherwise sidestepping people or situations that have proven hurtful. We *get* it. When we feel threatened by, say, a woman who reminds of us of that evil colleague who sabotaged our promotion, our amygdala might kick into gear, and we may find ourselves responding "irrationally," or with intense emotion. But we may also have spared ourselves some serious heartache, for, as Dr. LeDoux notes, "social situations are often survival encounters." We assess risk, size up, and survey the scene as part of our overall survival instinct. Not surprisingly, social anxiety is thought to involve overactive nerve cells in the amygdala, a notion that some might find convenient: You know, when in doubt just blame it all on the old hyperactive amygdala.

It's clear that some find it awfully tough to break the emotional cycle of anxiety and avoidance when confronted with the object of their fears. Consider a study of harassed, overweight kids out of the University of Florida. Researchers were puzzled to find that as the rate of weight-related bullying increased, the kids exercised less. Why? The bullied kids avoided the scene of the crime like the plague. They had little desire to revisit those situations and settings where they were most often singled out as punching bags—gym class and sports—even as those were, ironically, the very situations and settings that could benefit them healthwise. All bets were off, sadly, when fitness became synonymous with "emotionally unsafe." The powerful, negative associations simply blew it for them. Sound familiar?

It's one thing, after all, to fear spiders and heights and dark, cramped spaces. Those are a little easier to avoid than people. The sad thing is that while we'd *like* to view girls and women as perfectly harmless, it's clear that a lot of us have pasts that don't really allow us—or, more specifically, our brains—to relax. Our avoidance responses can be perfectly reasonable coping mechanisms for women who have been burned by other women. And it all functions pretty brilliantly when our evolutionary devices instruct us to do things like avoid Dr. LeDoux's bloodthirsty predator at the water hole. That is, until we take it too far. When our amygdala prompts us to overgeneralize, and we start viewing random females out there in the wild not as sources of trustworthy, "tend and befriend" comfort, but as threatening, potential sources of harm like the menacing predators our ancestors confronted, we're paying a pretty high price. As UC Irvine's Dr. McGaugh explains, when fear becomes anxiety, anger becomes hatred, friendship becomes envy (and, presumably, avoidance of, say, other women calcifies into withdrawal, loneliness, and isolation), our emotions have actively started working against us. At that point, our otherwise useful fear-based memories have ripened into deep-rooted anxieties or social disorders—troubling territory indeed. For as we'll see, extreme social avoidance can beget social isolation, which is not only a dismal way to live—it endangers one's health. As James J. Lynch, Maryland-based psychologist and author of books like *A Cry Unheard: New Insights into the Medical Consequences of Loneliness*, and so many others have argued: "Loneliness is simply one of the principal causes of premature death in this country."

To be sure, a new study conducted by experts at the University of Chicago, the University of California, San Diego, and Harvard contains all sorts of fascinating, if grave, conclusions about the broader societal impact of isolation and loneliness. After interviewing five thousand participants from the Framingham Heart Study over a ten-year period, researchers found that "people with few friends are more likely to become lonelier over time, which then makes it less likely that they will attract or try to form new social ties." So isolation not only makes us feel lonelier, the authors explain, it also makes us feel more anxious, self-conscious, socially inept, reserved, distrustful, and defensive. The same study warns that loneliness can actually spread like a disease among a given person's social network. We'll be looking at the concept of social contagion and interconnectivity later but, suffice it to say, one can "infect" or transmit a sense of loneliness and unfriendliness to others, eventually causing even those connections to unravel. As psychologist John Cacioppo, one of the study's authors, explains, it isn't just about the loneliness of one person at that point; it's about society generally:

> [It] is more like an indicator of the social health of our species on the whole—a temperature reading, if you will, of how well—or not so well integrated we are as a population.

In other words, just because avoiding women might be *understandable* in a particular woman's circumstance doesn't mean it isn't having grim health consequences for her, contributing to an unhealthy, disconnected dynamic within the gender and, ultimately, impacting society as a whole. As Dr. Cacioppo explains, we've "evolved to connect deeply with other human beings," and "our awareness of this fact can and should bring us even closer to one another." A person might become lonely for a number of reasons, even good ones, sure. But for our purposes, that's precisely the problem: We need to stop the *underlying* behaviors that so often lead to the avoidance and, ultimately, the loneliness and isolation.

DRESSING DEFENSIVELY: CLOAKS OF ARMOR, VEILS OF SUSPICION, MASKS OF CHEER

The duck-and-cover strategy isn't just limited to the Walking Wounded, by the way. Even if you haven't actively opted out of the sisterhood, you still might walk with those who take a less extreme—but no less cautionary—approach to women out there. Whether one has endured a single knockout blow, cumulative indignities, or sheer annoyance from a lifetime of milder femalecentric slights, a whole lot of women are admitting they just aren't feeling inclined to open up and expose themselves to judgment and rejection in today's social climate—or wanting to take the time to let new friends into their lives. They just aren't feeling the love. These women don't actively "distrust" their own per se, but they've seen and experienced enough of the dark side to keep them from readily forming new bonds. Like their more ailing sisters, it can take a grand leap of faith before they'll trouble themselves, go out of their way, and forge new friendships.

Sure, some women are completely happy with what they have—end of story. But, I find it disturbing to hear hundreds of women say they routinely hang back, circle one another, size one another up, assess risk, audition, and even "sell" themselves as worthy friendship candidates to other women because of past experience; or say they can't be bothered with any of it and do nothing at all. In their survey commentary, too many women are using words like *cautious* and *careful* to describe dealings with, as one put it, "new, unknown, and unproven commodities." Often, they're "keeping things light," holding other women at arm's length, and "feeling a situation out" before deciding whether to put their real selves out there.

Cynthia, a fifty-one-year-old Boston tax attorney, says she actually conducts "a lengthy audition prior to admitting a woman into" her inner circle—not because she thinks she's anything special but because somewhere deep down she fears the rejection and feels that a lot of women are exclusive and judgmental. Anne, a cabdriver in her forties, thinks that most women move on from their earlier troubles of youth, but for her the memories "have permeated my adulthood." She lays low and says the friends she has are "enough." Usually, these women say, they'll keep things pleasant and shallow, put on a good "show" when they must, or offer up only bits of their real selves. Really, it seems as though women are having to prove themselves to each other like never before just to get a foot in the door.

Other women say they hang back because of what they call the more "unwelcoming spirit" among females these days. They're feeling turned off and turned away and—because all of us are busy and already have a friend or two or more—figure it's just "easier." Some women say they're feeling threatened, intimidated, unwelcome, or thrust into "ridiculous" competitions. More than one hundred respondents told me specifically they've adapted by perfecting the art of arm's-length intimacy. They remain highly discerning about who they'll pass time with, reveal limited personal information, don protective layers of cynicism and sarcasm, and project bravada, defensiveness, or aloofness, sometimes without even realizing it because they're so used to relating this way. And, of course, plenty of them are doing what I used to do: pretending or convincing themselves that none of it matters. Again and again, women told me they could no longer lightly bestow trust in other females—at least beyond the immediate circle of BFFs with whom they've grown comfortable or "known forever." They conveyed all sorts of stories about betrayal and having learned their lesson to explain why they now keep their guard up and are more careful in their interactions. Somewhere along the line, I stopped counting the number of times women used the phrases "Once bitten, twice shy," "Fool me once, shame on you, fool me twice, shame on me," and "Burned too many times."

It sounds to me like there's all sorts of under-the-table stuff going on. A whole lot of women are, apparently, limiting instead of broadening their circles, taking less time for basic civility, and plain not bothering with those they don't know well. They've got their core girlfriends, they say, and that's enough. Others are just staying home, avoiding high school reunions, book clubs, groups, certain "types" of women, gatherings with new or unknown women, or any other situation that might remind them of past trouble or trigger another round of emotional turmoil and heartache. Dozens of women explained away this behavior with that worn refrain "Who needs it?"

Again, you might well be enjoying your circle of girlfriends and on the whole feel just fine about the state of women's relationships in our society. If you find your needs are being met, you're happy, and you're behaving responsibly and remain at least somewhat open, civil, and hospitable to other women, I see nothing wrong with that—in fact, I think it's wonderful. On the other hand, maybe the broader ramifications of all this haven't occurred to you before. If you really pay attention, I suspect you'll notice at least some women around you quietly retreating, making excuses, becoming more exclusive, and even gliding through their everyday social interactions with an inauthentic, detached, or vaguely numb engagement. Or maybe you'll see how you yourself are contributing to this kind of environment. As we'll be discussing more in part III, we're an interconnected species. Our individual behaviors on some level really do contribute to the overall culture—the culture that nearly every woman responding to my survey says needs an overhaul. Even if you're feeling personally content, stay with me here: I think it's worthy of at least some consideration.

It isn't just American women living in the States experiencing this, by the way. A couple dozen women I heard from were expats, or grew up in other cultures, or experienced other societies in depth. They went out of their way to offer commentary about what they call our more "unwelcoming," "challenging," or "ultimately inauthentic" culture of women relative to others they'd experienced. Another half dozen or so said as much to me in person. They spoke of the obstacles, difficulties, and inordinate lengths of time it has taken them to make genuine friendships here compared with other countries, as well as challenges their daughters have encountered in trying to infiltrate our Girl World. American expat, Irish, Spanish, French, Filipino, Thai, Bangladeshi, Brazilian—all sorts of women told me they've gotten the impression that our society of women can seem pretty and shiny and enviable on the outside, but exclusive and sometimes superficial on the inside. As one Polish woman working as a nanny and painter in Chicago put it, "It is easy to find many faces to know here, but very hard to find souls to know." Everyone's path is different, of course; it depresses me to even write this. And, to be fair, we have no way of knowing if the problem for these women can be attributed as much to language and cultural barriers, general transitional challenges and pressures, or any number of other factors as it can to the purported incivility of the American female. Personally, the women I know from other cultures seem to have integrated beautifully—and many acknowledge similar conditions in other countries. I've seen it myself here in Thailand, where I currently live. But shouldn't we at least consider what these ladies say they've experienced? To my mind, they're offering some eye-opening, telling observations from a unique vantage point worthy of at least some degree of reflection.

In any case, with so many of us viewing the sisterhood as less than hospitable or steeped in a vague negativity—the precise antithesis of that unified, nurturing, evolved society of souls we desire and perhaps even assume we're all enjoying—it's hardly surprising to learn that even the Socially Supercompetent sometimes back away and keep things superficially airy. Think of the social butterfly who fully indulges, charming to all, ready for action. She navigates the female world with enviable ease. We think she's doing just fine. But according to some of these women themselves, they're the hardest-working gals in show business. Beneath the facade, many are treading with caution and admitting to feeling a hollow uncertainty about who their real friends are, thanks to sustained levels of superficial chitchat, reflexive put-downs, status jockeying, exclusionary games, and other unpleasant airs they've inhaled (and exhaled) through the years. Several women who place themselves in this category acknowledged their ambivalence. Their all-too-common mantra? "Aside from a few close friends, I'm not really sure where I stand."

One self-described "prominent, highly social, and well-connected" woman told me that despite her very full dance card and ostensibly charmed social life, she's tired of the posturing and isn't at all settled about her female friendships. "If I'm going to be really honest here, despite all that I have and all who I know, it's still an issue of depth," she admitted. "I can't really say who my true friends are. People would be *shocked* to know this about me, though, I'll tell you that."

Heidi, a twenty-seven-year-old travel writer, is one of those sturdy, seemingly confident, above-it-all gals who initially told me she didn't get the fuss; things didn't at all seem grim out there in Women's World. As we talked, though, she became more reflective and said that she actually did feel a vibe of unease among women she knew. By the time we finished chatting, she was laughing and acknowledging that she's pretty much always been in the business of keeping things light with women, a way of relating so entrenched that she hadn't given it much thought:

> I guess it's really true. I've never generalized and thought my friends were like the offending and annoying women of my past, and I haven't shut myself off from new friendships. But I'm *definitely* guarded and careful, which I guess isn't a great thing for women, is it?

Nicole, a middle school guidance counselor, feels less charitable, saying, "I cover my discomfort with a paste of friendliness and outgoing cheerfulness in the hopes that it's all in my head." Buying into or going along with the inauthenticity, she figures, is the cost of admission for "playing with the ladies." Sabine, a twenty-six-year-old paralegal, agrees. She calls it a game women absolutely expect other women to play: "I'm very cautious about friendships with new women now, but I play along because it's expected. I offer little, though. Who knows whether the personal information you share will get back and hurt you? The unfortunate result is that most of my relationships aren't deep. I can't really count on most of these women I call my 'friend.'"

Meanwhile, Jill, a twenty-seven-year-old personal assistant, thinks she's mastered the "routine" quite artfully.

You'd probably never know it. I can be very charming. But I'm *always* guarded and a little suspicious. I'm a big believer that women can be each other's best allies or worst enemies. We're the more manipulative gender, so I need to get to know a woman and her motives, focuses, and goals first before I'll trust her. She goes first. My comfort level depends on my perceived level of trust of another woman.

Like a lot of women, Jill sounds matter of fact and even "okay" with this unnatural style of relating. Trouble is, it isn't just Jill. It's others in Jill's orbit and beyond, too, and this is what concerns me. Sooner or later, it seems, this limiting, vaguely suspicious, inhospitable climate continues to radiate outward; we become more complacent in our existing girlfriendships, more exclusive, and less integrated and congenial. This seems particularly probable given our multitasking, mobile, increasingly fractured, scattered, and tech-reliant society. What will society be, eventually? Will it come to resemble some futuristic sci-fi setup, where we all become a bunch of busy, emotionally closed off, inhospitable shells who take only passing, superficial, and suspicious interest in women outside our immediate, carefully selected orbits—with little trace of the more connected, supportive, nurturing, tending, and befriending creatures who once roamed the earth?

A lot of us, meanwhile, are coping with our ambivalence by simply limiting the type or extent of information we give up, since, as Marion Underwood has warned, the shared confidences often come back to betray or hurt us later. Colleen, a thirty-nine-year-old pilot, explained how her "secrets and sensitive personal stuff were so often thrown back in my face in a negative light that I learned it was foolish *not* to keep my cards close to the vest." Keeping an arm's-length distance, these women say, minimizes the risk that their ego, psyche, and self-confidence will take a hit. It also, unfortunately, injects their relationships with a more hollow and inauthentic air. Take thirty-three-year-old Brenda, a physician in Kansas, who admits to "keeping it light" socially and giving precious little of herself to other women:

I'm much "tighter" now with my heart, less trusting. I'm hesitant, afraid to be honest, nervous. I don't feel like I "truly" know any of them and don't feel like they "truly" know me. I'm not sure I want them to know me. I'm afraid it will give them too much power over me . . . But I hate being superficial too, so it's kind of lose-lose.

To be sure, one of the most compelling bits of ancillary feedback I've received in working on this project, as I laid out in chapter 3, is women's increasing frustration with fake and inauthentic social situations and "all the bullshit"; they're tired of going through those motions. Dozens spoke of a subtle pressure to wear smiles at all costs, even as they're feeling anxious, self-conscious, or plain disinterested, even when things aren't all that great, even when it's all hanging by a thread. The irony, a couple of them noted, is that they're not to seem *too* perfect or happy. As one anonymous survey respondent puts it, "Vanilla. Keep it middle-of-the-road vanilla. Not too happy, rich, or perfect, not too whiny or frumpy."

Some refuse to play along. Ally, a literary agent, knows it isn't the best work tactic, but in her personal relationships, she just can't bring herself "to fake kindness to the women who are fake. I'd rather have no relationships than fake relationships." Sometimes, Ally and these other respondents lament, it just takes too much work not to be yourself and too much effort to have to prove yourself worthy to other women just to advance to the next level, particularly if they already have girlfriends, family, or other sources of comfort and company to turn to. Dozens of women told me how refreshing—and surprising—it is when they come across a woman who keeps it completely real. And all I can think is, *Wow, it's come to this: refreshing and surprising to find a woman being real?*

Avoiding certain situations, holding women at arm's length, and keeping things light are certainly some of the more common strategies women say they use to cope with their annoyance, frustration, and distrust of women. As we'll see, though, sometimes it's not so much about all women but more about the *type* of woman—or number of women—that can scare us off.

CHAPTER 6

TRIBES AND PACKS
AND CLIQUES, OH MY!

Groupthink turns otherwise normal girls and women into hideous, evil hags. Just say no!
—Adrienne, fifty-four, television producer

Literally hundreds of women told me they weren't bypassing female intimacy altogether as a result of past trouble, just the situations where women congregate in packs. Thought you all were cozy at that last book club? Maybe, maybe not. Sororities, book groups, fitness class, Mommy & Me, women's writing salons, philanthropic socializing, the cocktail party circuit, PTA, feminist forums, the pick-up/drop-off spot at school—you name it—women in your midst are citing all of these as potential mine fields of bad memories, anxiety, and unpleasant groupthink. Scores of women, even those who are otherwise comfortable with females one-on-one, said they recoiled from group camaraderie. This isn't surprising when you consider that nearly 60 percent of my survey respondents said they'd suffered from group or clique cruelty at one point or another. As one woman responding to my concerns wrote on the website Jezebel:

Large groups of women—post–high school—scare the crap out of me. Someone has to be the "est" in a group: skinniest, fattest, richest, poorest, oldest, youngest, etc. It makes me break out in hives trying to avoid all the comparisons and judginess. My handful of great girlfriends is all I need.

Many of these women said they actually avoided optional group activity whenever they could, preferring to indulge in a more one-on-one brand of relating. Several echoed the sentiments of Michelle, an agricultural lobbyist in her late twenties who told me she's quietly harbored "semi-posttraumatic types of issues around groups of women" for years thanks to bad high school memories. She says the women in her line of work tend to only reinforce those fears. Rose, the woman still carrying remnants of her 1970s sorority nightmare with her, says she's moved on with her life but "joining groups of women is a big decision for me, giving me pause even thirty years later." Nancy, meanwhile, an engineer in her early forties, say she's "extremely selective" in deciding who she spends time with, habitually avoiding women's clubs, exercise classes, and any volunteer situations that would put her in contact with groups of women, because they make her uncomfortable "every time," she says.

Amy, a thirty-six-year-old middle school librarian, says she can't think of a group female experience that *hasn't* been unpleasant to some degree. Discussing the women she knew in college, she says that those who made it into certain circles of exclusivity and popularity seemed to become "different people altogether," doing what they felt "they must" to preserve their status. "It was usually anything but pretty behavior," she says. Kelsey, a woman responding to my *Times* piece on the blog Feministe, says she just can't stomach or embrace the catty and ugly dynamic that so often pervades a group setting:

> As a child, I attended an all-girls summer camp and had the time of my life until A Certain Age, when cattiness and malice seemed to blossom from a void in space. My tent-mates and then my entire "tribe" decided I was a lesbian and stole my things, filled my sleeping bag with shaving cream, and constantly made a point to keep me an outsider and laugh at me. Through junior high, high school, and still into college, I have a hard time relating to young women in groups.

Given that I'd written about my own traumatic sorority experience, it's not surprising that I heard from over one hundred women about sorority life in detail, as well as all-girls schools and summer girls' camp—stories of sisterly love at its best and sisterly love gone very wrong. Like me, many say they recognize in hindsight that the particular brand of group identification they were going for just wasn't the right fit for them. Hilary, a middle school teacher, says her sorority beat up on her for having the "temerity to be the sole advocate, in a secret, mandatory meeting convened by the sorority's president," for a sister who they'd unfairly victimized. She was accused of "undermining the group's values and its image within the Greek community" and to this day feels comfortable with women only on a one-on-one basis. Don't hate the messenger here, but more than a couple dozen women insisted that they'll never allow daughters to pledge sororities or attend girls' camp.

Still, let's be clear: Groupings of females aren't inherently toxic entities. By their very nature, it's pretty hard to get close and enjoy great substance or depth with another person in a group setting, whether all female or otherwise. It's also important to recall that female tribes, clans, and packs have enjoyed a healthy and positive evolutionary significance that probably still drives our herding instincts. Group identification has, after all, yielded crucial dividends like a sense of belonging, intimacy, protection from predators, and access to resources, along with psychological bonding, security, and other support that's helped us survive in the wild. As Judith V. Jordan, a clinical psychologist at Wellesley College's Stone Center for Developmental Services and Studies, has explained, even the dreaded cliques aren't in and of themselves bad. They can lend a "strong sense of bonding and mutual support" and be important, if magnified, manifestations of our "intense desire to connect." Plus, as most of us know, convening in packs can be great fun. Just ask any community quilter.

In fact, I'm thinking seriously about finding a quilting group for the communal aspects and health benefits alone. I've spoken with more than a dozen quilters now, and although this is pure speculation, might those who quilt together be the most peaceful, satisfied, and fulfilled women in America? It's like they've found an answer to the madness without really trying—by going back to basics. Think about it: As we've dispersed and gone more mobile with our careers and personal interests, we've become so much more fragmented and isolated, our ties so much more attenuated, even with cellphones and Skype. In the midst of it all, these women—friends and family of all ages and generations—come together to share their art, creative self-expression, and positive camaraderie in a calm, supportive, all-female ritual. Of course, being a quilter isn't necessarily the *reason* these women are good to one another; quilters probably have their sinister, petty side just like the rest of us. Maybe they secretly resent the master quilters among them. Maybe the women of the Gee's Bend, Alabama, quiltmaking collective let fame go to their heads and nearly unraveled after all the fuss. But I've certainly heard none of that. Really, it's hard not to admire the built-in support, nurturing, mentoring, welcoming spirit, familiarity, and shared accomplishment these women say they enjoy. It sure sounds like the kind of sisterhood I'd like to be a part of.

Meanwhile, back at the ranch. As many of us know firsthand, groups can and often do turn sour and become petri dishes of wickedness that make *Lord of the Flies* look tame. They become toxic, Dr. Jordan explains, when the focus is on excluding others, which often arises when individuals within the group worry "about how loved or cared about they are." I would add that any group that rabidly emphasizes the "Greater Good" at the expense of the individual presents an always-dicey proposition. Indeed, exclusive clusters of females can be hideously intimidating to both the insider and the outsider. Even those who seemed to be the socially savviest among my survey pool said they'd experienced groupthink to be "scary stuff." Excessive loyalty to the group—joined together and reinforced not just through identification of who they are but by who they are *not*—is inherently problematic. You sure wouldn't want to lose your hard-earned status and be rendered a have-not. Or worse: an outsider.

Look at Elaine, the main character in Margaret Atwood's *Cat's Eye*. Once she found acceptance with her group of girlfriends, Atwood writes, she became "terrified of losing them." So she does what a lot of us do: whatever is necessary to avoid committing "irreparable sin" and getting herself cast out. A sound strategy, perhaps, for as evolutionary psychiatrists have emphasized, rejection from one's clan has for centuries been considered one of life's greatest emotional disasters—a threat to survival and a very death sentence to some. For humans, rejection is, in fact, understood to feel just as bad as physical pain. A UCLA neuroimaging study of people who had endured social exclusion revealed that the areas of the brain activated by this kind of emotional pain were the very same areas affected by physical pain. This, researchers say, helps explain why it literally "hurts" so very much when we lose social support and meaningful human connections in our lives. Experts at the San Francisco organization No Bully also think it explains why exclusion can cause even greater lasting damage than physical violence, placing the excluded person on a path toward isolation, depression, anxiety, and further social conflict.

I can certainly relate to all this. At age eighteen, my desire to find a niche or community at a large university two thousand miles from home is what initially drove me toward sorority rush, a process I knew absolutely nothing about beyond a brief notice in university welcome materials. I wanted to fit in, sure, and gain some sort of status from these "popular" young women. I was willing to conform to the extent necessary. I can forgive myself now for trying to get these things from the particular sorority house (or "institutionalized clique," as some have called them) that, for whatever reason, seemed alluring at the time. It might have had something to do with the beer and boys—but I've no doubt it was more about the women. Whatever the case, I craved acceptance from them, willingly adhered to their customs and mores, trusted them, and relied on them for reciprocal nurturing and nourishment. Then reality intervened, I made the mistake of drinking too much one night, bad things happened, and groupthink reared its head. I was deemed dirty, unworthy, unwanted, and was summarily banished from the very tribe I'd hoped and even assumed might comfort me during a difficult time.

It all sounds so dramatic now. And so it was. Yes, I was an idiot for getting drunk at a frat house, but I'm not going to sugarcoat things: These women behaved abominably in adjudicating my fate, like holier-than-thou hypocrites. They left me shell-shocked and cowering—at the time, I imagine some of them probably hoped for that. It has to be the closest you can get to the torch-wielding mob of *Frankenstein* in real life. And yet, despite my residual discomfort with women, I haven't carried around a corrosive bitterness or resentment toward those girls. I was a willing participant, after all. I booked a room at the slaughterhouse, happy to dance attendance on their every whim pursuant to their arbitrary, mostly silly rules. The majority of those girls were decent people one-on-one.

Sadly, I can't even sit here and assure you with 100 percent certainty that I wouldn't have done the same to another girl in my shoes. I'm inclined to think not, but, as my former philosophy professor reminded me recently, peer influence and group identification can be omnipotent, blinding forces, especially when you're young, feeling lost, and searching for an identity—and there's no one stepping in to set things straight. It can create a perfect storm for mayhem and, as humans, we're going to behave and react in some less-than-admirable ways. Leaving aside the issue of rape and men for now, all I know for sure is that the hopes and expectations I brought to the sorority banquet set me up for a loss of innocence and one colossal letdown. The casting out obviously cut deep and left me with the kind of scar tissue I wouldn't wish on anyone. Skittish around groups? Yes, I definitely get that.

But, again, what did we really know in youth? Were we thinking of anyone, really, besides ourselves and the group? We thrived on status and power. In our frenzied rush to find acceptance and bond with other insecure souls, most of us probably didn't have a clue that we were trampling on others. Jodi, a forty-six-year-old architect, says she's not all that apologetic for the so-called sins she may have perpetrated while among the young and the clueless:

> I think the reason I never apologized as an adult was that I felt it was something that happened when we were kids and not necessarily in control of our feelings. There was a group mentality that was bigger than us, one we didn't know how to handle. Many of us were struggling with pressures or issues at home. In some ways, I think we were dealing with our feelings by taking out our aggressions on each other. Not cool, but that's cliquethink for you.

We certainly shouldn't excuse or write off the evils of groupthink, but recognizing that the membership of most any tribe is often comprised of the misguided, confused, and frightened goes a long way in helping us understand and forgive the nefarious happenings that occurred on the group's watch. A culture of hurtful exclusivity, bile, and ugliness shouldn't stand, but, at the same time, bitterness among the fallen ones is hardly productive. In other words, it's complicated.

In the final analysis, maybe I should have known that the culture of the particular sorority I joined was more frivolous, hedonistic, and punishingly elitist than the others on offer. Though it was the eighties, and really bad things raged seemingly throughout college campuses everywhere, I think that's a distinct possibility. In my hindsight brilliance, sure, I'd love to reach back to the young Kelly and whisper, *Oh, no, no, dear. This one isn't quite right for you; it'll undermine the essence of who you are. Let's look elsewhere.* But, alas, for most of us, youthful indiscretion, bad judgment, and poor choices are almost inalienable rights.

TYPECASTING

After avoiding groups, steering clear of certain "types" came next on the list of common ways that women say they've adapted or managed in the wake of intrafemale negativity. Now, to be clear, sometimes we just have less in common with a given woman. Maybe we fail to make a connection and gravitate elsewhere. No harm, no foul. And, clearly there is a lot of unsavory generalizing going on when you're fingering an entire species of women as objectionable. (The sheer number of times the term "girly girl" came up in survey responses was pretty depressing. I'm not even sure I know what a "girly girl" is, exactly.) Still, the links between past trouble and present views and attitudes about females and the patterns I'm seeing among women's responses are undeniable. The most recurring "categories" or "types" women said they avoided with regularity, in order of frequency, were:

- Girly girls
- Aggressive, power-obsessed alpha women
- Stepford types: women fixated on status and material things
- Pretty cheerleader types, trophy wives, or cliquey women
- Flashy, unserious, or frivolous women
- Women who are thinner
- Wealthy women who conspicuously flaunt it
- Anyone who makes me feel frumpy or dumb

Really, I have to believe that most of us appear on this list some-where. The bottom line, it seems to me, is that any woman who re-minds us of past unpleasantness is, in the drama of our own minds, guilty by association and a potential trigger of trouble. Anyone who reminds us we're not quite measuring up in a way we'd like is likewise threatening: These women confirm our worst fears by their mere ex-istence. It's been pretty surprising to hear women admit so candidly that, fairly or not, they just plain avoid any woman who strikes them as smarter, thinner, prettier, wealthier, better educated, better styl-ized, better traveled, better read, or more accomplished because it makes them uncomfortable and feel "less than." By the same token, it's demoralizing to hear women so blanketly dismiss other women (or categories of women) as dumb, frivolous, uncultured, or otherwise in-ferior before they've even given them a chance—the old judging-the-book-by-its-cover tic. But, again, that's the beauty of offering an anonymous survey for women to come clean and vent. They don't hold back.

Julie, a thirty-two-year-old stay-at-home mom of three, thinks that our insecurities really have the potential for bringing out the worst in us, turning us into "petty, judgmental shrews." Rather than giving a woman the benefit of the doubt or a chance to show her col-ors, we too often assume the worst, dismiss her out of hand, and turn away. It can be completely irrational when we think about it—we know that. But it's far easier, for example, to avoid one's perceived nemesis and the attendant sense of inferiority than to deal with her or let her prove you wrong. Sandy, who moved capably and rapidly through the ranks of her male-dominated banking firm and enjoys her male friendships, illustrates this conundrum. Being around those in her neighborhood women's club, which is filled with "gorgeous, personal trainer–sculpted, stay-at-home moms," she says, brought up things from the past and left her feeling crummy about herself every time, just as she had back in college around ultra-attractive women. The gossip and backbiting she encountered among them didn't help matters. She "didn't need it," she figured. Sandy convinced herself that she was on a higher intellectual plane and found the fix easy enough: She simply made excuses and stopped showing up. The other women, quite understandably, eventually stopped inviting her. Sandy calls it "a blessing and a curse," since she thinks it would have been nice to connect. Though she does have her regrets ("Yeah, it was irrational. Most of them are probably great women"), she says she hasn't dwelled on it too much. Still, it's too bad; sounds like a lose-lose scenario that didn't have to be.

It does strike me as perfectly normal, of course, to feel awkward as a newcomer, anytime we don't know someone, or anytime the surrounding women seem already bonded in some way. What is unusual, though, is the tenor of women's commentary. There's so much unabashed stereotyping, disdain, generalizing, and dismissiveness flowing forth, much of which women attribute to past dealings with a particular type of woman. There's also, as we saw with Julie, some underlying elitism and self-congratulatory back-patting seeping through. Fran, for instance, a math professor, believes she's more the "thinking" type, someone who boasts superior values compared to the superficial girly girls who drive her crazy and with whom she can't be bothered:

> I'm girly, but I get uncomfortable around real girly girls. I find they normally don't mesh with my personality due to my more nonsuperficial values. I mesh best with girls who aren't superficial or drama oriented; my best girl friends all match this description. I just can't have an authentic female friendship with someone who's a stereotypical girly girl inside and out.

Debbie, a department store clerk in her thirties, says she'll never forget the "popular" girls who teased and excluded her incessantly in middle school. No doubt about it, she says, it's the "pretty, well-dressed, social types" who have invariably intimidated her into and throughout her adulthood. She figures it's now "embedded self-consciously into my brain that those types of girls just are out to get me." She copes by staying away.

Again, I am not endorsing, accepting, dissing, or otherwise judging these women's personal feelings one way or another. I aim to merely illustrate the insidious, divisive thinking that goes on beneath the veneer—just another unfortunate manifestation of the fallout from our shadow-side tendencies. Which brings me to the "unthinkable": preferring to fill the void by passing one's time with those of the male persuasion.

OPTING FOR THE COMPANY OF MEN

Another common, if definitely controversial, adaptation strategy involves throwing in the towel with females and turning to men for friendship. Now, certainly some women just prefer the company of men in the first instance. But we're talking about something else here. Hundreds of women—even those who haven't entirely given up on their own gender—told me that thanks to their negative dalliances with fellow females, they're finding liaisons with men more straightforward, authentic, less complicated, appealingly low maintenance, and simpler all around. Lucy, a twenty-seven-year-old waitress, puts it this way: "There's none of the bullshit with men. You always know where you stand." Tilda, an "underemployed" writer in her thirties, says much the same:

> In my sixth decade, I still favor the companionship of men over women and have stayed very much at arm's length from cliques or clubs of ladies . . . I guess I just have more trust in the way I'll be treated by a male.

Laura, a network news producer, tells me that middle school and a "backstabbing coworker" put her on a path of distrust when it came to females and a preference for men:

> Though I do have close women friends, I too have sometimes felt more anxiety about women than men, particularly women in packs. I didn't last long in a group of new moms, mostly sit with the dads at soccer games, and still stay away from all-women book clubs and Pampered Chef parties.

Mari, meanwhile, says that even at the tender age of seventeen, after all the travails and high school girl drama, she just finds it "easier to enjoy myself when in the company of boys." There are a lot of Maris out there. These young girls say that even though they may have girlfriends, hanging with guys can be refreshing because they "don't feel judged the way they do around girls." (The irony here is that some girls will judge them all the more for the time they spend with boys.) Many respondents say they're tired of walking on eggshells and feel emotionally safer with guys, though at least a quarter of them admit that it's a less filling substitute for a girlfriend. Collie, an MBA student, tells me the reason she didn't say female friendships were "extremely" important on my survey was because after being burned by women, she's finding herself enjoying male companionship equally as well, or even better:

> I didn't say "extremely" because I would rather hang out with my boyfriend of two years. We have a very relaxed relationship free from a lot of petty drama. It's also nice to have girl time. But to me it is not the end-all . . . Too much girl time gets to me, personally. Males and male relationships (friends or boyfriends) sometimes give you a good mental break from the chaos.

Others are turned off by what they call the petty or "frivolous" behaviors and interests of women, so they believe they just have more in common with guys. As one anonymous blogger put it in discussing my *Times* piece:

> Girlfriends can be so high maintenance. Sometimes, at the end of a long day, I'd rather just bro-down with the boys and a beer rather than listening to one of my girlfriends prattle on and on about the same dude who has done her wrong, and she's still dating him, and yada yada yada . . . I guess I am just very selective. If that makes me a hater, well, so be it.

Another woman commenting on my article wrote on Jezebel that despite her placid sorority experience and girlfriends, she'd be the first to admit she prefers guyfriends:

> Less drama, less competition, less whining about stupid shit and less emotional wah-wah overall. Maintaining female

friendships takes a lot more energy than I'm willing to exert for the most part . . . I hate to say it, but there are very few normal, down-to-earth, interesting women out there to be friends with. Sad but true.

Other women described a subtle, perhaps subconscious, tension that grips them when they're in the company of women, often because they've been judged or sized up so brutally in the past that they don't know how to conduct themselves naturally anymore—so, again, advantage men. In *Cat's Eye*, Atwood sums up this sensibility in Elaine. She's curious about other girls, she's read about them in books, and she wants a girlfriend. But she isn't used to them; she doesn't yet know their social code. Once they surround her, in the flesh, she's self-conscious and uncomfortable:

> My relationships with boys are effortless, which means that I put very little effort into them. It's girls I feel awkward with, it's girls I feel I have to defend myself against; not boys.
>
> . . .
>
> I know the unspoken rules of boys, but with girls I sense that I am always on the verge of some unforeseen, calamitous blunder.

Sadly, these are the very same types of worries the fictional Elaine—and the vast sea of women who've shared similar anxieties with me—still utter years later in adulthood. But, as one might imagine, hanging with men doesn't sit well with some. The online lifestyle guide DailyCandy has a defined term for it: "GhaG—n. Acronym. Girl-hating Girl. The one whose only friends are guys." Even Anna Quindlen has weighed in on these "man's woman" types:

> There is a kind of woman, usually called a "man's woman," who always seems to see other women as competition or furniture, whose orientation is always toward the XY chromosomes in the room. Maybe all of us become that kind of woman for a time.

The actress-director Drew Barrymore says she plain doesn't "trust women who don't go to their girlfriends." Kara, a twenty-one-year-old student and painter, agrees:

> I've know a few women my age who claim they "hate girls" and mainly hang out with dudes. However, it's not like the men bring them intimacy, emotional support, and other things that we women have been conditioned as experts in. How can you instantly hate 50 percent of the population? I understand this behavior as a defense mechanism, but it seems like these women are the ones who "start it" with other women in the first place; at least in my experience. By claiming they hate other females, they're just placing other women in the social setting "below" them. It's a domination tactic, it's hierarchical, it's poisonous, divisive, and sad.

It shouldn't really matter to anyone that you prefer to hang out with guys, women, or even animals. If people are content in their friendships, fantastic. Still, shouldn't it bother us that a considerable number of women have grown so uncomfortable, have been so hurt, or are so frustrated with the darker or "frivolous" intrafemale dynamics that they're feeling squeezed out or otherwise forced to look elsewhere for companionship? It bothers me. Too many women are saying the same things here. It doesn't sound to me like they—most of them, anyway—are turning to men because they "hate" women or feel superior to them. In this respect, the snap judgments of Drew and Kara may well be missing the mark for a lot of these women. To me, it's just another unfortunate manifestation of sisterly love gone wrong and our quiet attempts to cope.

CHAPTER 7

REMNANTS OF DENIAL, DISTRACTION, DEPRESSION, AND WORSE

I am trying to stop living in "fear" but truthfully wonder whether I'm really living—or just hiding. It's amazing how quickly those feelings can transport you right back to the past. I just don't want to go there again.

—Carla, thirty-seven, computer programmer, San Francisco

Through this process, I've learned that you really just never know who among you might be feeling quietly anxious, self-conscious, frustrated, annoyed, or plain turned off by their female peers. More often than not, though, it's that charming ad executive, seemingly unflappable litigator, or happy-go-lucky mom in your book club. Several women have come clean with me—and with themselves—by admitting that they've mastered the "cover-up" or convinced themselves it doesn't matter, all the while trusting females less and less and turning away from them more and more. At least a hundred women gave me separate, specific commentary on this issue alone, saying they realized as they took the survey just how much they'd consciously or unconsciously denied, buried, and distracted themselves from their gender-based hurts and ambivalence. Terry, a woman in her sixties, wonders whether that means "we end up being more self-sufficient and less needy," or whether we're simply building stoic shells of protection and keep ourselves moving—with less real intimacy and fewer connections to show for it. It's a valid question.

SECURING PANDORA'S BOX WITH . . . BAND-AIDS?

Like any other unpleasant experience we try to forget or outrun, women are revealing a kitchen-sink array of busying activities, everything from work, exercise, and travel to marriage, kids, religion, and vigorous intellectual and professional pursuits—whatever's distracted them or helped them forget about it. They've moved away, run away, denied anxiety, denied the past, and hoped to hell the Band-Aids stay on for the sake of the kids, their marriages, and themselves, all the while getting little in the way of substantive friendship with other women. Remember how 43 percent of all survey respondents said they actively suppress or even hide their "anxieties, fears, difficulties, struggles, and/or true feelings about other women"? Well, several of them elaborated on that thought, explaining that it's not *just* about embarrassment or shame—it's about not getting stuck and simply getting through the day-to-day. Some women explained a sustained need to keep their ghosts, skeletons, and unhealed misery reined in. Plenty of others said they hadn't really looked at their life paths this way before but, in thinking through the issues, could indeed see how their run-ins with females may have played a role in some of their life choices.

Again, we're not talking oddball recluses here. Most of these women sound like they're perfectly sociable and "just fine." They're accomplished, admired, well-liked people who by all appearances "have it together" and are excelling in other areas of their lives. They tell me they haven't advertised their anxieties, worn them on their sleeves, or actively dwelled on them. Instead, by their own admission, they've masked or shelved their struggles and awkwardness behind busy lives and superficial social maneuverings. Some are embarrassed by the notion of feeling tentative within the gender and take great comfort in learning there are others out there feeling the same way. Take Maureen, a self-described lonely but wary thirty-three-year-old photographer, who says she yearns for the kind of female friendships she assumes "every other woman" enjoys but, thanks to past troubles and residual insecurities, finds it hard to reach out and open up. She says she settles for anonymous, surrogate intimacy via online women's blogs and is certain there's "something wrong" with her. But she also sounds relieved to know there are others experiencing a similar ambivalence, something she "never would have imagined." I know the feeling. As another woman from my survey puts it, "I know I feel a lot less like a freak now that I know it isn't just me" feeling uncomfortable beneath the surface.

Katherine, the university professor we visited earlier, says she *knows* her past experiences with women have messed with her confidence in completely "irrational" ways and left her feeling hypersensitive around women. Like so many others have said, she knows she'd benefit from probing the origins of her distrust and what she calls her "borderline social ineptitude." She knows that putting herself out there and creating new, more favorable experiences with women would help erase the bad. She admits to feeling lonely and wanting greater depth to her female connections. But, she says, she's too busy. She also sounds adamantly reluctant to risk clouding current relationships and productivity by pausing to really think about it. So she plods along.

The psychotherapist and newspaper columnist Polly Drew has explained how distrust and denial can affect even the most solid and best intended among us. In the *Milwaukee Journal Sentinel,* she wrote how some hurtful and embarrassing incidents among women she considered intimates "turned [her] world of girlfriendship upside down" and planted seeds of mistrust with women for the long haul. Even two years out, she found herself feeling shy and careful. "Rather than trying to navigate the voyage of new friendships, I took a pass," she admitted. The self-described "pro-woman" Drew says that although she still had female friends to turn to, she nonetheless felt alone, wary, and easily hurt around other women. Her coping strategy of choice—denial—rings all too familiar:

> I told myself that having close women friends was overrated, that "women always being there for each other" was bunk made up by Hollywood and Hallmark.

Chantal, a fifty-year-old personal organizer, is the kind of outwardly put-together woman most of us would admire and consider fulfilled. She and her husband are financially sound, just completed construction on the lake home of their dreams, are "best friends," and enjoy close relationships with their two successful kids and grand-child. It sounds ideal, except that Chantal's lonely and admits to want-ing "greater depth in relationships with women." She says she's never really had girlfriends—no walking partner, no book clubs, no lun-cheons, no pal to ring up about life's ups and downs and little noth-ings. And yet, like Katherine, she says she can't imagine indulging these feelings much. She's too busy with family and life in general to deal with her wariness, reach out, and find women she can trust and open up to again. So she goes without.

Then there's Lila, a gregarious realtor in Miami, who says she'd probably benefit from probing the origins of her distrust so she can forge more authentic and intimate female relationships. She admits, though, that it's very hard to talk about and worries that even pausing to acknowledge her past—beyond "taking the hour on an anonymous survey"—could cause a meltdown. Serena, a pastry chef, confided that she felt embarrassed just *taking* the survey. She started typing "No" to all the questions relating to intrafemale trouble and lingering emo-tional issues and considered just quitting. Then she realized she "was kidding myself" and actually went back to amend her responses to better reflect the truth. Like many who took the survey, Serena says it was "weird" to realize just how much she'd actually written women off on the emotional front in her effort to preserve appearances and all-around momentum in life.

Other women said they didn't know they had a phantom anxiety, or didn't appreciate the extent of their unprocessed wounds, until a triggering event or ghost from the past forced them to confront them. When those ghosts and triggers do rear their heads, though, it can be overwhelming. Happiness and living well won't necessarily safeguard us from the emotional assaults that reopened memories can deal. Take Nancy, an unemployed teacher, who thinks it's amazing how "you can go through life and do good things and be happy and suddenly be re-minded of your past, cut down to nothing again, and made to feel like an insecure nothing from a Podunk town." Or Alicia, a self-described seemingly got-it-all, twenty-nine-year-old radiology fellow, who found that her hard-won successes and professional stature didn't in-sulate her from the insults of online social networking more than a decade after high school:

[It] didn't stop the inevitable heartache and vomit-inducing stomach gripes when Facebook reared its ugly head and all these ghosts from my past started looking me up, wanting to be "friends" with me—or worse, still not wanting to be friends with me and having to experience the rejection all over again.

Leora Tanenbaum reveals an important truth in *Slut!*, a book that conveys the experiences of girls and women stigmatized as "sluts" at various points in life. Tanenbaum says that what hurt her most when she personally endured this brand of harassment was how "girls were the first to point a finger at me." She coped by sequestering herself in shame and feeling haunted by it all for years, donning baggy clothing, avoiding eye contact and social encounters, crying a lot, seeking therapy for depression, and, eventually, throwing herself into her studies. "I began to tackle each assignment with vigorous determination . . . [and] retaliated by insisting that people regard me for my intellectual worth," she says. "My intellect became a form of damage control."

Dozens of women echoed Tanenbaum's reflections through their own stories. One doesn't need an epic life trauma to feel motivated to succeed, of course, and plenty reported the opposite fate. Still, it was surprising to hear so many grounded and accomplished women say that their difficulties with females actually motivated them to transcend their past by "doing better," working or studying harder, or chasing their personal definition of success all the harder. Cynthia, the Boston tax attorney, thinks this has to be a common trajectory with women like her. "The way we're treated by our female friends has such a profound and lasting effect on our self-esteem. I wonder if there aren't a lot more women like me who choose to become professionals in an effort to regain control after being crushed by girls."

Cynthia may be on to something. Among the dozens of women who shared accounts of early brokenness and struggles, many revealed themselves to be so-called driven, type A, professional types. While none of them would want to repeat the experiences or see a daughter endure the same twisted path to success, more than a few attributed their drive to this rising-from-the-ashes brand of motivation, explaining how they'd gained quiet satisfaction by regaining the control they'd relinquished to others in the past. A couple of them do seem to harbor a rough, somewhat vengeful edge about it, revealing a sort of "living well is the best revenge" or "I'll show them" catalyst. Claudia, for example, a fifty-two-year-old school administrator, says she "developed a thick skin and strong cynicism" on her path to success thanks to her troubles with other females. Most, however, at least *sound* as though they've adopted a more positive, goal-oriented mindset, intuitively recognizing that *they* were the ones holding the power to reinvent themselves and dictate the terms of how others would view them.

These Pandora-like struggles are something I certainly relate to. After my sorority 86ed me, I mostly kept to myself, hiding in the stacks and carrels of libraries (sometimes studying, sometimes messing around and reading magazines), or hiding between the headphones of my Sony Walkman—anything that allowed me to escape socializing or the potentially critical eye of fellow females. I could have called on my family or Teri, who quietly stuck by me throughout my ordeal, but I felt exposed even with them. I made some friends here and there but invariably kept them at arm's length. I'm still not sure why I didn't just pack up, transfer schools, or head home. Instead, I changed majors, took up a more rigorous course of study, buckled down, and burrowed in. Looking back, I'm sure I subconsciously hoped that by hitting the books, becoming a lawyer, and, later, immersing myself in domesticity and a multitasking "be it all/have it all" frenzy—balancing a demanding job with traditional roles of wife and mother of four, obsessive world travel, and all the suburban trimmings—I might legitimize my life, silence the lingering doubts and insecurities, and bring closure on my eviction ordeal. Truly, it tires me out just thinking about it. And it's my own life.

I now have the clarity of hindsight and maturity to see that for nearly two decades, I rushed about like the proverbial headless chicken, hoping to forget and outrun it all. But, as Ricky Fitts wisecracked in the film *American Beauty*, "Never underestimate the power of denial." I got away with it for a good long stretch, all right, but only until I bumped into one of my former sorority sister-tormentors at a local Gymboree store twenty-odd years after the fact. Neither my defensive armor of wit and cynicism, nor the otherwise fulfilling life I'd constructed, could stave off the rush of suppressed shame in that moment. I suppose I'd just been postponing the inevitable. In the end, I'd have to agree with the mental health professionals who insist that one's "stuff" does tend to catch up with you.

INTO THE ABYSS

And still, some women definitely don't "get" women who feel burned and wary. They're unable to grasp how anyone can get so hung up on how other women view or treat them. Others don't understand why we all just can't relax, move on, and view the whole of womankind as rosy and fabulous—as if willing us to be one big, happy, unified community of souls or pretending it to be so actually makes it so. To some, it's a black-and-white scenario: The world is full of keepers, grab the good ones, dodge and sever ties with the bad, move on. Sounds straightforward enough. But, again, if I've learned anything through my own continued struggles and the voices of all these other women, it's that few who've wrestled with gender-related troubles want to hold on to it or deal with it. Few of the women I heard from seem comfortable with these lingering anxieties. In other words, it's not the security blanket one might think. You yourself might be an uber-resilient, hardy soul, but please try not to judge so fast. For a lot of women, it isn't always a simple matter of picking oneself up, dusting off, manufacturing an instant trust or social prowess, and skipping along the merry path of female intimacy.

Again, we've seen Phyllis Chesler, Cheryl Dellasega, Lyn Mikel Brown, Rachel Simmons, and many others in this field forecast the likelihood of hidden and lasting fallout from relational aggression. They've cited the possibility of enduring anxiety, depression, eating disorders, loneliness, and, tragically, suicide. And now, along with all the compelling research on the long-term effects of childhood bullying that has emerged, my survey results certainly seem to confirm their fears. As anyone who probes the issues will find, these ordeals affect females of all ages, types, and backgrounds. Consider the author and former *Washington Post* columnist Leslie Morgan Steiner. She's written beautifully about women and plainly enjoys extremely loving relationships with them. But she's also been honest enough to admit that she's been through the emotional wringer with them, too:

This competitiveness of the female tribe led me to a teen-age bout with anorexia, endless hours wasted trying to get a 360° view of my butt in the mirror, and four years at Harvard proving that I was smart even if I'd failed in my quest to be physically perfect. It's not the kind of interior monologue that makes one feel particularly fine about the fairer sex. But I've never been able to rid myself of this need to judge women, including—perhaps most of all—myself.

I think it's useful to consider what it's like to stand in the shoes of one of the truly broken-spirited women who revealed her pain to me, just to gain a firsthand appreciation of how someone who suffered near-knockout blows to her self-worth might have difficulty pulling herself out of it and trusting women again. The stats and stories are deeply demoralizing and, in some cases, nothing short of chilling. You'll recall, after all, that nearly half of the women from my survey pool who reported female trouble also acknowledged that their gender-based suffering might rise to the level of lasting distress, pain, trauma, and/or emotional scarring. These women have endured low self-esteem (73 percent), isolation and loneliness (63 percent), lack of motivation or concentration (21 percent), vulnerability or feelings of exposure with other women (42 percent), and feelings of shame or worthlessness (42 percent). Many of them call these wounds "deep and profound." Few have discussed these issues openly—ever.

Nearly one thousand women said they have struggled with short- or long-term depression and/or sought counseling as a result of in-trafemale trouble. In a survey of three thousand random women, that staggers the mind. Another several hundred said they've blunted their pain through eating disorders, substance abuse, self-mutilation, and even suicidal fantasies. I'm sitting on stories from women who say they've self-medicated and numbed themselves with everything from Ben & Jerry's, to illegal or prescription drugs, to red wine benders—and gotten up the next day to make class, argue a motion, get the kids breakfast, or close a deal just like anyone else. Some refused themselves any depth of emotion for years. And while almost none of these women sounds bitter—to a large extent, they've internalized it all—many sound hopeless.

It's tough for me to adequately convey and for most any of us to truly grasp the depth of these hidden wounds. Consider Kendra, a successful ad executive, who says that after being wrongfully labeled a tramp by her sorority sisters, she hit rock bottom as a "promiscuous, self-hating alcoholic" and dropped out of school before clawing her way back, reclaiming her life, and learning to trust women again. Georgia, a thirty-four-year-old communications manager for an express mail company, found my survey on Craigslist. She says she suffered emotional abuse to the "nth power" thanks to women and isolated herself on the social front for years. After some initial struggles with bulimia, she ultimately turned to Vicodin and wine to take the edge off. It wasn't long, she says, before her lonely weekends consisted of mind-numbing drinking sessions, blackouts, and car wrecks. Although she's in therapy, she seems to have pretty much given up. She admits to having "a deep hope for a woman friend I can trust" but insists it's a very distant, fading hope and it's probably "too late." She worries nobody would want to befriend her anyway, since she'd just "come off as desperate and weird." Serena shared a similar story of cruelty at the hands of female coworkers. Like the others on this end of the spectrum, she also sounds deeply scarred and, ultimately, hopeless:

> I have spent the past five years hating myself and alienating myself from other women. When I am forced to talk to them, I try very hard to appear friendly and kind, but if I don't have to do it, I will clam up and stay away. I am alone.

Dozens of respondents ascribed their long-term depression to other women's (and, I have to believe, men's) obvious disdain for their weight, acne, or general appearance—and the shame, exclusion, isolation, and loneliness that flowed from that. As my young son said to me not long ago in a moment of utterly innocent perception, "I think the hardest thing to be would be a girl who is fat. Or maybe a girl who is black or Hispanic or lesbian and fat." Marcia, a forty-five-year-old overweight executive recruiter, would agree. She says she's "still overcoming depression and anxiety issues. It's horrible, and I wouldn't wish these feelings on anyone. No one deserves to have to constantly question themselves, but that's what we do to each other."

Here's a familiar tale: Christine, like me and too many others, lost her virginity to a fraternity party rapist during the 1980s. Like me, also, she found her sorority sisters pushing her away rather than supporting her, a scenario that for decades has left her feeling distrustful of women, her faith in them shaken:

> I suffered through a few months of insanity, drinking heavily, crying in public, getting into wrecks, and almost failing out of school. Eventually I picked myself up. I went on to succeed wildly, but it's not a fully happy ending. In order to pick myself up, I had to shut a part of myself down. I didn't allow myself any deep emotion for a long time. I still find it difficult to trust women in any way beyond the superficial. My only close female friend today is one who I knew before the Horrible Thing happened.

Psychotherapy is, obviously, one source of comfort for women in this predicament. Among those who say they've struggled with the more serious gender-based fallout, however, only about 20 percent told me they'd sought assistance from mental health professionals— a somewhat paltry number when you consider that so many women are linking depression, feelings of shame and worthlessness, low self-esteem, eating disorders, and even suicidal ideation with their female-related troubles. But seeking analysis for struggles with other females isn't necessarily an intuitive or obvious course for these women. For one thing, not all of us can afford it. For another, not all of us are conscious of or in touch with the origins of our inner conflicts and anxieties. Mainly, though, we're busy. Most of these women are doing their best to muddle through it all by drawing on a host of other less time-consuming, less invasive coping strategies. Others are self-medicating or brushing it aside. It's the best they feel they can do.

Those who have sought counseling or therapy told me they found it extremely helpful in processing the whys and whats behind the events, building up resilience and trust, desensitizing themselves, and helping them stop viewing women as a general threat to their emotional security. Meg, a professor in her forties, said it took several years of therapy before she was able to let go of the "shame and shakiness that accumulated over the years" thanks to the "searing, ego-shriveling" attacks of other women at work, but felt it was worth the grind. Others told me that because they never felt comfortable discussing these issues with anyone else, simply having someone to listen to their hidden, unprocessed hurts without judgment helped them regain the confidence they needed to cultivate trust and open back up to women again. Hanna, a thirty-six-year-old chef who said she hit rock bottom after some very serious girl-related struggles, put it this way: "$30,000 in therapy later and it's all good :)"

The world of girls and women might not look like this to you at all. Your world might be sunny and bright and filled with shiny, happy, supportive girlfriends, open and welcoming neighbors and coworkers, and well-behaved daughters. But this isn't a "messed-up-Them" versus "well-adjusted-Us" issue. The fact that so many girls and women are quietly struggling within the ranks of our gender, I think, really should matter to each of us. It's a matter of sisterhood, yes, but also of humanity, something that ultimately reflects on us all.

CHAPTER 8

THE VICARIOUS STRUGGLES
OF MOTHERS WITH DAUGHTERS

It was agonizing to see them exclude her and make her feel so unworthy. It was like watching a movie of my own life except it's probably worse as a mother, actually. It's bad to admit this—they're just kids—but I couldn't stand those little witches.

—Harriet, sixty-one, museum docent

It's really no mystery why I'm viewing the matter of incivility among girls and women more urgently than ever. In an ironic twist of fate, I have three daughters. Over the years, I've watched my girls, ten, ten, and fifteen, bask in the joys and muck through the mine fields of Girl World. Seeing them form solid, loving friendships has proven doubly rewarding for someone with my history, and I've tried very hard not to taint their journey by projecting my own anxieties. I know I can't stop the male- or female-inflicted hurts from visiting them. I know conflict is an inherent part of the human experience, one that will help them grow their emotional and social survival skills. But as someone who reluctantly hauled her gender-based baggage into adulthood, I can't help but feel concern sometimes; I know what's out there. And, thanks to the survey, I know now that a lot of other mothers are feeling the same way.

One of the many poignant observations Rachel Simmons makes in *Odd Girl Out* is this recognition that a mother really has no choice but to deal with her daughter's experiences and suffering through the lens of her own. And, indeed, the mothers I've heard from appear to find that their daughters' challenges in navigating the tumultuous terrain of adolescence often awaken and agitate old wounds of their own. Of the women who responded to my survey, 47 percent said they have at least one daughter. Of these mothers, 70 percent said they worried with some regularity about their daughters' relationships with other girls and the way they treat one another. The 1,450 separate comments I received from these women confirm that many are feeling doubly vulnerable on their return trip to Girl World. To varying degrees, they've unwittingly carried the disappointments of their own adolescence into motherhood, with many reporting a sort of vicarious vigilance when it comes to their offspring's hardships. A few admit to growing a bit *too* involved in their girls' lives, behaving, as one put it, like an overprotective schoolmarm. Many say they're simply desperate for a little reassurance and guidance given what they've seen for themselves.

I even heard a couple dozen women say they feared having daughters altogether. Katy, a thirty-one-year-old mother of a toddler, told me she was initially "desperate for a boy, simply because I didn't want a girl to suffer the way I did . . . I didn't want to pass on to her my insecurities and make her suspicious of women and their motives." Katy says she's delighted with her daughter, naturally, but suspects the anxiety will kick right back in once she approaches school age. Kathleen, another attorney-mom, says she's been fortunate to have found a few female friends to trust and confide in after her past run-ins, but it's been tough. She has no kids but says she's already "scared that when I have them I won't be able to make friends with other mothers because I'm so hesitant to get close." Anna, meanwhile, a thirty-six-year-old elementary school teacher, told me she thinks her past problems with girls and women "prompted the universe" to give her two sons. She wasn't joking. Tina, a forty-four-year-old receptionist at a car dealership, says that after all the trouble she's heard from her sister about her nieces and their friends over the years, she's sure she "dodged a major bullet" by having boys.

This raw, extreme honesty might seem unusual or even startling, but, to me, it's no longer so surprising given everything else I'm hearing from women. Still, I have to believe that most of us with girls are genuinely thrilled, no matter how awful our own struggles have been. Personally, I've found the dividends and challenges of parenting to be distributed pretty equally among my male and female offspring. I do think, however, that mothering girls comes with its own unique and distinct set of hurdles, especially if you've had a rough go of it yourself. When things get difficult for a daughter, it can wholly consume and permeate the mom's existence, too. In my survey, mothers of all types shared heart-wrenching stories of daughters suffering in Girl World, including girls who shut down emotionally, went "goth" or "emo," began cutting, tuned out the world through music, booze, boys, and drugs, stayed in bed, and ditched or dropped out of school in favor of homeschooling on account of the girl-related pressures and disappointments they faced. Only a handful of moms with school-age girls said they *didn't* worry about their daughters' female relationships with some frequency, a truly remarkable commentary on what's going on out there. What are we mothers worrying about? Our perspectives and degree of concern may vary from topic to topic, but when I asked these mothers what specifically troubles them, here is what they had to say (in order of frequency):

- Excluding, rejecting, shunning
- Group or clique cruelty
- Criticisms and judgments
- Gossip, spreading rumors, talking behind another person's back
- Jealousy and competition
- Shifting alliances
- Ridicule, humiliation, shaming
- Manipulation
- Bullying
- Betrayal and disloyalty

While most moms said they were concerned about their daughters getting mean-girled themselves, I did hear from some, like Constance, who are equally and actively concerned about their own girls being inconsiderate, mean, or aggressive.

I sure hope she won't turn out to be a mean girl. I would bring down some major consequences if I ever found out she was treating anyone this way, especially because this is something we have talked about many times.

Even women who have warned against emotional enmeshment and overinvolvement in their daughters' lives admit to struggling vicariously themselves. Take Judith Warner, the former *New York Times* columnist and author of the bestseller *Perfect Madness: Motherhood in the Age of Anxiety*:

> On the days before school projects are due, I hide out in my office, vibrating with anxiety. Social rejections—theirs, not mine—bring on a black rage.

Like me, these mothers yearn to spare their daughters the sometimes crippling ugliness they fear, and may know firsthand, lurks out there. Most of these women don't sound like paranoid, helicoptering neurotics; they come off as quite reasonable and realistic, actually. They know they can't insulate their girls from all evil. They're trying hard not to project or pass along their own fears and distrust. But they also want to arm their daughters with an awareness of these hostile propensities and teach them how to deal with them.

In *Best Friends: The Pleasures and Perils of Girls' and Women's Friendships*, the psychologists Terri Apter and Ruthellen Josselson detail just how difficult it can be for a mother to perform the "double act" of understanding her own formative experiences with females while trying to support a daughter through the same:

> My adult life is peppered with responses that are not too different from what my adolescent daughter experiences, moments with friends that make me worry about whether I have misunderstood the nature of my relationships, whether I have trusted too much and am about to get clobbered.

. . .

As adults, we may look back ruefully at the struggles of adolescent friendships, yet we fool ourselves to think we have ever really escaped them. The dilemmas remain, and what we learned about friendship in those trying years forever after colors our sense of self and our responses to others.

You don't even need to have a school-age daughter to worry about these things. Plenty of mothers with younger girls told me that they're already concerned. In the words of Erin, a sociologist with a pair of wee little ones, "Even though [the girl is] only two, I do worry about every single item listed in this questionnaire. Truly, after what I've seen, I'm petrified for both my son and daughter." Other women made distinctions between everyday slights and actual hostilities:

> I'm not really concerned about her getting hurt; that is part of growing up. But I would hate to see her suffer the real cruelty, like I did in eighth grade. My sister got a lot of that too, and I saw how terrible it was. Actually, I guess I'm concerned enough to have purposely sent her to a small school where they really watch that kind of thing and try to teach kids kindness and compassion from the start.

These can be truly trying times for moms who thought they'd moved past this kind of thing long ago. It's like what Al Pacino's Michael Corleone says in *The Godfather III:* "Just when I thought I was out, they pull me back in." And from what a lot of these mothers are saying, it stinks just as much the second time around. Lena, forty-five, a former flight attendant, says she's looked on helplessly as her shy daughter, Katie, has gotten out of the car at school drop-off. She says she's seen other girls give Katie the once-over and flashes of obvious disapproval. She admits to buying Katie a new wardrobe to "boost confidence" and better position her to fit in with the very girls she herself has come to disapprove of—and simultaneously curses herself for doing it: "She should be accepted on her own terms, as is, and not have to do backflips and be like them to get their approval," she complains. Heartbroken, Lena tells me she worries that Katie's already ending up "unpopular" and lonely, just as she says she was back in high school. A separate group of mothers, meanwhile—those who say they were fortunate enough to have sidestepped much of the adolescent maelstrom—now find themselves utterly confused and pulling their hair out for the first time as they confront what one called "all this bizarre mean-girl crap" with their daughters.

Lisa, a mom in her fifties, seems to concur. She says she's come to feel wary of other women the "hard way," mostly by watching her sister live through it for decades. She worries about the self-loathing that other girls have prompted in her middle school daughter, who she describes as "slightly chubby." Like Lena, once Lisa caught "the look of disdain on another girl's face as she glanced over my daughter's unfashionable hair and scruffy clothes," she "went out that weekend and spent three hundred dollars" on new ones. She worries about the confusing messages she might be sending, but she also wants to give her daughter a leg up.

It might be easy for a woman who isn't dealing with these issues to scoff but, really, it's hard to blame these moms. They're in a tough spot. I think for most of us the genesis of our vigilance is pure: We love our girls, we've been there, we want our daughters to navigate the delicate maze of adolescence with trust and openness and to emerge empowered, spirit and mojo intact. We want them to reap the unique dividends of female intimacy, but we also want to protect them, to spare them the crippling venom that can arrest their healthy ascent and development on a dime. We want all kids to behave themselves, to respect others over fleeting interests and alliances, and to squash the cruel habits that can inflict lasting distress and self-doubt. More than anything, we don't want our girls to hurt as we have.

Things can get pretty extreme out there, though. Gwen, a mom in a Detroit suburb, unapologetically admits to declining requests for second playdates across the board with her nine-year-old daughter, Taylor. She does this because she doesn't want Taylor getting "too close" to girls Gwen has sized up as potential threats or "mean girls." She's not alone. I've now heard almost one hundred mothers say things along the lines of "my daughter has a mean girl 'friend' who I am desperately trying to minimize contact with."

Other women related stories of growing up with distrustful mothers, stepmothers, and grandmothers. Interestingly, having a guarded mother who had few friends, while perhaps tragic and trying, doesn't necessarily indicate future trouble for oneself. It certainly can for some, and, indeed, I heard from women who trace their distrust and arm's-length approach to women directly back to their mother's indoctrination—a tough legacy. Sandra, a thirty-nine-year-old hair-dresser, falls on the other side of the spectrum. She shudders as she recalls her mother's warning that girls were essentially lying in wait to betray her. "It took a lot of effort to overcome that type of upbring-ing," she assures me, but she was determined not to repeat the cycle. Kathy, a thirty-one-year-old paralegal whose mother had "no close female friends," thinks it absolutely inspired her to cultivate strong girlfriendships, "mostly because I saw how it made her so lonely." She took it upon herself to do a complete 180-degree turn from her mother's style of relating and says she's always been especially solici-tous and generous with women. What I love especially about Kathy's story is the way she took responsibility for her own choices and rela-tionships rather than simply blaming her mom, a concept we'll be pushing a great deal in the chapters ahead.

PART III

NEXT STOP, PARADISE?

CHAPTER 9

GIVING THE BLAME GAME A REST

There comes a point when we have to stop blaming "the
patriarchy" and recognize ravening bitchery for what it is.
—"Alsojill," blogging about "My Sorority Pledge? I Swore
Off Sisterhood"

It strikes me that a lot of us women aren't exactly owning up to our shadow-side tendencies. We can cite a number of reasons for that, but, in some sense, we haven't really *had* to own up. Legitimately or not, many of us have grown pretty comfortable shifting blame to the other culprits out there—particularly men and the media. While it's obvious by now that I'm a card-carrying member of the personal responsibility police, I certainly wasn't expecting so many other women to feel likewise. They might disagree about the degree to which cultural and systemic forces influence us, corrupt us, throw down barriers against us, or actively harm us, but 94 percent of them feel that, for the most part, we're ultimately responsible for ourselves. We can't improve the lot of females in this country in any meaningful way if we continue to let ourselves off the hook for our own bad behavior.

Nearly one thousand women shared impassioned commentary with me on this issue. Most of them feel that girls and women are perfectly capable of discerning right from wrong and exercising restraint, just like any other rational, free-thinking, free-choosing creature.

Like me, these women appear convinced that we'll be mucking about our own self-defeating sludge in perpetuity if we don't commit to cleaning our own houses. Glossing over our internal antics and dysfunction, giving one another a free pass, and perpetuating inflexible shifts in focus toward other people or institutions won't help curb our own toxic inclinations. To a lot of us, it seems, the blame game has become an inappropriate, outdated, and even insulting cop-out that does little but shut down meaningful discussion and problem solving.

IT'S NOT JUST ABOUT MEN

When I first outlined this book, I admit I was hoping to dodge that sticky wicket issue of feminism. I didn't then and still don't quite feel qualified to parse through the failures and victories of feminism or to celebrate the amazing journey of women as those issues bear on our internal relationships. Plus, in my yellow-bellied funk, I worried that delving into these inherently controversial matters would upset women no matter what I said, thereby undermining my credibility on the more central issues of this book. Ultimately, though, the patriarchy's influence on female culture is a factor that bears on our infighting. It's part of our story. And, besides, it isn't like I have to rely on my own theories. I have a pretty impressive group of more than three thousand twenty-first-century, living and breathing women out there ready and waiting to be heard.

Toward the end of my survey, I asked women whether they thought a culture of mean or negativity existed within the gender. For the 88 percent who responded "yes," I included a follow-up: Did they think male-dominant, sexist, or similar sorts of influences caused or contributed to that culture? I know, I know—this topic alone could fill an entire book. But in posing the question, I have to admit I assumed that most women would roll their eyes, check "yes," and forgo the commentary, making the issue a tidy, straightforward one for this book's purposes. As it turned out, I was way off. The majority of them said things like, *Whoa! Not so fast!*—and gave me 1,543 meaty comments to consider.

Traditional feminist thought, you may recall, goes something like this: Patriarchal forces and institutionalized sexism have historically objectified and marginalized women as second-class citizens. The patriarchy controls access to everything we need and want, keeping us "down" and confusing us by sending mixed messages about who we should be and how we ought to conduct ourselves. We're expected to be well-behaved girls who get along, on the one hand; but we're anxious about those expectations, since we have to compete with one another for limited resources like jobs, men we can mate with, power, and financial security. Thanks to this setup, we have no choice but to turn on one another.

To some, it's that simple. And it's gospel.

It sounds like a lot of us, though, are rethinking the creakier planks in that platform. Fact is, only a handful of the women I've heard from feel that male-dominant forces remain the primary, moving cause of all evil. Ruth, a retired law office manager, is one of them. She believes that the "historical repercussions of sexism are very much alive," leaving women to fight one another to gain self-worth by "acting out self-fulfilling prophecies and living up to men's expectations." Donna, a Florida social worker, agrees. "Male dominance is a constant part of how girls grow up. We haven't yet broken out of our own stereotype, so it affects the way we view our place in society and act toward each other."

Nearly 30 percent of the women I heard from don't think men have much of anything to do with our infighting. Fifty percent say these cultural influences might play *some* historical role in our infighting—but most aren't convinced that lets us off the hook. A couple hundred other women, meanwhile, seemed to be outright shrugging their shoulders, admitting they had no real sense of how operative and relevant the so-called corrosive patriarchal forces remain. Dana, an architect in her thirties, summed up a common sentiment: She can "imagine that the roots of bullying between women go back to our previously second-class status," but she doesn't think it excuses the bad behavior of females today. Really, there was no consensus here. Even those who graduated from all-girls high schools and colleges couldn't agree. About two dozen women assured me that the differences in culture without men around to "spoil" things was like "night and day," but an almost equal number said precisely the opposite.

In reading the mostly thoughtful commentary of all these women, it's plain that the vast majority of them reject a fixed-blame perspective; they personally haven't felt "oppressed," held back, or lacking in opportunity. As Tonya, a forty-four-year-old AIDS researcher, explains, "I can't blame men for this one. There's incomparably less domination than fifty years ago, yet girls and women seem meaner now than I imagine they've ever been." Tonya's in good company. Nobody seems to be suggesting that things are perfect. But if you look around, you'll find plenty of reasonable "experts," people like the esteemed Penn anthropologist Peggy Reeves Sanday, offering us compelling reasons to at least reconsider the myopic male-dominance ideology and refrain from neglecting or ignoring the power that women *do* enjoy. As one anonymous woman commenting on my *Times* piece suggested, patriarchal forces "can only be blamed to a degree. When does it become men or women just acting that way because they are fuckwits?"

I've found it particularly intriguing to hear from women in their middle years and beyond, women who've experienced far less favorable conditions and even fought for change themselves but who nonetheless refuse to play the blame game. Take Elena, a retired judge who has seen elements of progress unfold over the past decades and says she was the first woman in her law school class:

> We live in a society markedly different than that which our elders were born into. If you're a woman living in this country today, you just can't buy this [patriarchy] stuff wholesale anymore. It's pointless complaining. We have some work to do yet, certainly, but we've come a long, *long* way, and that should be acknowledged.

Wanda, forty-six, a photographer, also thinks true equality remains a work in progress. But the concept of blaming men or society offends her as "a poor excuse" that undermines women's attempts to move forward. "We'll all be better off when women get over the past and start to own our feelings, inadequacies, and behaviors," she asserts. Until then, "it's just one step forward, two steps back." Hannah, a twenty-seven-year-old writer who says she's a feminist "of sorts," put an even finer point on it: "Sure, sexism might be a *contributing* cause of our competitions, but not the main one. The main problem is us. Period." Jackie, meanwhile, an account executive in her thirties, feels it's all a matter of perspective. "Male dominance might play a role in one's life, but there are so many more opportunities for women now. You just have to get out and explore and not use men (or other women) as an excuse."

Love them or loathe them, women as varied as Sarah Palin and Maureen Dowd have expressed rare agreement on this question. Asked about the so-called whining of women when it comes to sexism in our society—notably before she ran for vice president—Palin responded, "Man, that doesn't do us any good, women in politics, or women in general, trying to progress [in] this country." Dowd has said much the same: "[W]hen you use sexism as an across-the-board shield for any legitimate question," she cautioned, "you only hurt women. And that's just another splash of reality."

Having been dealt the luxury of a mid-1960s birth, all this ambivalence I'm hearing resonates loud and clear. On the one hand, I have great respect for the pioneering efforts of women who came before me, the ones who secured the advantages, opportunities, and choices I've enjoyed all my life. I admire what old-school feminists managed to accomplish when they rallied around a unified, coherent, and timely theme. I don't take the advances of first- and second-wave feminism for granted. I wasn't around to fight for voting rights or reproductive rights. I didn't march for liberation and equality, fight against exploitation, or, I gather, do much of anything to help anyone but myself. My nest came pretty nicely feathered.

And yet, I have to admit, it's awfully challenging to identify with or recognize myself in the old-school or more extreme versions of feminism. Hell, it's challenging to identify myself with any group these days. Growing up in the comfy bosom of Minnesota suburbia with my strong female role models (and the generous support of men too), it just never occurred to me that I wasn't getting my fair share, didn't enjoy true parity with males, or was somehow living a life driven and controlled by the Man. I grew up on Debbie Harry, Madonna, and a mother who raised five kids but went on to kick butt in an exclusively male profession on her own terms—all while rocking the "ladylike" heels and clingy St. John Knits she favored. My dad respected his girls' femininity but also figured it was worthwhile to teach us to ride dirt bikes, mow the lawn, change the oil, appreciate the spaghetti Westerns of Sergio Leone, and believe without any hesitation whatsoever that we could do or be anything in this world. Girls in my town were free to choose Little League *or* softball, and many of us did both. Male dominance and inequality? It just wasn't my personal reality— as a kid, in college, in grad school, or at my power-chick-strewn law firm.

Do I resent or feel compromised by my somewhat premature domesticity? No, I don't. I didn't feel boxed in or backed into any corners. I knew going in that sacrifice was an inevitable component to parenting. I do recognize this is a tough issue for many: We could use some serious enlightenment from both the public and private sectors on these issues, particularly for women of lesser means who aren't dealt the luxury of choice. But personally, I can't complain too much. I've had the good fortune of straddling both the working and home-front worlds, with respect and support on each end. The decision to have children and, ultimately, stay home with them surely involved sacrifice, unexpected transitional turbulence, and serious financial pressures, particularly now that we're running our large brood on a single federal government salary. But it was one I made willingly, eyes wide open.

Truth is, before I quit working outside the home, I was physically and emotionally craving more time with my kids. Child care was obscenely expensive, especially for four. At some point, it just made sense to try to make a home life work for us and, for better or worse, my husband, Steve, didn't come equipped with a womb or a lactation device (nor, sadly, a trust fund). He just didn't feel those same pangs of parental guilt and longing. I suppose I could resent him for letting me bear the predominant burden of our family's weighty work-life challenges. I could get stuck in the dance of anger or bitterness over it. I could rage at the cost of child care, the dearth of meaningful part-time gigs, and the seemingly all-or-nothing constraints for so many working mothers out there, but, for now, I'm doing the best I can. And, in any case, I'm just not willing to shift responsibility for my own family predicament elsewhere.

My husband can certainly play the role of Clueless Dude at times. But like most men I know, he came pretty gender-enlightened. And he's long pulled his weight on the home front, whether I was clicking my heels down San Francisco's Market Street or working the mommy-nanny-maid-laundress-cook-accountant-secretary-gardener-writer shift at home. He doesn't look at any of this as something I *had* to do as a mother or a woman. If he had his way, I'd still be practicing law and bringing in what he calls "easy money" to help us stay financially afloat. To him, it just isn't about gender. If it were, he'd be in trouble. Because not only must he respect and answer to me, three daughters, and a lovely mother—as a diplomat, his ultimate boss is Hillary Clinton. I'm hardly exaggerating when I say the man would turn cartwheels and backflips to carry her briefcase (or purse). So that's where I'm coming from. I'm not tone deaf. I realize others haven't been dealt the same luck, support, and gender-neutral experiences. But, then, from what a lot of women out there tell me, many in my generation and beyond actually *have.* Are we all naïve simpletons who fail to see the big picture? It's possible, I suppose. But when all is said and done, we can't manufacture patriarchal obstacles and suffering—many of our lives just haven't been as obviously defined by them. And, to me, that's something to be celebrated, not dissected into meaninglessness. As the feminist writer Sarah Seltzer wrote not too long ago, "Even for those of us focused on battles for the future, it's not a bad idea to pause and note how far we've come."

And speaking of generational tensions, it sounds like a whole lot of twentysomethings out there would also like to retire the *It's the men, stupid!* mantra. Pilar, a twenty-four-year-old fine arts student and nanny who told me that while she embraces the essential tenets of feminism and regularly trolls feminist websites to stay in the mix, she thinks that a lot of the arguments have been overplayed. She's deeply skeptical about "chants of female unity" and male bashing, especially after seeing so much anger, discord, and dismissiveness within feminist culture itself. She and many other young women complain that the across-the-board blaming that goes on just keeps women stuck in a victim stance, perpetuating that sense of helplessness we all loathe. I was surprised to learn that my twenty-year-old friend Leah feels this way, too. She's a scary-bright, already-accomplished playwright who spent the bulk of her young life buffed and misted in the feminist hammams of Berkeley, California. And yet, reflecting on the strong, accomplished women of her generation and the more radical perspectives of women on these issues, Leah rolls her eyes in glum solemnity and says, "They're just losing us with that bullshit."

Jennifer Baumgardner, coauthor of *Manifesta: Young Women, Fem-*

inism, and the Future, says she sees younger women running from the word *feminist* without knowing why—or even what the word stands for. It's a legitimate lament. The women I've heard from aren't conveying any real sense of shared predicament, history, or cause to rally around. But these are confusing times. I've seen so many variations of "feminism" and feminist thought out there that I couldn't possibly articulate what the word or the movement means in today's world, much less the spirit they're supposed to engender. I don't know if we're living in a third-wave society, a fourth-wave society, a postfeminist society, or something different entirely. Heck, maybe I'm advocating a different brand of "feminism" or "womanism" right here, within the four corners of this book. I certainly see the utility of working on a more basic brand of sisterhood before some of those other items on the agenda, one that promotes a more mindful civility and simple respect. Something that would help all women feel safer and supported. Ultimately, though, I'm not sure that today's women need a feminist label. When young women like Gwen and Leah seek to define feminism by living life on their own terms, when they feel they're enjoying rough social, economic, and political parity, and they've grown up observing pointless, almost reflexive infighting and negativity among their own, the unyielding cries of inequality, patriarchy, and sexism simply hold less appeal.

Ironically, one theory a lot of women do seem to agree on is this: Maybe what's causing some of our problems is our own desire to have it all and be all things in the more open and flexible society we've created through the successes of feminism. Jan, a gender studies student I spoke with, assured me that her peers "would kill" her for saying it, but she finds herself believing that our aggressions aren't so much about men but about women who are "conflicted and divided" about their roles and what they want in today's culture. Carrie, a thirty-five-year-old hotel concierge who's lived in a half dozen other countries, says much the same:

> I don't think a sexist society is causing this. As a matter of fact, I don't think women in the U.S. live in a sexist society. It's a society that gives women freedom to thrive. I think some American women have a negative, mean spirit because they

themselves are trying to have it all. That can be very difficult. But men's fault? No. I don't think so.

Some went so far as to call feminism itself the beast driving the evils among women today. How is it, these women wonder, that we can progress into a new age of female competence and greater equality, occupy a world previously more male oriented, and achieve more successes, only to find that our competitive spirits have deepened and we're tearing down one another as much if not more than ever? Something doesn't compute. Thirty-year-old Laurie believes the expectations we're placing on ourselves and one another are a "direct result" of feminism. "I think the feminist movement brought these kinds of problems, but worse," she maintains. "Women are expected to be modern superheroes: raise kids, have a career, keep house, be nice, smart, athletic, great moms, great wives, great cooks. And, by the way, look amazing and at least ten years younger than your actual age."

Few would trade the advances, but many sound frustrated. Sixty-three-year-old Thelma, a Wisconsin retiree, thinks that feminism came up short, let women down, and ushered in a new, troubling climate in which women just plain fail to respect one another:

Our society is engineered to create competition among us. The first and second waves didn't address this, in my view. Women going to work are pitted against women staying home. Women who can do both successfully are touted as the ideal. We don't respect each other's life choices. I'm tired of it.

Rita, a fortysomething stay-at-home mom who finds it challenging to try to accomplish and balance it all without turning bitter, says she sure wouldn't mind a little respect and support from her fellow females to ease the burden:

I honestly believe that the mean spirit has worsened over time and is due to women having more rights and freedom as our society has advanced. We now want to have it all: career, children, husband, house, and so on. It's hard for a woman today to balance it all, and you see them becoming resentful. I'm guilty of this behavior, but over time I've learned that I need to back off and let things be; for example, the house cannot always be clean. I stay away from women who are negative or powerhouses— I cannot relate. I have my own agenda, and I want to be respected just as I respect those who head up the career ladder full steam. As women, we must respect each other and realize that every one of us is trying to contribute to society in her own way. We should support that, not fight it.

While this is complicated terrain, I personally wonder if sometimes just *doing* and *being* amounts to a better strategy than overthinking things. I agree that we're trying to cover a whole lot of bases at once and placing some pretty unrealistic pressures on ourselves to master it all. And I agree with writers like Judith Warner, Allison Pearson, Lisa Belkin, and Leslie Morgan Steiner, all of whom have written compellingly about our frantic, neurotic quests to be perfect mothers, perfect employees, perfect wives, perfect period—the precise sort of frenzy fueling the comparisons, judgments, jealousy, status jockeying, and general competitions that lead to the ugly fallout at issue here. Life for a lot of us can get pretty stressful because of this, more so than I think we acknowledge. And, on top of all we're trying to accomplish, on top of all those competing demands and expectations and eggshells, most of us very much want other women to like, accept, and even admire us. We don't want to have to look over our shoulders and worry about the critical eyes of our own. It's a complex, tricky dance, one that few women can convincingly master. And it's why, I suppose, the art of self-deprecation has become so prevalent and socially effective: It preempts the judging and comparisons, puts other women at ease, and makes them feel good *enough* and, hence, emotionally safe.

I would never contend that things are perfect in this country, especially with three girls coming up through the ranks. But take me and my survey results out of the equation. Encouraging things *are* happening. The majority of women in this country seem to be enjoying a pretty full spectrum of choices. We're inhabiting previously unoccupied territories: operating on brains, flying to the moon, even fighting overseas. We made up 53 percent of the U.S. electorate in

2008, and our numbers dominate the greater workforce and class-rooms across the country. We didn't get a woman president or vice president last time around, but we have a female secretary of state, Speaker of the House, another U.S. Supreme Court justice, and scores of other women landing key, high-power positions in government and elsewhere. We're seeing beauty pageants ditch sashes and swimsuits—or shutting down altogether. And I don't know if I'd call this encouraging, but did you know that at least one in three online porn viewers are now female? Or that women have quietly been taking over the porn industry's executive arm? These ladies insist they're bringing a new perspective to erotica, ensuring better treatment for women in the business and taming the industry's misogynistic tendencies. Not my bailiwick, but undoubtedly interesting.

I think we should absolutely protest the misogyny and physical violence against women when it occurs. Fair game. We can rightfully complain about work-life balance issues and the fact that standards under the Family and Medical Leave Act lag behind those of so many other developed countries. We can argue that all those extra jobs women get are really just the crappier, lower-level, lower-paying jobs—although others will counter with competing data and explanations, some of which we'll have to admit are plausible. We can legitimately lament continued pay differentials, executive and senior management deficits, and other glass ceilings that remain, but we should recognize that plenty of other *women* feel that a chief part of the problem relates to our "timid" or inferior networking and self-promotion skills and other factors.

We can complain that women occupy only two of the Supreme Court's nine overstuffed leather chairs and the federal judiciary is way low on female representation, but shouldn't we also celebrate, say, the unprecedented, formidable swing vote power that Sandra Day O'Connor quietly held all those years? Or the triumph that is Sonia Sotomayor? We can make a fuss because President Obama shoots hoops and plays golf with men, because he filled only 32 percent of the "top-tier administration jobs" at the White House with women during his first year, or because women comprise only 17 percent of congressional representation. But these things are far more complicated than just a numbers game. We have to recall that few of us run in the first place (plenty of reasons for that, but still), that party affili-

132

ation plays a role, and that, like it or not, seniority lends benefits—an advantage for men, most of whom *have* been at it longer. And let's not overlook the substantive contributions and at-times decisive powers that the women who are there *do* make and wield.

We can, to be sure, pick apart all of the positive signs and perpetuate a glass-half-empty perspective in perpetuity just to ward off complacency. But, in the words of children's author Lemony Snicket, it all "depends on how you look at it." Though we can't talk victory or mission accomplished, I think we're talking unfinished business of a work in progress here. Shangri-la takes time; we do have a long, complicated history of inequality to overcome. A lot has changed and continues to change, but we're still evolving and redefining ourselves in the wake of that less pleasant history. Indeed, we can see similar trends with race and ethnicity in a lot of these issues: numbers creeping up, perhaps not as fast as we'd like, but often moving in the right direction.

Let's not forget, too, that a lot of women admit they aren't sure what they want; I know plenty of smart, successful women out there who nurture 1950s housewife fantasies, for instance. In the final analysis, no singular woman, group, or movement can presume to speak for all of us within the gender. It's a mistake to think that all women feel they're getting the short end of the stick—or take immediate offense when offered the odd "ladies first" perk. Perhaps, as Elena put it, we've come a long way and we have a ways to go yet. But, to me, it appears that most women think the antediluvian victimhood model is on its way out (or at least due for a tune-up). For, as many of us know firsthand and should see as a major takeaway from this book, the notion that only men can victimize, marginalize, and traumatize women is pure myth.

What also seems clear to me is that so-called sisters shouldn't be bullying other women under amorphous, stale auspices of a "feminism" that doesn't exist, as though the rest of us silly girls down here don't have a clue how bad we have it and, thus, need the unsolicited protections and guidance of others. As a whole lot of women seem to appreciate, that's just bogus. When 94 percent of contemporary women in a random survey say they ultimately own responsibility for their judging, competing, and negativity, it's time to pay attention. This isn't half-baked, androcentric tomfoolery, it's an evolved belief in the power, intelligence, and capabilities of today's female. Women are saying that 2010 is a vastly more enlightened moment in this country, one that warrants a tolerant, flexible, and less reactionary point of view—one that warrants a mirror as much as a bullhorn.

IT'S NOT ALL THE MEDIA'S FAULT, EITHER

The picture admittedly gets a little murkier for me when we shift our focus to the closely related specter of media and advertising. We can't do a full-blown analysis of media sexism and influence here, or get into things like Hillary and Sarah P. and that whole chest of drawers; such an examination lies beyond the scope of *The Twisted Sisterhood*. I think it's useful, though, to consider some of the specific ways that TV, film, and literature portray girls and women, and the extent to which those depictions might be influencing us, particularly in our relationships.

For nearly a century, books, television programs, and films have chronicled the dark corners of female camaraderie for our entertainment, from *All About Eve, Cat's Eye,* and *Carrie* to *Dynasty, Mean Girls,* and the current spectrum of cat-fight-based reality shows. Not surprisingly, the women who responded to my survey offered a tremendous amount of feedback about this. They don't agree about the extent to which the media's so-called sexist, salacious, and incendiary coverage fuels our female discourtesies, but a fair number of them think it serves up some pretty rancid and annoying stuff. Still, only about 45 percent feel media depictions *inaccurately* stereotype females. Less than half—43 percent—say television, movie, and other media offerings perpetuate the problem or make it worse, and a mere 28 percent feel they exaggerate the problem. In other words, as objectionable as some of the offerings may be, a lot of women concede they actually mirror back more of a reality than we'd care to admit.

Only about a dozen women in my entire survey pool insist that TV shows and films depicting mean girls or catty women are altogether harmless. (These ladies told me to lighten up for even posing the question.) Several dozen others told me they've actually found such offerings humorous, moving, and instructive. The film *Mean Girls,* for instance—based on Rosalind Wiseman's more serious examination of teenage cruelties in her book *Queen Bees and Wannabes*—

mostly survived scrutiny as an awareness-raising tool, though many deemed the reality series by the same name "exploitive garbage." Joan Collins and Linda Evans, meanwhile, might be delighted to learn that Alexis and Krystle's showdowns in *Dynasty* remain indelibly and fondly etched in the brains of many.

Over one thousand women, however, stepped up to condemn what's out there as sexist, demeaning, and manipulative, noting that it's all too "rare for the media to responsibly portray or discuss intrafemale negativity." For some in this group, the content does inappropriately depict female aggression because it perpetuates the problem, feeds a misogynistic culture for profit, and throws up terrible role models. Hundreds of women echoed the comments of Jay, a twenty-eight-year-old writer, who sums up a major point of my book:

> I wish more movies and TV programs showed the actual, negative results of this catfighting and competitive behavior. Especially in sit-coms, this serious problem is milked for canned laughter. It is disgusting and certainly exploits one of the most negative entities of our female being. Maybe if more women could see and understand the results of their catfighting and nastiness, they'd stop doing it.

Eliza, a thirty-six-year-old speech pathologist, feels the word *catfighting* itself is offensive because it minimizes bad behavior and makes it cutesy. "It's as if any time two women have a fight, it becomes either sexualized for the pleasure of men, or the women look like little girls with a frivolous disagreement." Dozens of others contend that the media plays too large a role in dictating to women— especially young girls—what's acceptable and desirable behavior, echoing Mary Pipher's warning in *Reviving Ophelia* that we are quite right to worry that these influences work to foster a "girl-poisoning" culture.

Now, anyone even marginally acquainted with me knows I'm not the righteous scold type. I'm not out to legislate what you watch on TV or expose your kids to. I won't judge you for your *Star* magazine subscription. I haven't become the modern version of Tipper Gore circa 1985 (although if another teenager exposes my little ones to Marilyn Manson, I may well get there). I could never make a convincing media watchdog. I crave all things Larry David and have worshipped far too long at the altar of *Family Guy*. I even find Gawker amusing. For better or worse, I'm afraid I'll excuse most anything dished up in the name of comedy.

But still.

I have to admit that I've been finding myself nodding along with those who find media content troubling these days, especially when it comes to kids' programming and the potential effects on young girls. Our girls are growing up in a different kind of media-saturated world. A lot of what's served up and developed specifically for little kids has such questionable value—but great influence. We seem to have reached the point where sassiness + selfishness + nastiness has become an acknowledged, if wrongly exploited, cultural norm. It's a proven formula that sells. Rarely do you ever see any hint of the actual effects or broader implications of our less than charitable behavior. *Hate* is a word we don't normally use in my house, but I really do hate how bitchiness, smugness, and sassiness are so often portrayed as "cool" and attractive, dressed up in the latest fashions and personalities of the most "popular girls," something not only tolerated but downright catered to and rewarded. The glammed-up rivalry scenarios one sees on TV, in particular, almost never come with a positive and humane context or realistic outcome.

I've heard all the arguments: *Get over yourself!, It's no big deal!, Turn it off, then!* I've thought about this a lot given my own viewing habits. I've considered the perspectives of people like the online gossip columnist Ted Casablanca, who defends the TV show *Gossip Girl* on the grounds that he "can absolutely guarantee that cavewomen were bickering behind each other's backs with grunting noises back in the B.C. days." I'm not so sure that's a legitimate reason for embracing the nonsense now, Ted, but no matter. And, yes, I do know what I'm sounding like right now. I remember adults like me when I was a kid—I thought they were crazy.

As a mother, though, I definitely worry that some of these influences trivialize the problem and encourage impressionable girls to think it's socially advantageous to behave like vapid, entitled, and narcissistic twits. Even if I avoid this stuff in my own house, kids are bombarded on all fronts; it filters down from above and bubbles up from the gutters. Nobody's making my job any easier. I am so pleased that that awful *Lizzie McGuire* show is mostly gone. Talk about your bad influence. Sorry, Tyra Banks, we're not into *America's Next Top Model.* I admire you and respect that modeling probably opened a lot of doors for you and others, but it's just not the kind of carrot I want my girls focusing on in today's culture. I could never name all those ridiculously insipid reality shows, but *Real Housewives, Dallas Divas & Daughters, Wife Swap*—are you kidding me? What are we, chattel? I'd even take *Prisoner: Cell Block H* over those any day. Anne Hathaway? Love her. I enjoy a good silly romp as much as the next person. Still, I found everything about *Bride Wars* just yucky: two best friends hell-bent on one-upping each other over dippy, high-end wedding plans? I loathed that Kate Hudson character and wanted her to just go away. And yet, despite poor reviews, the film sure found its target demographic: girls and women. It's grossed over $115 million and was even nominated for Best Fight—best *cat*fight, that is—at the 2009 MTV Movie Awards. The lesson, apparently? You can be self-absorbed, entitled, and hideously cruel to colleagues, your best girl-friends, and even your fiancé, but worry not: It'll all work out just dandy for you in the end. You'll get your man *and* your Vera Wang.

To be honest, I grew up on a lot of TV, but I don't even like watching it much anymore. Mostly because whenever I do turn on the set, something invariably annoys me straightaway. We're buffoons, we're clueless, we're infantilized, we're obsessed with shopping, boys, status, our looks. We hate each other, we're passive-aggressive. It's perfectly acceptable and normal for little girls to dress, think, and act like teenagers—or little women. I'm not an overly strict mom, but I have been somewhat vigilant about my kids' media diet. I think I've so thoroughly indoctrinated my twins about these issues, in fact, that they now almost automatically defend their TV viewing with the ironclad assurance, "Don't worry, Mama. It's not a sassy show."

I was so heartened a few months back when a positive item on the singer Beyoncé popped up on my Yahoo! home page. It cataloged the kind, selfless deeds she was racking up and included a tearjerker video of her singing "Halo" to a terminally ill little girl. The writer just had to point out that it was unlikely behavior for a "diva," and, sure, we might cynically suspect that Beyoncé's public relations team was just successfully manipulating us. But I couldn't help thinking about the power of that kind of media coverage. It was so inspiring. It left me feeling good about humanity: I found *myself* wanting to be more like Beyoncé. (And, guess what? I was left more likely to buy her music.) If you think about it, we do get the occasional, uplifting puff piece, but, generally, we really don't see enough of these positive, genuine female media moments. The fact that this one jumped out at me as so fresh is a testament to that. It's usually all about the latest celebrigirl screwup or home wrecker, gratuitous pot stirring, and invented gossip pitting famous women against one another—because they know we all enjoy a good catfight or long-running feud between the ladies, especially when it involves a man. It really does seem apparent that the men and women in that business lie in wait, day after day, hoping someone will fall on his or—more typically—her face. Drugs, booze, bad clothes and hair, hard times, illness, and death make for the best and most profitable news of all. Despicable, when you think on it.

The world of girls' literature isn't immune, either. Some of the books aimed at girls are probably just as culpable in fueling the fires as television. Again, I'm not some puritan out to censor or ban anyone's books. But I do find myself sympathizing with women who complain about the growing trend of too-sophisticated plotlines laden with those trusty formulas of girl-on-girl nastiness, entitled princess attitudes, vapid obsession with appearance and status, gossipy backstabbing, and other social manipulations. What troubles these moms most is that these works seem to be targeted at very young girls, who, in all their developing, vulnerable glory, are perfectly positioned to endorse and embrace this kind of dopey, mean, and catty behavior as the norm and even the ideal. A few moms complained that some of their old favorites, classics, and more age-appropriate works were getting bumped from the shelves at bookstores and even libraries to make room for these increasingly popular offerings.

Sammy, a mother of two girls in Falls Church, Virginia, pays close attention to her daughters' selections. Like me, she worries about all the glamorized portrayals of narcissism and evil "because it makes it seem accepted and normal without any hurt or consequences. I worry it will make them think all girls are like this, or expected to be like this, and so they should expect it and even conform." Apologies to the writers. I understand the importance of getting into the minds of young girls through their own vernacular and predicaments. My God,

I'm *still* grateful to Judy Blume. But, again, there's a fine line between realistically depicting Girl World and reinforcing and exploiting the very nonsense to which we object. Rarely do we see the crucial component at issue here: the palpable, lasting consequences of selfish entitlement and all those manipulations, cruelties, and general bitchiness.

I'm not asking you to agree with the most outraged of critics here. All I'm saying is let's think about these influences and start a dialogue. It's hard to see any real upside to this kind of "entertainment" when it comes to kids, particularly when the garbage is developed specifically for them. Even beyond the glamorized aggressions, gratuitous sexual innuendo, and limited variety of female types depicted, I think we should at least consider that a constant, steady assault of messages that tell us we must strive to be beautiful, desirable, and accomplished confections of perfection is partially responsible for our frenzied attempts to outdo one another. Can there really be any doubt that our girls are absorbing this and will inevitably feel shitty about themselves for every aspect in which they fall short? At some point, maybe we really are boxing our girls into believing this is their reality. Psychotherapist-author Susie Orbach thinks so. She argues pretty convincingly that Western standards for beauty have become so truly omnipotent that girls—not just here but around the world—are taking drastic measures to remake their own bodies and mimic those standards. We know about eating disorders and other manifestations of these pressures. But some girls are going so far as to surgically alter their bodies and faces toward the "ideal," frequently with their mothers' endorsement. Have we really become so used to it all that we don't find this appalling?

As we'll be discussing in the next chapter, parents obviously play a huge role here. I and so many moms I know try very hard to help their girls think independently, be kind, and not become so malleable that they'll follow the influence du jour. My girls do enjoy their pink, their femininity, and, yes, their Barbies and American Girl dolls right alongside their sports and wisecracking. They also aren't at all afraid to tell their brother to take a hike. We have open conversations about what they see on TV, in the school yard, and at others' homes. Sounds great, right? I'd love to say they're sufficiently hardy to withstand objectionable media and peer influences. Except, I kid you not: My husband and I have always been able to tell *immediately* when they've watched a certain TV show or played with certain girls; the little sponges begin emulating sassy swagger, parroting back the disrespectful, cool-seeming tones, and working the entitlement vibe straightaway. Maybe the influence sticks, maybe it doesn't, but in my experience, the messages can absolutely seep right on through to even the steadiest of girls.

And yet despite all this, I still don't think we can prima facie blame the media, i.e., the shadowy figures in Hollywood (not even those at Bravo and Disney), the "conscienceless" ad agencies, or the magazine editors women are complaining about. At the end of the day, can we really aim all of our outrage outward? If so, we're pounding some pretty hollow sand. The stuff sells, and we've been buying it; we're literally paying them to do it. It isn't just about twenty-eight-year-old men creating and drooling over the characters, dramas, and rivalries. Females have demonstrated a sustained interest in all of it and comprise a considerable portion of the audience that male and female media executives count on. We've proven ourselves to be willing, demanding, and paying customers who support pretty much everything we say we object to. In other words, we're compounding the precise problems of which we complain.

Take the gossip rags. Remember the olden days, when celebrities entertained us on the screen, stage, or field, and although they fascinated us to no end, we didn't feel an obsessive need to know their every intimate, real-time movement? I understand the interest in the beautiful and talented, but the manic, 24/7 celebrity gossip, paparazzi-driven culture of today is out of control. I really thought we'd learned our lesson with the stalking of Princess Diana. Such a public spanking, to my mind. And yet the readership of these publications is overwhelmingly female—and relatively affluent and educated too. Don't believe me? I can't tell you about online audiences, but 65 percent of the *National Enquirer*'s paper readership in 2009 was female; *In Touch Weekly* was 85 percent; *People*, 88 percent; *Life & Style*, 83 percent; *Star*, 77 percent; and *Us Weekly*, 74 percent. You can't dispute that we are feeding the machine. The people serving up this junk might be many things, but when all is said and done, they're also what's called clever business folk. If you're watching, buying, subscribing, and marinating in it, or worse—allowing your daughters to revel in this kind of entertainment and culture—you're *directly* reinforcing, subsidizing, and rewarding the culture. And the only certainty in that is this: More will keep coming. At some point, we have to convincingly vote with our pocketbook and a committed sense of restraint. Or just stop complaining.

I have to come clean here and admit that while I wrote this book, I took my little surfing breaks and scanned a few online gossip blogs. The Tiger Woods scandal was brewing and, I'm mortified to admit, I do enjoy ogling Angelina and Brad's beautiful brood. And, though it's invariably cruel to the core, some of the gossip bloggers are really quite witty. Not only that. When my sister Stacy and I get together, we've long practiced the shameful ritual of loading up on the glossies and papers at Safeway and thoroughly dissecting celebrities' lives into the wee hours. On the one hand, it's harmless fun and private bonding time. On the other, I can only hope that none of our six daughters has witnessed the carnage—talk about poor role modeling. Mostly, it's just mean. We're contributing to the culture, after all. As one woman who's also trying to "quit" suggested to me, maybe "we need to outfit ourselves with electric shock collars" to arrest these inclinations as they arise.

You don't have to accept my word about the media's questionable bombardment of us and our kids, though. Take a look at the compelling arguments in two of the better books on the subject, *Packaging Girlhood: Rescuing Our Daughters from Marketers' Schemes*, by Lyn Mikel Brown and Sharon Lamb, and *So Sexy So Soon: The New Sexualized Childhood and What Parents Can Do to Protect Their Kids*, by Diane E. Levin and Jean Kilbourne. While you're at it, check out the miniprograms comedian Sarah Haskins has done for Current TV's "Target Women." They are hilarious and so smart. Haskins strikes the ideal pitch in slaying those media and marketing dragons. She's thoroughly annoyed, that's plain. But she's calling *all* of us out, not just the creepy men running things from behind the curtain. Nothing's sacred: the parade of reality TV shows that demean us but exist because we willingly demean ourselves, the Lifetime network, Barbie, the beauty gadgetry and exercise programs we desperately fall for, our love of jewelry. She raises consciousness about important truths in a clever, funny, and painless way by smoking out the bs, deconstructing it, and leaving us to fester in our own silliness and culpability for buying into it all. It's effective. And the message, again, seems to be: Just say no! Simply because this junk is out there doesn't mean we have to buy it, watch it, and otherwise let it into our lives. Sure, most of us would like to see some changes in what the media is offering up. But as with anything else, I think it makes sense to pause and consider whether we might be at least somewhat responsible for what's being generated—particularly if we're mothers of impressionable children. If we're out there lapping it up, we really have little standing to complain.

CHAPTER 10

MOTHERS, IT'S TIME TO ENGAGE!

I think the apple very rarely falls far from the tree. But personally? I hated my mother's gossipy, shit-talking nature. I rejected it completely.

—Patty, forty-seven, magazine editor

An old classmate of mine recently told me how surprised she was to hear how I'd turned out. She said I always struck her as a Least Likely to Be Domesticated and Have Kids Anytime Soon kind of gal. A curious thing to say, but I guess it's sort of true. If you'd told me back in law school that within eight years I'd be married with four kids, assorted pets, a van, and a hideous suburban mortgage, I'd have written you off as a major wingnut. It just wasn't part of the master plan.

Don't get me wrong. I *love* being a mother. It's dealt me this life's greatest hits and pleasures, and, truly, it's a rare day that I don't feel (or try to feel) a dose of supreme gratitude for the four kind, healthy, and always-amusing people I've managed to spawn. *No one* is going to suck the joy out of this experience for me, no matter how tough things get. At the same time, though, I see no point in playing the role of stoic, ubercompetent master, or projecting an *Everything's Great!* facade to the world as I think we mothers sometimes feel we must. Let's be honest: On the other side of joy and hugs and kisses, the business of raising children can be messy, maddening, mind-numbing, and exhausting work—on both the son and daughter fronts. If you think about it, parenting really is the great equalizer. We get one shot at growing our young properly no matter who we happen to be, no matter what our status, no matter what our circumstances. If we're going to do this thing right, we can't be falling asleep at the wheel, outsourcing, or otherwise lying down on the job. We're *on* in one way or another—24/7.

Which brings us to the role of Mom. As you might imagine, I've heard a great deal from women about mothering, far more than we can delve into here. Since mother-daughter relationships are generally known for their inherently dicey nature, it was hardly surprising to hear so many women describe theirs as complex and challenging. Still, a heartening 57 percent called their relationship with their mom or stepmom "close, caring, or positive." Twenty-six percent said they've enjoyed a "somewhat" close connection, while about 15 percent gave me the resounding *Um, no.* (Two percent marked the question "Not applicable.") Given everything we hear about these fraught relationships, that's actually better than I expected.

THE IMPORTANCE OF MOM

This isn't the place to have a full-on nature-versus-nurture blowout; both sides of that coin have their merits, and even the experts seem to disagree. Still, the basic statistics and anecdotal evidence I've cultivated about the impact of mothers on their offspring is pretty tough to discount. When all is said and done, about 80 percent of the women responding to my survey think that the relationship they've had with their mother or stepmother has directly influenced their relationships with other women. Perhaps even more telling, a full 95 percent said they believe a mother's own behavior and/or role modeling shapes, causes, or otherwise contributes to a daughter's mean or negative behavior toward other females. Most of these women, in fact, consider Mom's influence to be the key indicator of whether a girl will be aggressive, petty, manipulative, or exclusive with her peers. I won't speculate here on the propriety of blaming *your* mother for how *you've* turned out. But, believe me, a lot of women out there insist they can. Girls are sponges when they're young, these women argue, and develop their core sense of self through their primary

same-gender role model, which is usually Mom. Sonia, a flight attendant I chatted with recently, puts it this way: "Who better to teach a
girl to love herself, respect herself, and then to love and respect others? A mother who fails to teach her daughter these things by example risks raising a mean, cruel, manipulative brat. And yet you see it all
the time."

I have to believe that most mothers, stepmothers, and other caregivers out there are—or think they are—doing the best they can. Just
as it isn't easy being a girl in today's society, I think the prospect of es-
corting our daughters through Girl World intact can be equally
daunting. One thing is blatantly clear from talking to different types
of women, though: Crummy role modeling is on the minds of many.
And, sadly, some mothers appear to be in serious denial about their
kids' behavior, not to mention their own. We might dupe ourselves
into believing our girls don't notice our insincerity or little impropri-
eties (or maybe we're convinced we aren't doing anything untoward),
but you'd be surprised. Gossip, put-downs, blowoffs, phoniness, apparent disdain, status obsession, materialism, entitlement—all of it—
seem to filter right on through to the kiddies, which, of course, helps
explain why the apple frequently falls not *so* far from the tree.

Hundreds of women offered up versions of the old apple cliche,
actually: "Monkey see, monkey do," "We live what we learn," "Mean
moms beget mean girls," "It all begins in the home," and just plain
"Come on, it's where it all starts." Even a few anonymous women who
identified themselves as psychotherapists or family counselors told
me they'd seen the phenomenon play out among mother-daughter
pairs. Yoko, a journalist and mother of two in her midthirties, says she
finds it "funny how the girls you don't approve of always seem to have
mothers using the kinds of parenting techniques that perpetuate the
problem." Kerry, meanwhile, one of the many teachers I've spoken
with, minces no words about the significance of maternal virtue:

> I'd say the major cause of increased meanness is poor parent-
> ing. Mothers and fathers must spend more time with their chil-
> dren and instill in them good morals and values. Today parents
> often ignore or excuse their children's bad behavior. Ask any
> teacher and you'll get an earful about this. And I have to say,

those three to four girls that I keep tabs on? Their moms are no picnic either.

A few dozen women cited the duplicitous, two-faced types of behaviors as a mom's most egregious party foul. Sherri, a French translator living in Manhattan, doesn't have kids but knows mothers "who gossip, judge, and criticize in front of their daughters, only to turn around and play sweet to their targets. Then their girls pull the same crap, and they're confused and shocked! It's crazy." Abigail, a stay-at-home mom who also teaches yoga, sounded similarly incredulous and joked that she needed to go meditate to calm down after merely thinking about all this:

> Parenting is tough. But, God, we live in this enlightened world, and I still see women shaping the way their daughters handle the world around them through lying and manipulation. How the heck can we ever get past it if we don't admit our mistakes and show them that it all works out better in the end when we're keeping it real?

To be sure, a lot of women believe that just as good role modeling lends a solid foundation, things like under-the-breath judging, criticizing, and inconsiderate digs place a girl on a fast track toward the same. It does make sense. If you grow up watching Mom or Big Sis behaving this way without any negative repercussions—or even bonding over it and benefitting from it—that's a powerful message about how the world works. You may or may not follow suit, but you're probably going to spend at least part of your impressionable life thinking it's a valid enough way to conduct oneself.

Lindsey, a twenty-eight-year-old writer and middle school teacher, thinks so. She says that whenever she comes across an aggressive or mean-seeming girl, she need only look to the priorities and values of Mom and the household she grew up in. "If her mother places great importance on looks, conformity, beauty, and the material trimmings, sure, she might do a full 180-degree turn and run the other way," Lindsey says. "But she's far more likely to be another mean girl, in my experience." Shireen, one of my favorite Peet's Coffee & Tea servers back in Berkeley, tells me that in her experience, "the bitchiest girls usually have the bitchiest mothers encouraging the behavior." To her and to so many others, the pattern is a no-brainer. Abigail, the yoga instructor, was another one who subscribed to the trickle-down theory of phoniness and snobbery (whether intellectual, social, or other):

> The snobbiest girls I knew in high school generally had snobby moms. Moms teach their kids either to be inclusive or exclusive, fake or real. I definitely think a mother's behavior can shape her kids to be sensitive to people's feelings. It makes a difference. And those who didn't give those lessons early? I think it shows.

Regardless of a girl's innate personality, I too have to believe that modeling authenticity, respect, empathy, and tolerance, refusing to indulge anything less from others, and refraining from the put-downs and duplicity after the guests have gone home go a long way in setting the moral compasses of our offspring. My own kids have sported extremely different personalities and relational styles since the day I met them; each sprang from the box a certain way and hasn't changed a whole lot since. On the other hand, we've tried to make respect a priority in our house, and they all seem to generally get it. It's a boundary they usually don't cross outside the home. Now, I can't tell you whether this is because of inherent hard-wiring, because my husband and I are such fabulous role models, or because our kids are sufficiently deterred by the looming penal consequences for acting otherwise. But I guess I have to agree with the advice a seasoned parent of five gave me: "You have your pleasers, and you have your free spirits who want to chart their own course—they come this way, so you do what you can to steer them straight along their own unique path, but always—always—insisting on respect toward others."

Only a handful of women I heard from—less than 2 percent—seemed to flat-out dismiss the importance of a mother's influence. They insisted that even if we *do* learn how to conduct ourselves by watching Mom, we don't have to act like her. Patty, the magazine editor who says she rejected her mom's less-than-stellar social style, argues that each of us has a choice to rise above the bad habits of our mothers, sisters, or peers. One ultimately decides to be a "carbon copy or the complete opposite," she says. Monica, an unemployed computer programmer, agrees that we can't so readily blame our mothers for how we turn out. Even the best of moms, she feels, can't always control a daughter's darker inclinations:

> We can do our best to teach our girls to be good, but in the end, they are their own person and must learn from their own experience. I do think a mother who is mean will greatly increase her daughter's chances of being mean, but, sadly, I think almost every girl is mean at some point.

Three percent of the survey respondents admitted that they had no idea how much Mom's example really mattered. Tamara, a geologist in her late thirties, says she *wants* to believe our girls come hardwired but, really, she isn't so sure:

> Nature versus nurture, anyone? I believe that a given individual's unique personality and general demeanor account for most of the choices they make and the impulses they act on. Yet I must also feel the mother has something to bring to the table, or I wouldn't be trying so hard to instill compassion, conscience, courage, and so on in my children! Since I can't be totally sure if the mother's influence accounts for 1 percent or 90 percent, I guess I'll keep plugging along here just in case.

Other women offered a more nuanced perspective, suggesting that, eventually, peers become the more powerful force, one that can, for better or worse, usurp much of Mom's influence. A few of them insisted that fathers, siblings, aunts, teachers, and others play just as crucial a role in a girl's life. Mostly, though, it's been a lot of chatter about Mom. In fact, women who boasted close relationships with their mothers almost uniformly credited this positive, baseline support for helping them navigate adolescence and understand the importance of treating people with dignity. Many who commented spoke with a touching reverence, praising their mothers for their gracious role modeling, for having the strength to follow through and hold their kids accountable, for just plain listening, and for helping instill that elusive gift of self-confidence. Danielle, a fifth-grade teacher in western Massachusetts, for instance, said she learned all about healthy *and* unhealthy female dynamics by watching how her mother dealt with it all:

> She was a stunning beauty and the envy of other women. This was her power in the world. As such, she never seemed to be concerned and always seemed secure even in the face of cruelty. She taught me to hold my head high, let my beauty and grace speak for itself, and let mean women roll off my back. I experienced her as a confident and secure woman in this way, and it shaped my ability to be the same. I have rarely, if ever, been mean or negative to females.

Silvia, a mom from the foreign service community, has lived around the world. She thinks that accountability, consequences, and follow-through were key to instilling respectfulness and confidence in her family growing up, and are the things she tries to pass on to her offspring—especially her two daughters, given the amount of "unusual girl drama" swirling about at their new school:

> My mother was a great role model for us in that she refused to tolerate it when we didn't treat our siblings or other kids respectfully. In my own household, we have the same: clear and immediate consequences for treating other kids anywhere near the disrespect line. They might do some other things I don't care for, but I'm proud to say I don't think anyone could honestly call my kids mean.

It might be tempting to blame Mother Dearest for everything a girl is and does later, but I think reality is rarely so clear cut. A mother's influence and your relationship with her can be key, no doubt, but there are many other factors and influences at play when we talk about what propels girls to become aggressive and thoughtless with their own. As with patriarchal or media influences, I'm not inclined to ascribe total blame to mothers and leave it at that. Having said this, of course, nothing will stop me from getting back on my soap box to awaken some moms out there from their peaceful slumbers.

O, MOTHER, WHERE ART THOU?

I've come to believe that if there is any objective truth sewn into the fabric of this universe, it really has to be this: Treating fellow human beings with dignity and respect is essential for a civilized society to thrive. Obvious but true. And where better to revisit this simple truth than with young girls? As psychologist, professor, and author Lyn Mikel Brown has written, the inhumanity among girls is precisely what "prepares the ground for more costly and high stakes social and political disconnections among women. So while I don't particularly endorse or relish the idea of judging other moms for the jobs they're doing, I'm hardly alone in thinking it's fair to call on us all to renew our maternal vows and more mindfully model the positive, healthier behaviors we women can be so good at. Michelle, a mother of three girls, who seems totally in tune with my message, thinks a lot of moms are just distracted or functioning on autopilot and, as such, simply forget that their kids are watching, absorbing, and, quite often, mimicking us:

> You ask what I teach my daughter about female behavior? So far, my only answer is this: My girl will learn from my actions more than anything else. My life and choices will be her lesson if I will let it be an open book before her and live by certain humanistic principles of respect, equality, and honesty in my own home. When she sees us thrive with these principles, she will not need the duplicitous and hypocritical ways of the female world, which I feel have evolved as coping and survival methods, albeit a lowly and self-defeating kind.

Michelle sounds like a really good mom. But let's take it a step further. Aside from teaching our girls these basic principles, I also think it's fair to call on one another to help improve the broader culture by more meaningfully stepping up, crying foul, and getting involved in the face of our girls' incivility when we see it. It can be uncomfortable, sure; it's far easier to ignore it, play polite, save face, and let these incidents go. Most of us dislike confrontation. And, let's be honest: We hesitate because we don't want to step on anyone's toes. Many mothers are plain closed for business when it comes to anyone uttering a peep about their kids, after all. Yet little troubles me more than seeing flaccid, impotent parents do nothing as their daughters exclude, gossip, and manipulate without intervention, as if it's just a phase, just part of her inherent nature, or just a manifestation of her wonderful self-confidence and otherwise admirable "leadership" skills. It drives me—and a lot of other women—nuts to watch mothers of girls disbelieve, shrug off, or stand by in silence as their little darlings pull the latest in Girl World thuggery. Time and again, I've seen distracted, exasperated, or mentally checked-out moms sigh, throw up their hands in mock helplessness, and utter the old *"I'm* not getting involved," "Ugh, these *girls,"* or "Well, these girls just have to learn to work it out themselves." This kind of thing makes me want to hit the ground, curl up, and go fetal. It's a pretty safe bet that these are the same moms who will resent any third party—teacher, other parent, anyone—who has the audacity to cry foul or try to do something constructive where their daughter is concerned. Denial is a tough nut to crack.

The truth is, avoidance and denial don't seem to be working. Our girls need our help. Ignoring bad behavior is the functional equivalent of accepting and condoning it—the message gets through to kids loud and clear. I'm not suggesting that we fight our kids' battles or micromanage playdates or engage in nonsense like demanding to know why Kitten wasn't invited to Claire's tenth birthday party. No one's saying we should allow ourselves to get sucked into our girls' everyday social dramas—the sort of creepy helicopter style of enmeshment and overparenting that's just as egregious as underparenting. No, to a large extent, I'm talking simply about moms taking a hard look at their own behaviors and paying a bit more constructive attention to what's going on in their girls' lives. From all that I'm hearing, it's absolutely key to making sure young girls develop a rich sense of self and a solid enough ethical foundation that will leave them less likely to play games and mistreat other girls, less likely to waste their own time and emotion ruminating about power, rank, and status, and less time wondering what's "wrong" with them when they're the ones mistreated.

I'm certainly not the first to say it, but I do worry that in our grand effort to build up our kids' grade point averages and athletic prowess—or as we simply scramble about to cover our kids' basic day-to-day needs—we're sort of forgetting to teach them how to empathize, control their impulses, realize the world doesn't owe them anything, and appreciate that their behaviors have a real effect on other kids' inner lives. You know, the fundamentals. There's virtue in raising competitive kids with great brains and thick skins, to be sure, but I'm thinking there's at least an equally urgent virtue in growing compassionate, tolerant, and cooperative people who can play, think, build, fix, brainstorm, innovate, connect, and coexist peacefully in a more integrated society, one that doesn't put up with inhumanity or indulge and reward those who disrespect others for sport. I think we need to hold girls accountable for their bad choices, but it's equally clear that we need to do a more convincing and committed job of parenting, mentoring, role modeling, redirecting, and empowering them from an early age. We can let our "kids be kids," leave them to fight their own battles, let them experience life and figure it out for themselves, but we should also try to lend a bit more guidance and help foster a more supportive playing field for them to launch from as well.

Despite my strong feelings about all this, I don't often make waves on the kid front. On the whole, I do try to let things play themselves out organically. On the other hand, I think, if we're going to bring children into this world, don't we have a certain responsibility to them and to society? We can't be burying our heads in the sand, even (or especially) with the little ones. Our girls are watching us, waiting for cues. And they do, quite frequently, need our help—not our denial or inaction. Sometimes you just have to bust out of the collusive parental silence and speak out. I've found myself in these types of situations a couple of times just this past year, and, no doubt about it, it's difficult. In one instance, I'd heard other parents literally speak ill of a little girl (let's call her Morgan) for years. My kids and I had little contact with Morgan, but other parents had essentially designated her the class bully and seemed to have already given up on her. From what I was hearing, she routinely showed up on the "Do Not Place My Child in a Class with This Child Next Year" request forms that certain parents submitted to school each spring. Yet nobody seemed to be coming clean and talking to the parents directly, possibly because it was socially awkward. They were highly visible, well-liked people in the community. The old cone of silence thing again.

I was walking our dog to school one afternoon for the usual pickup when, as fate would have it, I witnessed Morgan holding court and ridiculing my daughter of all people. "She's sooooooo bad at biking!" she shouted amid a group of girls. "Why does she even bother? She's so lame!" Yes, I could have said nothing and let the kids figure it out for themselves. No, I don't make it a practice to fight my kids' battles. But what about the larger picture? The poisoned culture that everyone had apparently grown to accept? It wasn't just about Morgan and my daughter. The ongoing, unchecked behavior of that kid—who was probably hurting in her own way—needed to be stopped in its tracks. Recalling the no-nonsense moves of my younger sister Tricia, the elementary school teacher, I got down on my knees, looked Morgan in the eye, recited the Golden Rule and all that, and told her the harassment had to stop. Then I called her parents.

Though taken off guard in a haze of mild denial, it didn't take the mother long to own it completely. She was lovely, actually. She said she'd been too distracted with work and family health issues to deal with Morgan meaningfully, hadn't realized that things had degenerated so far, and vowed to pay closer attention. I am definitely not patting myself on the back here; I felt stupid-guilty, worried I'd been too aggressive myself, and wondered if I came off as some sort of wannabe Girl World Enforcer just because I was writing this book. I know some experts might argue that I did my kid a disservice by injecting myself into the mix. For example, in the book *Girl Wars: 12 Strategies That Will End Female Bullying*, authors Cheryl Dellasega and Charisse Nixon say we mothers need to be extra careful not to overreact, get caught up in our own drama, and give our daughter the impression that she's "incapable of managing the situation herself" by intervening. They emphasize, as I have, that one of the reasons we pay so much attention to relational aggression among girls is "because moms respond from the heart" when they see other girls being hurt:

> It touches our hearts to think of another young woman being subjected to what we encountered ourselves. Every mom needs to examine her motives, though, and make sure unresolved emotions are not driving her to respond in unproductive ways.

This is solid advice. The same book contains excellent strategies for helping empower girls and build reserves of self-esteem and assertiveness so they can prevail on their own. Personally, though, I no longer doubt that I did the right thing with Morgan. Not in today's climate, when I'm hearing from hundreds of mothers feeling the same frustration with girl-on-girl incivility and exclusionary games, when girls are quietly and not so quietly hurting and hating themselves as a direct result of these shenanigans. I wasn't trying to parent Morgan. I wasn't acting out of some vicarious, childish, overly intrusive rage. And I doubt that I denied my daughter any precious life lesson or teachable moment, or passed along the "relational equivalent of math anxiety," as Lyn Mikel Brown has legitimately warned against. Really, let's not overthink this. The child was getting away with hurtful behavior repeatedly and had caused enough heartache. Her parents needed to hear it, the behavior needed curbing, and she needed to be called out and given a chance to refresh her image. She actually struck me as a nice enough kid who just needed some more fine-tuned guidance. What's wrong with kids seeing adults refusing to tolerate these kinds of behaviors? What's wrong with communicating with other parents in an honest, constructive manner?

I agree with Mona O'Moore, coordinator of the Anti-Bullying Research and Resource Centre at Trinity College Dublin, who cautions that "by not challenging bullying behavior, valuable opportunities are lost in shaping society's need for respect for each person's dignity." Nancy Mullin, executive director of Bullying Prevention, a consulting firm in Massachusetts, also believes it's crucial for adults to involve themselves more often:

> Bullying happens in front of or within earshot of adults most of the time, so they need to be the first responders, and they need to be effective. The sole responsibility shouldn't be dumped on kids.

I've actually found some of the so-called expert commentary on bullying pretty disappointing in that it's so often centered on the reactive. *Toughen up. Fight back. Walk away. Change schools. Don't let them get you down.* As with office bullies who are frequently allowed to roam this earth as they please, I think we need to try a little harder to teach kids to respect one another in the *first* place, to stop letting them get away with anything less, and to encourage them to appreciate the real and lasting hurt they're causing in other human beings. Bullying, harassment, possessiveness, and exclusionary tactics are pandemic among girls—this we know. And it is essential to recognize, Richard Holloway says in his book *On Forgiveness,* that "a single act of passion or thoughtlessness can destroy someone's future happiness." That's a powerful statement sadly grounded in truth. If we as adults don't step in and insist on a physically *and* emotionally safe environment in which young girls can thrive, we are a huge part of the problem.

I appreciate harmony, etiquette, and the school-of-hard-knocks ideology as much as the next person, but I say enough of the coddling and faux social graces. Let's not worry so much about depriving our young children of their "special" developmental moments. A 2005 U.S. Department of Education report actually flags bystanding as one of the biggest problems with bullying and social aggression. Did you know, for instance, that the involvement of bystanders frequently determines the nature, extent, and outcome of a bullying episode? We tend to focus so much on the aggressor but, according to Robert Sege, pediatrician and chief of ambulatory pediatrics at Boston Medical Center, bystanders are equally culpable in that they perpetuate or even intensify situations. Adults owe it to kids to more proactively upstand, get involved, and nip the nastiness in the bud so that perpetrators, bystanders, and victims alike know with all the certainty their developing brains can muster that hurtful behavior won't be tolerated. Our girls need to know that putdowns, exclusionary power plays, and gratuitous cruelty are not valid currencies in the world of interpersonal relationships, that it isn't a cool or acceptable way of relating, and it won't in fact make them popular or get them ahead. If nothing else, try to view upstanding as a public service from which we can all benefit. I can't put it any better than Rose, a mom of two young girls, who thinks that all of us, adults and kids alike, need to recognize the opportunities to do the right things as they arise. "In standing up for and preserving another's dignity, we might very well save our own."

A RENEWED CALL FOR RESPONSIBLE MOTHERING

When it comes to parenting, I have to agree with Elastigirl of *The Incredibles:* It's time to engage. A *Do as I say, not as I do* or *Let kids be kids* approach is not going to cut it with today's savvy kids. This book offers up a tall order of issues, but possibly its greatest contribution would be to inspire more mothers to meaningfully commit themselves to raising a more compassionate, inclusive, and integrated generation of girls, to give them the tools to define and feel good about themselves, and to help them protect and nurture that rather than look to others for self-worth and happiness. A girl's fragile sense of self is what leaves her vulnerable to the shadowy stuff, after all. I'm convinced that the more sturdy, independent minded, and confident we grow them, the less likely they'll be to cut down their peers now and into adulthood, the less likely they'll become victims of unhealthy self-narratives, and the less likely they'll find themselves stuck in a belief that they aren't worthy or good enough to follow their dreams and tackle life's challenges.

On the other hand—and I see no contradiction here—for the grown women among us who are accustomed to pinning their bad behavior on Mom or their upbringing at this stage of the game, I beg your pardon. I don't know your pain or past. I don't know what it will take for you to rise above it. But you're not operating on autopilot here—or at least you shouldn't be. Ultimately, I think that no one, not even Mom, can make you disrespect another human being. It might well be time to take greater responsibility for how you view and relate to others. Yes, Mom should have done better. But she didn't. Poor mothering doesn't entitle anyone to a lifelong Get Out of Jail Free card in the game of humanity.

I don't mean to imply that everything is doom and gloom out there. It's not. All I'm saying is that if you're a mother, I hope you'll consider stepping up and taking these issues seriously if you aren't already. Prepare yourself for more mindful heavy lifting. Here's what other moms are saying: Let's spend more time with our girls. Let's encourage them to be more inclusive, interested, and tolerant, especially with new and timid girls, nonconforming girls, or girls who are somehow "different" from them. Let's try listening to our daughters sometimes without the lecturing or second-guessing. (Now, *there's* something I need to work on.) One school counselor told me point-blank she thinks that not only are most mothers not engaged enough she thinks, "most of us are failing our daughters miserably. It's a lucky girl who has a good enough mother."

Even if you disagree with that sad assessment, it's clear from what I'm hearing that a lot of us could benefit from reassessing and strengthening our mother-daughter bonds in a real, personal, one-on-one way. Our girls need solid connections with an assortment of other people, too, like Dad, their peers, teachers, and extended family. They need to sense that safety net beneath their toes at home and out in their communities—to feel secure, like they belong, and will be liked and appreciated for their true selves. They need to be liberated from the constant threat of being slapped with those spirit-deflating judgments and disses that seem to lurk around every corner. And they need plenty of options for channeling their talents and building self-confidence, whether through sports, scouting, mother-daughter book clubs, girl-focused empowerment groups, community service, empathy or antibullying class, or all those other programs available at school and elsewhere.

A couple dozen women specifically cited team sports and acting as crucial to their healthy development of self, not to mention an outlet for avoiding some of the pitfalls of female adolescent nonsense. Kris, a college sophomore, says the strong, independent, supportive, and "logical" women from her crew team taught her invaluable, lifelong lessons about sisterhood and support:

> Indeed, we do experience "drama" and "bitchiness," but I would trust most of these women with my life. I would suggest you encourage your daughters to participate in sports. This is where women are forced to cooperate and think about how their actions affect others. It is also a way to bond and make girlfriends in a way that isn't founded on prettiness or wealthiness, but instead drive, work ethic, and similar interests.

It turns out there's some really wonderful grassroots stuff happening out there for girls beyond the usual sports, hobbies, and scouting activities. In addition to all the fine work that Wiseman, Simmons, Dellasega, educators, and others are doing with the younger set, I was thrilled to come across a nonprofit organization called the Kind Campaign while surfing the Web a few weeks back. Started by a couple of young Pepperdine grads, the campaign has worked with schools, sororities, camps, and other girl groups around the country to raise awareness about the crucial role of kindness, compassion, and understanding in female relationships. The point is to reduce girl-on-girl hostilities and the very types of lingering effects we've been discussing here.

Zanna, a mom-friend at my twins' former school in Virginia, recently turned me on to a terrific group that she and her daughter joined based on the book *The Mother-Daughter Project: How Mothers and Daughters Can Band Together, Beat the Odds, and Thrive Through Adolescence*, by SuEllen Hamkins, MD, and Renée Schultz, MA. The idea is to create a safe haven for a few girls and their mothers to come together and connect in depth in a nonjudgmental environment at regular meetings that occur, hopefully, over the course of several years. They meet for potluck, crafts, and other fun activities but also hold open and frank discussions on topics like friendship, fights, body image, boys, and all of those other loaded developmental issues. What a wonderful way for girls to stay connected with their moms and a trusted, safe posse of other females through those challenging adolescent years. (As long as things don't get too exclusive and clubby, that is.)

Antibullying efforts, meanwhile, appear to have really taken off. October now brings us National Bullying Prevention Awareness Week, and we've seen all sorts of celebrities and politicians pounding the pavement to "stomp out bullying" through organizations like Love Our Children USA. We're seeing bullying and cyber bullying workshops popping up with increasing frequency at schools and community centers, and more and more websites dedicated to bullying and relational aggression. Britain's Beatbullying website, for example, makes for an incredibly helpful resource, offering everything from "CyberMentors" who will listen to and counsel bullied kids, to lesson plans for teachers, to parent resources.

At the same time, pretty much everyone out there seems to agree that we need to be taking a closer look at our kids' texting and Internet use and talking about it with them, particularly since so much of the dissing that goes on these days spreads this way. It feels slightly creepy to do it but there's a lot of insight to be gained through a bit of responsible, within-reason oversight and sleuthing. It's important to remember that none of this is really "private," after all. I've seen the impulsive, mean, insulting commentary among teenagers firsthand on cellphones, Facebook, email, AIM, and the latest favorite, Skype. It's potent stuff. Really, it's not a thick skin you need—full body armor's more like it. I think we have to appreciate that not all of us have that toughness and resiliency, especially the developing, hormonally charged, sensitive, and impulsive youth among us. On this score, kids really are still kids. They need our guidance, our support, our limits, and, mostly, a more hospitable, reliably safe environment. As Mary Pipher explains in *Reviving Ophelia:*

> We can strengthen girls so that they will be ready. We can encourage emotional toughness and self-protection. We can support and guide them. But most important, we can change our culture. We can work together to build a culture that is less complicated and more nurturing, less violent and sexualized and more growth producing. Our daughters deserve a society in which all their gifts can be developed and appreciated.

Would you believe that Pipher wrote her wonderful book a full fifteen years ago—in 1995? Yet I sit here wondering what, if anything, has changed for the better in Girl World. Since we've been around this block before, I have to preconcede that any renewed enthusiasm I'm able to generate among women will all be for naught if more of us mothers don't assume a more convincing, proactive, and highly personal sense of responsibility toward our daughters. We may not be the entire answer, but we do play a significant role in all this. I think most of us would agree that getting our girls off to an emotionally healthy and confident start in life will only enhance their experience and save them a whole lot of trouble down the road, the kind of trouble some of us adult women have dealt with for years, even decades. None of us wants that for the next generation. What remains to be seen is whether we have the collective resolve to really shake things up this time.

CHAPTER 11

THE UPSIDE OF AGING?

It probably depends on the individual, but most women I know who are my age seem to appreciate that we really are in this together, that all the petty competitions and mind games were a waste of time. As we get older and hopefully more mature, I do think sisterhood starts to mean something to a lot of us.

—Jeanne, fifty-eight, retiree

The role of mothers was certainly one of the more central themes that emerged in listening to women suggest ways to improve the female culture. Another theme that emerged time and again was this notion that things generally tend to get better over the years—the so-called upside of aging. Of the women I heard from, 65 percent do believe that conditions improve with age and the passage of time—after we've worked our way through some of the various life stages such as school, the workplace, dating and marriage, mothering, hormonal changes, and more. They think *we* get better. Twenty-seven percent felt this was "somewhat" the case, while only 8 percent disagreed entirely. From where I sit, that is awfully comforting to hear.

It does seem logical that as we age, we shed the insecurities of youth, grow more comfortable in our skins, mellow out a bit, and become less concerned about conforming or fitting in. Older connections deepen, prospects for new ones open up to the extent we want them to, and we feel wiser, more mature, and better positioned to enjoy the richest friendships of our lives. Indeed, women confirmed this progression over and over. The stories of friendship I've been getting from those in their fifties, sixties, seventies, and beyond, in particular, are incredibly touching and inspiring—one can often detect an undeniable peace or calm radiating through their words. Many assured me that they have no interest in judging, competing, or one-upping other women, mostly because they've finally figured it all out: The payoff just isn't there. Others emphasized that their priorities have shifted, the superficial trappings no longer matter, and they just plain care less about how others view them. They think for themselves, and if others don't like it? "Tough" was an attitude I heard expressed more than a few times. Some, like Patty, who's retired and in her sixties, told me she's found that women in her age group really do seem to value the concept of sisterhood and, on that basis alone, tend to make better candidates for friendship:

> I think we gradually grow into our authenticity and finally shed the need to compete at the expense of the sisterhood. I just really think that most older women realize how detrimental it is to our sex to behave with negativity toward each other.

The increased wisdom and perspective, Patty thinks, is also what helps these experienced women feel more empathetic, accepting, and forgiving of others—and themselves. My own mother feels this way. She says that women her age seem gentler on the whole, more willing to open up, and less self-conscious and insincere in their dealings, "probably because they've been around the block a few times and know the alternative is pointless." This so-called mellowing seems to have ensnared even the most aggressive among us. Forty-eight-year-old Willow, a cosmetics company rep and self-described "reformed Queen Bee," feels she's outgrown her nastier tendencies and is "*much* nicer in middle age." She wonders who has time for such nonsense, a refrain I heard from dozens of like-minded women of every age group. Other women offered versions of what they call a more universal, "sobering truth" of aging: We don't just age, we grow up and, in the process, "realize the mean-girl stuff is just a silly waste of time." Deborah, a mom in her forties, feels that "time and life experiences teach women they no longer need to punish themselves or each other simply for being born female. We can only hope for them and for ourselves that this is so."

GIFTS OF CONFIDENCE, PERSPECTIVE, AND—HOPEFULLY—MATURITY

Women from my survey also frequently linked the concept of authentic, stable friendship with the self-confidence that so often comes with age and experience. Belinda, another woman in her sixties, who finds that both her long-term and newer friendships feel calmer and more satisfying, says she only wishes that she'd had that hard-earned confidence when she was younger.

> Absolutely, I'm more confident. Because we become ourselves in a way we aren't as children, we develop real opinions and real beliefs that are our own, and can share those with our friends. I have a confidence and certainty in myself that I never had as a child, which makes me a more stable friend to my friends as well.

Again and again, comments like these came in, suggesting that there might well be a silver lining to a woman's aging after all—the gifts of confidence, perspective, and maturity:

> It takes many years to finally figure out that none of us are perfect, that we're all struggling with the same things inside. Here's a tip: When women get to the point where they can laugh at themselves genuinely, that's when they start connecting with one another.

> You share more of the life experiences that matter (good/bad) together. Trust gets stronger. You learn to ignore insignificant shortcomings in your friends which would have previously bothered you. All of this makes the bonds more mature.

> As I grow older, I don't take the slights so seriously. I also care less about looks and the material things, more

> about life and thinking about others. I do think that
> women become less self-centered and start thinking
> about bigger things.
>
> Aging is the great humbler. There are fewer things about
> which to be competitive. No cheerleading tryouts, no
> competition for first chair in band, no competing for a
> guy, no competition over a job or who gets the
> promotion. I think we know ourselves better as we age
> and gravitate toward people we admire or who share
> common traits and interests.

Reading the inspiring words of these more seasoned women actually left me a little envious—in a good way. Not that I need to accelerate the aging process any more than nature's already insisting, but I think we can learn a great deal from what it apparently took these women years to master. How incredibly liberating to finally relax into oneself and more easily filter out the bad noise, to let go of the nagging uncertainties and inner dialogues and prizeless competitions, to just sit back quietly and enjoy life's main attractions. If only we could bottle that confidence, wisdom, and self-love and gift it to ourselves earlier. As Deborah puts it, "Gosh, imagine if all that learning and wisdom came at a younger age; the trouble it would have saved us! Some of us sure could've used it."

All of this does sound idyllic, but then, not everyone agrees with the "upside of aging" perspective. Not everyone gets cozier, more gracious, and more civilized as they age, after all. And not everyone heals, gets a personality overhaul, or suddenly opens up to trust and friendship. In fact, some of the 35 percent in my survey pool who questioned this model argued that many of us just grow all the more bitter, isolated, and entrenched in our negativity. Alice, a fiftysomething legal secretary, thinks it depends completely on the woman and her level of maturity going in:

> I see a lot of hatred and venom between older women that
> shouldn't exist. I think we *like* to think we get wiser with age
> but if you don't have good relationships early on, you'll be
> more likely to put up defenses that'll keep you from making
> them later.

Yessha, a woman in her fifties, offers another thoughtful perspective about our female culture as a whole:

> For the most part, I think it's true that female relationships get "better," but I'm not altogether convinced of this. I see a lot of isolated women out there and think it is a flaw of our culture. I think women of all ages would benefit from authentic, stable, reliable, and emotionally intimate relationships early on in life. It's too bad it takes a long while to figure this out.

A few other women, meanwhile, shared some downright calcified views. Take sixty-seven-year-old Cora, who says she's seen it all and "knows with certainty" that women remain the crueler sex no matter the age:

> We're still catty and talk about each other behind backs. We still concern ourselves with who's prettiest, thinnest, happiest, and has the nicest clothes. We're on the lookout for someone who's uglier and fatter or unhappy so we can feel better about ourselves. And we all still obsess over who's having lunch or vacationing with whom. Better? Lord, no.

Regina, a forty-four-year-old cleaning woman, doesn't buy the "with age comes maturity" optimism either, saying, "Females can be jealous, nasty, snotty, and competitive at any age." Cora, Regina, and a fairly distressing number of others insist they've known few women who *haven't* participated in this behavior to some extent, even in their golden years. Others say that while our responses and coping mechanisms might improve with age, our core personalities don't—you know, the old leopards-don't-change-their-spots view. To them, skittish, reserved women tend to stay skittish and reserved their whole lives, while "nasty girls just grow up to be nasty women." Shirley, a fifty-three-year-old gift shop owner, says she thinks women take even less time to form relationships as they get older. She tells me that her eighty-six-year-old mother confronts the same nonsense at her assisted living facility that she's encountered anywhere else at any other time in her life. She says women can actually be seen shifting meal trays around to discourage and exclude unwanted dining companions who are, invariably, other women. Like those sneaky female professors we spoke of earlier, the image of this would have an almost comical quality if it weren't such a grim and painful reality for real live women out there.

FOR SOME, TIME REALLY DOES HEAL THE WOUNDS

Women from the "gets-better-with-age" camp also spoke to how the old dents and dings that once nagged them ceaselessly tended to attenuate through the years, despite the tenacious, stubborn memories. Marilyn, a seventy-four-year-old living in Rossmoor, California, says that after enduring various episodes with women who "broke her spirit" and kept her anxious and always on her toes, she eventually relaxed into what she calls her "old age" and "got lucky with a nice group of women who seemed equally relaxed, accepting, and ready to be themselves." Despite all those years of wariness, discomfort, and skepticism about the intentions of females, she says that the wounds and vulnerability faded substantially, and she now feels deeply attached to her girlfriends.

Diane, a fifty-eight-year-old retired elementary school teacher and Fulbright scholar, told me she had trouble with triangles, possessiveness, and hurtful secrets even before the "in" group from high school ganged up and made fun of her for her "thick ankles" and family status. She calls all this the "unfortunate roots" of her lifelong battles with self-esteem on the female front and says she never felt too sure of herself around women; never felt she could just be herself. "It always stuck in my craw, that nagging doubt that I wasn't good enough or attractive enough for other women to like me—wasn't worthy, really, in any way." She spent decades feeling uncomfortable with her own, always putting up a good front at work and at home through the veneer of confidence, clowning around, and her considerable professional accomplishments. It wasn't until she got through the work and child-rearing years, she says, that she finally began feeling less judged and on display. After decades of avoiding women, she now actively socializes with them and rarely finds herself feeling intimidated or unworthy as she did "virtually every day" in her earlier years—a seemingly happy ending. Like many others from this age group, Diane attributes her current comfort level to the gradual lessening of insecurities among women and within herself.

Other ladies who said they'd nursed some serious wounds over the years cited the healing properties of plain old time. Maria, fifty-three and a patient care coordinator, feels that the benefits of aging include maturity but also the gradual dulling of those "awful" memories:

> The piquant nature of the pain has faded with time, regardless of the level of heartache that I initially felt. This has been one of the many benefits of aging: increased wisdom with lessened pain.

Eighty-two-year-old Beverly agrees. Time might not heal all wounds, she figures, but it does help. She told me it was a "long, slow" process letting women back into her life after her husband's affair, the death of her best friend, and her constant feelings of inadequacy around other women, but time helped blunt her fears. Still, she says, "I can probably count the total number of truly trustworthy lady friends I've had in my entire life on one hand." And, of course, some women reminded me that age and maturity are two very different things. As Lila, a seventy-one-year-old painter, explains, "If a woman isn't confident in herself, regardless of her age, there will be limitations in her ability to be a true friend—or to accept one."

A few dozen other women, meanwhile, told me they'd grown savvier about choosing prospective friends through the years, learning how to weed out the toxic ones and bypass the unhealthy alliances for quality connections. Many admitted that they figured this out much later in life, unfortunately, after years of senseless shenanigans, hurt feelings, and self-flagellation. Still, several boasted that they now enjoy a ripened ability to "spot the kinds of women—and men—who are toxic and superficial" and not let them linger too long in their lives. Ann, who is in her sixties, says she no longer feels drawn to the types of women who don't bring out her best or respect her "truth." Nor are there the work and parent obligations compelling her to spend her time with them:

> I think it's a natural process to start weeding out the bad seeds as you get older, and hopefully wiser). You feel more free to be nicer to everyone else, I think, but also free to be more selective with those you'll choose to keep close.

Marilyn, the Rossmoor retiree, says much the same:

> I pick and choose the positive people I want to be around today, unlike when I was younger and felt trapped or forced to associate with certain women. I don't have the energy or inclination to fight or be petty or judgy anymore or be around those who do. I am only close to those I genuinely love and who really have my best interests at heart. Life now really is looking too short for anything else.

Constance, a fifty-six-year-old retiree, says she's "entered the land of wisdom on my gleeful journey to cronehood" and thinks opening up to the possibilities, trusting her instincts, and, again, choosing wisely helped her rise above all the negativity. If you behave honestly and respectfully, she insists, "that is exactly what you'll attract in other women." Peggy asserts that one still has to be picky in choosing one's girlfriends, but for the right reasons—not the frivolous or superficial ones:

> I've taught all three of my nieces to never keep friends around who aren't supportive, loyal, and honorable. If they gossip about you once, they'll do it again. There are very good women to pick and choose who you reveal your deepest secrets to. As I've gotten older, I've been better attuned to who has good character and who doesn't. You just learn to pick carefully.

The passage of time can help with any residual regret a woman happens to be harboring, as well. Several women told me they'd carried vague parcels of guilt and sadness with them for years over their past nastiness, thoughtlessness, and broken friendships—not in an active, troubled-soul way but in a quiet, regretful, and remorseful way. Some wrote that they felt a quiet restlessness for years and hoped to find a way to make amends for their behavior, or to otherwise repair relationships that had ended badly. This isn't terribly surprising. It's only natural for us to want to make amends, I think, especially if you buy into the women-as-nurturers-and-peacemakers perspective. Take away the stoicism and drama and sideshows, and many of us find such loose ends troubling. We want to gain closure and a peace of sorts by coming clean, settling up, and atoning for our "bad." In other words, most of us do have a working conscience.

THE PEACE THAT COMES FROM ATONEMENT AND CLOSURE

This, it appears, is where confrontation, apology, and forgiveness have come into play—often unexpectedly. Now, I have no illusions that we're all going to fan out, locate the women we wronged or who wronged us, and proceed to confront or apologize. Nobody's advocating a global primal scream here, where we actively drum up the past and reignite old hurts. But to the extent that these opportunities arise and the players are available, what's to stop you? As Richard Holloway explains in *On Forgiveness*, the act of forgiving is one of the most "astonishing and liberating of the human experiences." True, our victims might have already forgiven us and moved on, but unless we can admit to the trespass, "the value of [that] forgiveness will lie there like an uncashed cheque." So shoot that email or Friend request. Pick up the phone. At the next reunion, why not tell someone you made an immature mistake, that you're sorry for hurting her, that the truth of the matter was you envied her, admired her, secretly found her intimidating or threatening (or were just being young and stupid)?

Consider Diana, whose "distressing behavior and treatment" of a dear old pal drove a wedge between them, fried the friendship, and kept them and their families apart for years. Diana says that although she never admitted it, she always felt terrible about it and never really shook the guilt and regret.

> Then she moved to the West Coast, so distance kept us apart. Somehow we found each other again, and I apologized. She was very gracious, and although I didn't think I deserved it, I appreciated it. Definitely a relief.

Marilyn, a news reporter in her thirties, said she couldn't just do nothing when she was trolling Classmates.com and "ran into" a girl she and her high school compatriots had ostracized mercilessly:

Years after we graduated, the girl put a comment on Class-mates.com that said, "To all of you who were mean to me, I'm successful and happy, so take that." I paid the fee so I could send her an email and apologize. It makes me very sad to think she just so badly wanted a friend, and I made things worse for her.

For some, confronting one's oppressors and targets can be a real watershed moment, bringing the type of peace women say they've quietly craved for years. Writing for *More* magazine, the writer Rachel Cline recently illustrated the power of lasting guilt and remorse—and ultimately forgiveness—from the vantage point of ag-gressor. She says the glories of Facebook forgiveness are what finally put the "mean little girl" Rachel squarely on the path to peace and atonement, a path that had eluded her in her twenty years of therapy. Cline did terrible things to kids as a kid, a true bully, she says. The school suspended her, but she never did apologize or make amends to her chief target, Didi. Life went on, but she didn't exactly forget. For years, in fact, she went out of her way to avoid bumping into the Didis of the world:

> [W]hen I was back home, if I spotted anyone who resembled her—even if that person was a child—I would cross traffic to escape. If I was introduced to an adult Didi who had the right approximate height and hair color, I couldn't look her in the eye.

Flash forward all these years later and, in an "adrenaline-driven state of fear," Cline logged on to Facebook, coursed through the ghosts of her past, and eventually found Didi. "There was no option but to write to her and beg forgiveness, which I did, that very night at one AM." Didi replied within minutes and said she'd forgiven her long ago, though "not without some effort." The emotions Cline de-scribes are quite intense:

> The knot in my heart unraveled. Relief set in, followed by tears . . . As of that moment, Rachel the mean little girl could

leave the building—there was nothing left to keep her after school.

I've now heard a lot of Rachel-and-Didi-like stories, their tales differing in detail but always highlighting the power of memory and the gratification that reaching out, having an open dialogue, apologizing, and forgiving can lend in broken relationships even years later. Zoe, a grocery store clerk in El Paso, Texas, told me that her traumatic junior high memories had mostly faded until she was reunited with the culprits a decade later. Though the old, shameful feelings came rushing back, she used the opportunity to talk about it and detail for those women how their pointless taunting and excluding clung to her for years:

> Long fruitful discussions were had with a few of these ladies and the air was cleared, finally. Amends were made, and I think we have all felt a lot better since. It was like this giant weight, one we couldn't see, but definitely felt, had finally lifted.

I had an interesting, almost surreal experience along these lines when a couple of old fraternity and sorority members read my *Times* article, remembered bits of the decades-old mess, and wrote to extend their support and regret. While I never meant for my writing to operate as a hit piece on the Greek system or anyone in particular, I found this type of acknowledgment and gesture incredibly meaningful. One woman who'd treated me poorly said she was ashamed to see pieces of herself in my story after all this time. She wrote a warm and apologetic email for her role in the ordeal, for being "clueless," and for failing to stand up for me when we "shared the pledge floor." It absolutely blew me away; still does. She lived nearby and asked if I wanted to meet up and talk it over with our dogs—a prospect that left me conflicted and ruminating for days. Ultimately, I told her how much the apology meant to me and explained that I wasn't even sure *I'd* have done the right thing had it been some other girl being ejected from the tribe instead of me. I wasn't standing in judgment, I assured her. But I also admitted that I had a tough time seeing people from that period of my life—and promptly wiggled out of setting a date.

We never did get together, and, frankly, I was relieved to escape the situation by moving away. Part of me, I gather, is still reluctant to go there even after all this time. Part of me probably still isn't ready to trust her. And, truly, part of me doesn't want to put someone standing before me in an awkward spot for something that happened so long ago in our clueless youth; the prospect of it feels forced, inorganic, too Maury Povich. We all have kids now. We've mostly moved on in life. So I'm not even sure what good would come of it. I found it so cathartic to write it all out and acknowledge what happened and how it affected me. It feels good to try raising an awareness about these things now. But opening it all up again in real time with the actual players? I'm sure the psychologists out there would have a field day with this, but for me, personally, I'm sorry to say that I'm just not sure I need to do more at this point.

Trust is a tricky thing, after all. Allowing others access to one's inner self after a flogging or two isn't easy, even (or especially) with the passage of decades. I don't care how much older and wiser you are. When push comes to shove, it remains an extremely delicate matter to muster faith in oneself and in others, to come out of hiding, open up, and take those risks again. Some tell me it's been an all-out battle to allow themselves any kind of vulnerability, to go the distance, beyond arm's length, and get over the soft, quiet fear of returning to that abyss of disappointment and hurt. Still, you can find plenty of women like Ellen, forty-four, who describes her earlier experiences with women as "devastating," but who, in the end, puts a positive spin on her difficult past:

> My trust and friendship, for a long time, went to men instead. For many reasons, it felt safer and I felt more in control. I think I just got lucky, and over the years a few women managed to befriend me in spite of my wariness, and slowly, with their help, I healed. It took me a long time to trust women again, and I wasn't always successful. Sometimes I still managed to make bad choices but quickly recognized it and got out of those friendships. I think the wounds I suffered will never go away. It is a deep-rooted damage. But the joy and friendship I am blessed to have eventually allowed into my life more than

make up for it. Though we can't change our past, we can change our future.

I'm almost, though not quite, with Ellen. For me and some of the other Walking Wounded out there, time has healed much, but it's still hard to get to that point of complete trust even when we want to. I still embellish my interactions with humor and excuses and other well-honed defense mechanisms. I give scraps of myself to most people but invariably hold a lot back. I've grown so accustomed to this style of relating that most of the time I don't even know I'm doing it. I'm no longer closed for business and, like Ellen, do have a wonderful, core group of girlfriends I'm grateful for—the kind of people "I'd let change my diaper," as one mom I know describes the true test of friendship. But other than family, I've probably felt truly comfortable and revealed my real self, secrets and all, to only two women in my entire life. Nothing wrong with that in and of itself; it's the reasons behind the reluctance that are unfortunate. The genuinely intimate connections we make in life are indeed rare, and it sure feels good when you get there, but it's a doubly tough proposition for some of us. I'd be lying if I painted things any rosier than this. As Ellen said, it's a deep-rooted damage, I guess. Still, after all those years of hiding, I'd say I'm in a pretty good spot and glad to be sharing if it might at all help others see the benefits of reassessing their relational styles and those broader concepts of sisterhood.

CHAPTER 12

BETTING ON THE POWER OF FEMALES AND "SISTERHOOD"

Get that cease-fire in place, and other things can start to happen. Without that cease-fire, we are still trapped in the quicksand.
—Colin Powell

So is pining for a more open and collaborative spirit among women unrealistic or hokey? An outdated pie-in-the-sky dream? Sadly, many women seem to think so. Some of my own friends have given me the old eye roll when I've gone into my sisterhood spiel; they find the mere utterance of the word cringe-inducing. "It's polarizing," they'll say, or "It makes me think of some militant, fringe crusade." But I think it depends on how you define it. The word *sisterhood* means different things to different people, has been co-opted for all sorts of purposes, and has unquestionably come to turn off or intimidate many—much like *feminism* and *solidarity* have, I suppose. Sure, rallying girls and women to behave in more sisterly fashion is a noble goal, the holdouts admit. But as one woman explained, "It's somehow more real when no one calls it that. And anyway, it's about actions, not words."

Exactly. Call it whatever you'd like or nothing at all. Just please work with me here. Because, to me, it's actually pretty elementary; even basic dictionary definitions nail what I'm getting at. *Merriam-*

Webster, for instance, calls sisterhood "the solidarity of women based on shared conditions, experiences, or concerns." That's not so intimidating or objectionable, is it? Women have all sorts of shared conditions and experiences, after all, particularly when it comes to our relationships with one another. From what I'm hearing, most of us do, in fact, feel conflicted and share concern about the way we're viewing and behaving toward one another. Most of us are concerned about an undercurrent of negativity and incivility. Most of us are experiencing some ambivalence and really *would* like to coexist in a more peaceful and welcoming society of women. Some told me they wished we could behave, literally, more like "sisters in the truest, best sense of the word"—like partners rather than rivals. They *want* to trade the judging and competition and skepticism for basics like respect, support, and kindness. Who wouldn't?

But women are wondrously complex beings, to state the obvious. Most of us are doing our best on all fronts, full throttle, every day, amid competing demands from multiple sectors. I know this because I live it. Writing a book about our darker side is inherently controversial work no matter how you go about it. It's emotional terrain, there aren't any across-the-board truths, and I'm bound to upset people no matter what I say. Again, though, this isn't about dwelling on the past or advancing blame with a side of bitterness, it's about examining these issues in a different light, owning our conduct, and taking the reins to improve conditions for girls and women from the inside out. It's a naked appeal to conscience and compassion and, in the purest sense, a quest for genuine sisterhood. Utopian, yes, but I think most of us still believe in basic human goodness, especially in the realm of the female. It's there, within us all. The levers for change are there too. With a better understanding of the fallout, maybe—just maybe—we'd feel more inclined to pause, think twice, restrain ourselves and, yes, behave more sisterly toward one another. And if we happen to stoke some good old-fashioned guilt and shame along our road to progress, I have no problem with that. I'm a product of the School Sisters of Notre Dame nuns. Whatever gets us there.

I can be as cynical as the most accomplished cynics out there. But, really, what's so cheesy or sinister about renewing our attentions to female relationships, where the highs are so wonderfully wonderful but the hurts and resulting fallout are often so horribly horrible. As Sarah

Seltzer wrote in the *Jewish Daily Forward*—amazingly enough, the very week I am finishing this manuscript—now is absolutely the time for us to be reconsidering notions of sisterhood:

> [Women] may dismiss the idea of a giant sisterhood or the no-
> tion "we're all in it together" because it sounds too hippy-
> dippy, earth-mothery or gender-essentialist—and it doesn't
> take into account important differences in the way class, race,
> culture, and religion inform feminist goals. Still . . . there may
> be real value in promoting some modified vision of sisterhood
> and a connection between all women (including those who
> identify as women), because clearly we don't imagine ourselves
> in each other's shoes right now. Once we do, we may be more
> effective at changing the law and society for the better.

I couldn't agree more. Too many women, to my mind, seem to be throwing in the towel, turning inward and away from one another, bunkering down in smaller, safer, more exclusive clusters of known-commodity girlfriends, and creating buffers of distance away from the rest of us. Sheila, a math teacher in her thirties, sees it this way. She says she's read every book that has ever come out on female relation-ships because she finds the continued lack of collaboration and sup-port so deeply demoralizing. Like a lot of us, she wants something better for her daughter: "It's made me view women as machines that work against each other, when we should be working together. It's as-tonishing that females so often won't offer support and do these neg-ative things to each other so regularly."

Cathy, a college junior, says pretty much the same after observing the unpleasant rivalries and other quiet-ugly dynamics at her school, a place where she wrongly assumed women would have outgrown it all:

> I do have great friends but to this day I remain shocked by the
> utter lack of female solidarity. I have a crazy-difficult time mak-
> ing and trusting female friends. Gloria Steinem always said
> that we shouldn't aim to raise our daughters like our sons but
> to raise our sons like our daughters. I'm not so sure.

I don't want to get back into the controversial issues of patriarchal influence here but, catfight-spectator jokes aside, most men I know really don't understand or enjoy the discord. They'd like to see the women in their lives feeling stronger and more secure in themselves, to stop with the criticizing and backbiting and comparing themselves to other women. I know this isn't true for all males, but I ran into a man's online comment recently that mimics precisely what I think a lot of today's men—our brothers, husbands, bosses, and fathers of girls—are feeling about the females in their lives:

> A woman who believes in herself and has sufficient confidence doesn't feel threatened by other women, even those with greater confidence. A woman of true strength and character doesn't attack another out of spite or jealousy to build up her own self-esteem. Competition, jealousy, and disrespect are all signs of insecurity and weakness. Even men don't get it: Women are mean to each other because they're slaves to their own overblown insecurities. It's in your nature and it's your greatest weakness.

This kind of in-your-face diagnosis of our female culture might rub you the wrong way but it's hard to disagree with this fellow, really, given what I'm hearing from women themselves. In any case, I'd hardly put him in the same league as, say, the writer H. L. Mencken, who once defined *misogynist* as "a man who hates women as much as women hate one another." To me, the guy sounds more concerned and frustrated than hateful or pruriently entertained.

So here's the thing: We can't really improve conditions—as many of you say you'd like to—or fire up the full spectrum of female-based resourcefulness in this society if more girls and women, including you and me, don't resolve to join the party. What we're lacking, it seems, is some form of collaboration on a new social contract, a proactive, mindful commitment to civility so that we can at least try to "minimize the antagonisms," as Leora Tanenbaum puts it. Please don't be alarmed: I don't envision us joining hands, gathering in a circle with candles, and singing rounds of "Kumbaya" to the heavens. I don't see us donning polka-dot Rosie the Riveter bandannas and chanting "We can do it!" through the streets (though I'd be up for either of those if it would help). I'm not talking about linking arms to protest inequality and the Man, or any other issues that may or may not feel relevant to your life. This isn't about embracing your pesky neighbor, Mrs. Kravitz, the one who drives you crazy, or putting up with a female colleague who isn't carrying her load and is dragging down the whole operation—just because they're your so-called sisters. You won't find me suggesting you should vote a woman into public office whether or not you agree with her politics or philosophy of life. I don't subscribe to that way of thinking.

All we're really talking about here is civility and respect, making the culture safer and more hospitable for girls and women to thrive. Nicholas Christakis and James Fowler report, in their compelling book *Connected: The Surprising Power of Our Social Networks and How They Shape Our Lives*, that we humans bond so that we can face the world more effectively. A major point of their research and book is to get people to "come to terms with the idea that no man or woman is an island. People are connected and their health and well-being are connected."

Christakis and Fowler aren't messing around here; you can't so easily dispute or cast aside their findings. When we band together as a more cohesive, collaborative group, they say, we get things done; the "synchrony in mood or activity" benefits us individually and collectively in all sorts of ways. And when we lose that connectivity, they warn, "we lose everything." Liz, a financial analyst in her forties, seems to agree:

> I think women will never rule or really thrive if we don't learn to work better with each other, collaborate on business opportunities, and support each other. We don't always have to like one another, but we should always respect and help each other out.

These principles apply to all humans, obviously, but for our purposes, let's stay focused on us girls and women. *Each* of us stands to benefit from feeling connected by nurturing a more open, hospitable, and tolerant society of females. And each of us has the ability to spread that juice through our own, everyday interactions. Again, we don't have to adore one another because we share the same pair of chromosomes but, as a matter of decency and human dignity, we shouldn't be going out of our way to adjudicate one another's choices, rip each other apart, sabotage one another's ascent, or dismiss each other out of hand, either. I find it utterly demoralizing to think that we might already be so disconnected, so busy, or so complacent in our comfortable clusters that we'll casually swallow as our fate the broader girl-on-girl cruelty, workplace disharmony, social sniping, and all those other off-radar slights and manipulations that we complain about but eventually blow off—as if there aren't any real consequences or alternatives to these behaviors. I have greater faith in us than that, and I'll bet you do too.

THINKING BEYOND OUR PERSONAL PLOTS IN THE FEMALE GARDEN

Female disunity has broader implications than we might be appreciating. If we take a look beyond our own little plots in the garden, we can see that girls and women both here and around the globe continue to be seen—often through their own eyes—as irrelevant and invaluable less-thans, human beings worth perhaps no more than the market price of two billy goats. The evil that continues to visit our fellow females simply because they had the bad luck of being born female grips my conscience, as it should yours. They're being beaten, sold, enslaved, mutilated, raped, marginalized, ignored, denied education and medical care, or simply left to die. Even if you aren't on board with trying to improve the status quo among those in your immediate orbit, consider this: While we continue to bet *against* ourselves, feel smug or content with our personal situations, or waste one another's time and energy with our self-defeating nonsense, some of the most well-respected, brilliant, and powerful minds in the world are betting *on* females and the broader horsepower we could all be bringing to the table. They're saying we need to wake up and recall that when you discount, oppress, mistreat, and hold females back—no matter *who* happens to be doing the discounting, oppressing, mistreating, and holding back—you squander a precious world resource: us. It's time, these people say, to renew and strengthen our commitment to female welfare, relationships, and empowerment at all levels the world over because we are, quite literally, *the* most promising mechanism for improving global conditions on all fronts, be they cultural, social, or political.

Indeed, if you keep an open mind, you'll see that promising things are brewing for the greater sisterhood both here and abroad. During his first two months in office, President Obama appointed a new White House Council on Women and Girls to ensure that our federal policies and programs promote equality and fairness. This is unprecedented. Secretary of State Clinton, noting the "absolute link" between women's issues, foreign relations, and even our national security, launched the new State Department Office of Global Women's Issues to keep these matters central to her foreign policy agenda. California senator Barbara Boxer is leading a new Senate Foreign Relations subcommittee on women's issues, while other entities like the United Nations, the Bill & Melinda Gates Foundation, the Clinton Global Initiative, and the Vital Voices Global Partnership are stepping up nonpartisan efforts to harness female power in all sorts of ways.

An illuminating report from Maria Shriver and the Center for American Progress, meanwhile, entitled "A Woman's Nation Changes Everything," is creating new dialogues among government entities, businesses, the media, and faith institutions to get people to acknowledge and adjust to the cultural upheavals and growing economic power of women. Also, how can you not appreciate the tireless efforts of people like Pulitzer Prize–winning journalist-authors Nicholas D. Kristof and Sheryl WuDunn, or playwright-author-activist Eve Ensler, who have devoted themselves to assisting and empowering females worldwide, who remain convinced that girls and women are among our greatest natural resources, and who believe that unlocking female power and potential is the very antidote to global poverty, political extremism, and other societal ills.

Clearly, my homespun crusade is of a different sort and scale. But it too derives from a core belief in the power, resourcefulness, and essential goodness of females, and the recognition that you can't unlock the best in a girl or woman who is feeling physically or emotionally unsafe and unsupported. As Leora Tanenbaum writes in *Catfight*, some women don't see how a "poor black married woman in Somalia share[s] any common ground with a white lesbian Internet editor in San Francisco." But many enlightened people would argue that, at some level, all of it is interconnected and interdependent; *we're* interconnected and interdependent. I am certainly not equating inhospitality, general negativity, or the mind games that go on among American females with the atrocities in Somalia or eastern Congo. But on some level, doesn't it ring just a little bit curious that as we rightfully deplore what's going down elsewhere, many of us continue to run roughshod over each other right here? At the end of the day, it all boils down to matters of humanity, dignity, and respect. And on some basic level, a male's inhumanity—or a female's inhumanity—to a female remains just that: inhumanity. As we work to improve matters for girls and women around the globe, let's make sure we aren't also stifling the horsepower, prospects, and quality of life of our fellow females here too. Because from the sound of it, that's precisely what a lot of us are experiencing.

Few would take me for a starry-eyed idealist, but I've come to crave a new default mode for my daughters and for me, one in which females a priori tend toward openness and propping one another up versus dressing each other down. Imagine the possibilities with a more welcoming, cooperative, and integrated society of females at our backs. Doesn't it stand to reason that more of us would be operating from positions of confidence and strength? Without the gender-based distractions and petty sideshows dragging us down, wouldn't we feel more comfortable and better positioned to put ourselves out there, dip toes in risky waters, showcase our talents, reach full potential, enjoy true parity with the Man, and make the full spectrum of contributions to the world around us? Wouldn't it be better to feel safer, more supported, more *connected* in this way? When we feel good and confident in ourselves, and are surrounded by others who are respectful and encouraging, we needn't waste time looking over our shoulders, keeping our heads down, walking on eggshells, or operating from crouched defensive postures—all the things women say they're feeling compelled to do. When we're feeling unsupported, under siege, and insecure around one another, it's bound to manifest in less than optimal ways. And if we continue to feel that way because of how other females have treated us in the past, then we've gotten ourselves into a pretty bad cycle. We're not going to readily give many women a chance to prove us wrong, win us over, or reset our trust-o-meters.

Imagine an environment where we view one another more openly, as teammates or at least creatures of the same species. Where put-downs, comparisons, subtle blowoffs, and other discourtesies that seem to come so easily to some of us no longer feel right and welcome, get attention, or operate as a valid bonding adhesive. Where younger girls and women alike see, feel, and know that these behaviors simply aren't a cool, tolerable, or socially rewarding means of relating. When we begin to see that our unkindly ways are no longer met with laughter, tacit endorsement, reinforcement, or reciprocation—when we see that ridiculing or gossiping or excluding doesn't provide a springboard to acceptance or personal empowerment—doesn't logic dictate that we'll be less likely to engage in it all? I'm betting so.

Given the demonstrable influence and sway that girls and women have over one another, I think there's little question that a more spirited, proactive effort in this direction would rub off and eventually radiate outward. Indeed, the phenomenon of social contagion has been receiving all sorts of exciting buzz lately thanks to Christakis and Fowler's research. In *Connected*, they explain that, for better or worse, our habits and social behaviors can spread like disease among those in our social networks. Smoking, diet, emotions, laughter, gardening, study habits, politics, fashion sense—even accusations of witchcraft— can work their way from person to person via a socially contagious chain reaction. Without even knowing what happened to us, we can take on our buddy's happiness, agitation, and virtually anything else just by being exposed to it. The influence is perhaps more subtle than that Faberge organic shampoo commercial in which Heather Locklear told two friends about it, and they told two friends, and so on, and so on. But it's apparently no less effective.

I'm going to go out on an armchair, social scientist limb here and suggest that the infectiousness of mindful civility is just as plausible. If we can make each other smoke, gain weight, wear horizontal stripes, or feel depressed simply by hanging out with folks who smoke, are overweight, flaunt their stripes, or feel depressed, I have to believe we can nudge each another toward being more decent too, with a minimal amount of effort. Just as nastiness, gossip, and violence breed nastiness, gossip, and violence, and just as happiness breeds happiness, so too can kindness beget kindness and become, say Christakis and Fowler, a palpable, powerful "force for good" over bad:

> [A]ltruism tends to spread and the benefits tend to be magnified . . . When a person has been treated well by someone, she goes on to treat others well in the future. And, even more strikingly, all the people in these new second-round groups are also affected in the third round.

Susan, a former sales manager now teaching at a woman's fitness boot camp in South Carolina, is one of many who told me they never understood why women gravitate toward or put up with the kinds of "friends" who only mirror back their own negative behaviors:

> I want to surround myself with women I admire and feel have a good handle on their behavior. I would look to those to learn from. I can now recognize destructiveness in women's behavior and always gravitate away from that.

I think Susan's tapped into what is so essential here: surrounding ourselves with kind and genuine women who inspire and help lift up our own behavior. I think of the authentic and graceful souls who always bring out the best in me when I'm around them. You know the type. Like my friend Michelle: kind and welcoming and in the mix, but never speaking ill of others or engaging in the stealthlike judging, comparing, status jockeying, and other nonsense to which many of us are so vulnerable. Women who seem to see the world through an entirely different, more forgiving lens and move to an entirely different rhythm. You wouldn't consider flicking the ash of gossip or judgment their way because you know they're just not into it; you'd feel ashamed before the petty or negative remark even skated past your lips. It feels good to be with these women. You want to be more like them. You want whatever they're having. You want to be better.

It doesn't even have to be a good friend for you to benefit from basic civility. Who doesn't feel great after a simple, honest, and pleasant exchange with another female, whether it's your best friend over the phone, a smiling woman on the subway who takes the time to ad-

mire your necklace, or the intimidating "has-it-all" neighbor who finally notices you, says hello, and asks you about life? I used to see my
own day lifted whenever I bumped into this one woman at the dog
park in Virginia. Like me, she was a busy mom in her forties, I'd
guess. Realistically, neither of us had time to get to know each other—
these were quickie dog walks sandwiched between family and work
obligations—but the way she was always beaming, remembering my
name, always ready with the "Hey there, how's it going?" Nothing
too obtrusive; just genuine and sweet and real. Seriously, I always
walked away with an extra spring in my step. (And was probably nicer
to my family for at least a few hours afterward.) Again, pretty basic
but undoubtedly powerful stuff.

SO, NOW WHAT?

The point is, even if you aren't buying my program, there's a real, sci-
entifically proven power to our connectivity and influence over one
another, one of the "smile and the world smiles with you" variety. You
might not be feeling the negativity so much or engaging in it yourself,
but I can absolutely assure you that plenty of other women and impressionable girls out there are. Some are wading in it up to their ankles or necks; others are quite drowning. So what do we do now?
Much of it is ludicrously simple, to my mind. Each of us holds the
power to contribute toward a more positive culture, starting now, this
second, with our neighbors, that reserved coworker it would be simpler to ignore, the awkward-seeming mother at our kids' school, our
daughters, and even our girlfriends. And if all of this idealistic rallying
is beginning to sound vaguely reminiscent of a sappy infomercial or
vintage Miss America pledge for world peace, as a couple of women
joked, I'm sorry. When you have daughters or when you examine this
dark stuff up close and personal for months—really live it, breathe it,
and pay attention to the struggles of other females instead of turning
away or blowing it off as Other Women's Issues—you begin to feel a
sense of shared responsibility. You can beat on as usual, sure, or you
can, as Gandhi suggested, "Be the change you want to see in the
world." (Yes, I just quoted Gandhi.)

The stories I've been hearing aren't fiction, and, believe me, these aren't parlor games we're playing. Girls and women all around us are getting hurt and taking major hits to self-esteem, health, and overall life prospects. Others are simply pulling back and feeling burned, turned off, and closely guarded about who they'll let into their lives. Too many women are speaking of a distance and disconnect among females today. One believes "we're witnessing the decline of civility itself, and this is what our generation of women will be known for; we just don't know it yet." I won't go that far, but the notion that the behaviors driving our distrust and ambivalence have somehow become so commonplace and prevalent that they're expected and even *accepted*—as fair-game fodder for *Family Guy*, no less—should trouble us all. It's time to consider the net effect: an increasingly fractured, disconnected, inhospitable, and dysfunctional society of women. Less happy women. Less productive women.

Again, I think you can't effect social change without true resolve and commitment. We have to collectively want to strengthen the social fabric. The wherewithal has to come from somewhere within ourselves. Like anything else in life, it's pretty tough to motivate people to change behaviors we've all grown accustomed to and accepted as part of existing culture. And it's doubly tough to quit behaviors that are routinely encouraged, validated, made light of and excused, or downright rewarded by peers, parents, the workforce, and the media. I see a whole lot of moving parts here, but I think that if more of us would just pause and consider the lasting implications of our less than sisterly conduct, if more of us would rally and embrace the notion of a cease-fire, it really could result in an organic, contagious change for the better.

A HANDY TOP FIFTEEN

Today's horoscope in the *Washington Post* offered some pretty compelling admonitions about giving people the benefit of the doubt and treading gently: Plato's old "Be kind, for everyone you meet is fighting a hard battle." I'm not normally a Plato-quoting kind of gal, or even a horoscope-following gal, but isn't this precisely so? Most of us have so much going on and shoulder enough burdens in our day. We don't need these distractions, these extra worries, these little nuisances that can nag us and take up so much real estate in our inner lives. Life deals us enough challenges, pressures, disappointments, and conflicts as it is. So many of us seem to be second-guessing ourselves and spending unnecessary time, energy, and emotion on the negativity. Others—let's face it—aren't bothering to think much beyond themselves and their immediate cocoons. Instead of actively adding to one another's loads, shouldn't we be more consciously lightening them through a more proactive civility?

Well-meaning intentions aren't enough. Eleanor Roosevelt had it right when she said that it "isn't enough to talk about peace. One must believe in it. And it isn't enough to believe in it. One must work at it." We've been talking and talking and paying all sorts of lip service to the *fact* of our infighting and insecurities, but little has changed. We have work to do. Each of us really can play a role, simply by practicing daily kindness, tolerance, openness, respect, conscientious role modeling, and, as much as anything, restraint and self-control. It's about taking that extra moment to think twice and do the right thing—or nothing at all.

Since I launched my investigation, a number of women have conveyed the hope that I might seize upon the silver-bullet antidote and send them on their merry way with a laundry list of tips for improving the culture of girls and women. As you might imagine, I've resisted that kind of thing. First of all, I've always been skeptical of those tidy, simplistic, half-baked ten-point lists; you know, the pithy, surefire prescriptive tips that purport to tie messy and complex human issues together with a pretty red grosgrain ribbon? My goodness, my grocery lists aren't even that clear cut. More fundamentally, though, this book is about raising consciousness and creating a dialogue. I'm not so sure I'm qualified to be your self-help guru—certainly by now you can see that I'm a work in progress myself.

On the other hand, as I've emphasized all along, the fundamental antidote to curbing some of these shadowy tendencies isn't all that complicated. And since I happen to be sitting on mounds of wisdom and experience culled from specialists and thousands of women who care very deeply about improving the status quo, I'm persuaded that it's worthwhile to distill their thoughts and offer a few sound bites to consider as we set out to improve our collective lot. It's a start, anyway.

Consider the lasting effects that your words and actions might have on other females, the very type of fallout discussed in this book. Don't forget it. Those seemingly innocuous digs, crafty blowoffs and slights, and everyday bits of negativity or can't-be-botheredness often sting more than a given woman will acknowledge or ever permit you to know. As unlikely as it may seem, and as stoic and invulnerable as another gal appears, you may hold a very real, if subtle, influence. With a single careless whisper, you could seriously impact how she feels about herself—in the short term and, possibly, the long term. Show some compassion. Use your fem powers responsibly.

Curb the gratuitous meanness and negativity. Really, if you have nothing positive to say, think back to what we all learned in kindergarten. Exercise some self-control and don the muzzle, if necessary. The next time a woman, even your best friend, floats one of those dangling invitations to critique or gossip, don't take the bait. Give her a blank stare, change the subject, end the conversation, or call her out. She'll feel mildly ashamed and get the message. That's okay. If she doesn't, you've taken the high road and a step toward greater virtue. Well done. And, bonus: There's a strong chance she'll follow your lead and find your goodwill and generous spirit infectious.

Stop supporting the very cultural influences you say you object to, the ones that feed the negative climate of which you complain. There's a reason this stuff is everywhere, poisoning even our most legitimate media sources. It sells, and we've been buying it. Sorry, but this might even mean canceling your *Star* magazine subscription or turning off the mind-numbing TV shows that reinforce the female dark side and our attendant insecurities, perpetuate the vapid, catty vibe as our reality, and just plain exploit us. If you simply can't do it, by God, at least keep it away from your daughters.

Be more inclusive, less *exclusive*. Cultivate existing friendships by checking in and showing up but consider expanding that comfortable cluster of friends, too. Be welcoming, hospitable, and genuine toward women you don't know well or even have time for. Smile. Open up. Reach out. Have a coffee. Take a walk. UCLA and Harvard researchers say you'll be healthier and possibly live longer for it. They're smart people. Believe them.

Mothers, take 1: Please quit judging. Now. You are not a better mom just because you opted to stay home with the kids. Nor, working mothers, are you smarter, more valuable, and all-around More Important People because you didn't. Get over yourselves. Paddle your own canoes.

Stop fretting so very much about your looks, your body, your self. There is always someone more beautiful, intelligent, and fabulous than you. And that's okay. The happiest women (and men) I know are those who might not score *conventional* 10s in those departments but have long accepted themselves, are secure in their skins, and remain blissfully unconcerned about how they measure up vis-à-vis other females. And, by the way, these are the women who often seem to make terrific mothers, bosses, and girlfriends, too.

Mothers, take 2: Awaken from thy slumber. Girls do *not* figure it out for themselves. Pay attention. Intervene. Practice zero tolerance when you see them excluding, gossiping, and otherwise wielding their manipulations. Check out what they're texting and saying on Facebook. Don't let them get away with mean-girling anyone; rein them in, hold them accountable, follow through with consequences. Get to the bottom of why they're doing it. *Listen* to them: They're dealing with all sorts of pressures and do, in fact, need you. Worry more about being the responsible adult and less about saving face, being polite, avoiding confrontation, or hoping other parents and children will like you.

Strip the automatic smug, snark, cynical, and nasty from your vernacular. You are actively feeding the negative vibe out there. And guess what? You're perfectly clever, savvy, and interesting without it. No more knee-jerk attacks on any female who thinks, acts, looks, or just plain moves differently than you—not with your girlfriends, not online, not even in your head. We're not talking about a sisterly love-in, voting women you don't support into office, or hiring an unqualified female because you share a pair of chromosomes. We're talking about giving another woman a break because it's the right thing to do. Regardless of appearance, status, weight, education, or religion. Why *not* start with women? We could use it. We constitute more than half this country's population and hold unique and profound sway over one another in ways we often don't with men. A new social contract that rewards open kindness and compassion over exclusivity, inhospitality, and outright cruelty will serve all of us more constructively.

Respect. Tolerate. Support.

Try to forgive yourself *and* the women who have sliced and diced your psyche. Try opening back up. Come clean. Write. Create. Do yoga. Meditate. Take social risks. Put yourself back out there. Smoke out the gems in your office or neighborhood. Find a higher purpose and volunteer somewhere. Get some therapy or whatever else proves helpful. Appreciate that any ugliness you encountered was almost certainly borne of insecurity, fear, bad judgment, or forces of youth, peer, or group influence. You might not gain closure, but realizing that it's more about them than about you or your perceived shortcomings might save you some heartache and help bolster your confidence.

Working women: Seriously, please chill. I am shocked by what I'm hearing. You are nice and accomplished people who are better than this. Stop backbiting and sabotaging your female colleagues' achievements and ascent. Stop the petty disparaging of women for everything and nothing. Even if you aren't leading the pack, stop being the audience that feeds the beast. Maybe it helps distract you from the daily drudgery. Maybe it's just a habit or handy bonding ritual for you and your office compatriots. But it's ugly and, ultimately, demoralizing for all. Again, this kind of stuff drives the undercurrent of negativity in our culture and keeps women down. Consider the possibility that you're acting out of jealousy, insecurity, or sheer boredom. Start supporting your female colleagues, mentor them, show them the ropes, guide them through. You will feel better about yourself—believe me. It truly takes more energy to tear someone down than to support them or help prop them up. It'll pay off in the end. There really is enough pie for you both. And if there isn't, you can join forces and make more pie.

Bystanders: Please start upstanding. Do something. Don't just sit there, for crying out loud. Experts say you are actively contributing to and exacerbating the problem. Remember: Silence + inaction = tacit consent. Just because you're not hurling the actual stones doesn't mean you're not a player.

Mothers, take 3: Please take your job seriously if you aren't already. Strive to be a more committed, active role model. Show your girls what respect, tolerance, dignity, and empathy look like. Stop teaching them that two-faced shenanigans, gossiping, judging, and other less-than-charitable moves are okay. And less focus on the material, please; you *know* it isn't what matters. All of this filters right on through to little Susie; she sees right through you. Let's assure our daughters that they needn't be perfect. Foster kindness and confidence. Get them thinking positively about themselves for the right reasons, but also thinking of others besides themselves, too. Try involving them in community service for the service aspects, not just because it's a school requirement or résumé builder. Nursing homes, hospitals, libraries, animal shelters, homeless outreach, environmental organizations, and food banks abound with volunteering opportunities for kids. Help foster healthy self-esteem through sports, Scouts, hobbies, and programs like Empower Girls, Club and Camp Ophelia, the Mother-Daughter Project, Girls Leadership Institute, Girls Inc., the Kind Campaign, and antibullying workshops—anything that helps solidify a proper sense of right and wrong, shows them it's actually cool to be kind, and helps ensure that their self-perception and personal narratives aren't based solely on what their *peers* think of them. Fill that undefined space with something positive as a fallback for when friends aren't being so warm and accepting. You can find these offerings at school, online, and throughout your community. The websites of Rosalind Wiseman, Rachel Simmons, Dr. Robyn Silverman, the American Academy of Pediatrics, as well as Stopbullyingnow, Kidscape, Hardy Girls Healthy Women, Kidpower, and Beatbullying are just a few of those with a wonderful array of resources and links.

Even if things seem just fine on your side of the pond, keep an open mind about how you—and other girls and women—might be contributing to a negative or inhospitable culture. The notion that only men, the media, Mom, and other world forces can victimize, marginalize, traumatize, demotivate, and otherwise hold females back is pure myth.

Once again, with feeling: *Pause. Think twice. Restrain thyself. Support.*

author's last stand

As you set aside this book, I can only hope that you aren't as exhausted as I am. Then again, I should probably hope you are because that would portend good things: It might mean you're willing to work with me here.

During the time I put this book together, I found myself riding a rather topsy-turvy roller coaster in real life, one that, fittingly enough, has left me appreciating my hard-won girlfriends all the more. My husband took the overseas job of his dreams and, after twenty years in the Bay Area, we pulled up stakes to join the ranks of official global nomads. While he spent months learning an exotic new language at the not-so-exotic Foreign Service Institute in Arlington, Virginia, I sold our house, packed up, shipped pets, bid adieu to friends and family, gained twelve pounds, drove our overstuffed Odyssey minivan to Washington, D.C., unpacked, hung out for a few months, packed up, shipped pets, bid adieu to friends and family, moved to Southeast Asia, unpacked, and exhaled.

In the midst of all this, I parted with one of my best friends over something that should have been a trifle (a dog this time, not a belt) but ended up taking on a stubborn life of its own, as these things so often do. I watched bits and pieces of girl drama unfold in my twins' circles, fretted over alliance shifting and manipulation among the teen girl set, and dealt with plenty of teenage boy turbulence too. I read the works of Madonna, pretty much every nonfiction book on girls' and women's relationships (including Leora Tanenbaum's *Slut!*, which I must have defended to my son a half dozen times), and dissected the prose—and music—of my new favorite neuroscientists. I bought Chrissa the American Girl doll and her must-have accessories. And I wrote.

A few nights before we left California, I was treated to a ladies-only farewell fete that can only be described as an attend-your-own-funeral kind of wonderment—a night that still leaves me *verklempt* when I allow my thoughts to meander there. It was an evening of friendship, of memories, and, of course, some not-so-discreet tears. I still can't claim to feel completely at ease around women, even those I hold most dear. There are moments when a reclusive life in the Maine backwoods still holds a very real appeal to me. But I left that night knowing I was lucky. I've come a long way thanks to the fine collection of authentic, honest, supportive, and extremely interesting women I've managed to befriend and hold on to.

The truth is, I've spent too much of this life ducking for cover, keeping you all at arm's length, and pretending it didn't matter. Like so many others I've now heard from, I've always *wanted* to open up and feel safer, less judged, and more welcomed. I've always wanted women to like me. That may be a Minnesota thing. It may be a female thing. Maybe it's just a human thing. Whatever it is, I've spent a lot of time wishing we could all be a little more real and let our guards down a bit more convincingly, wishing we could take the time to more meaningfully reach out to one another, and, yes, wishing we could all just behave.

I still have plenty of work to do, but I'd like to think I'm in a better place as a result of this project. I do think I'm less judgmental of other girls and women and far less vulnerable to the negative tendencies that only leave me disappointed in myself. I wouldn't exactly call it a born-again renewal, but I'm definitely more mindful. Ridiculously enough, dear reader, this is the same old lesson plan and generosity of spirit Sister Marilyn peddled back in the second grade.

As they say, better late than never.

I am beyond humbled and heartened to report that several women have conveyed a sense of enlightenment, concern, and inspiration just by taking the survey and thinking about these issues in the context of their own lives. Many said they appreciated the wake-up call. Others felt encouraged to hold their daughters tight or take a closer look around them and see if there was room to forge deeper, more authentic connections with women. And some just said things like "Right on, sister." I liked that.

The Twisted Sisterhood is, without question, an unabashed attempt to rally the troops. At the end of the day, though, it's just another book, one you'll return to a shelf, recycle, toss, lend to a pal, or, if you're like my friend Wendy, maybe even beat against the side of your head. You won't relate to or agree with everything I and the women who contributed to this book have said, but we're covered: We've spoken from the heart. My straightforward, if lofty, goal is that we might open the door to collective reflection and dialogue about the hidden and lasting trouble we females are uniquely capable of dealing one another, and tender a salve to the "closeted" among us who didn't know there were others out there nursing the same frustrations and struggles. If nothing else, I do hope more of us will consider casting a fresh eye on our relationships and help redraw the status quo by keeping it real, thinking twice, and consciously practicing a more gentle civility in our day-to-day—for ourselves, our daughters, and the next generation of women. It's going to take a village.

acknowledgments

The irony that it took a posse of enlightened sisters to make *The Twisted Sisterhood* happen never escapes me. On that score, I'm chiefly indebted to my brilliant agent, Andrea Barzvi at ICM, for pulling me from my complacent slumber and putting me to work, and to my extremely patient and gracious editor, Marnie Cochran. Marnie's belief in this project and always-keen instincts made the book exponentially better than I envisioned. I feel so fortunate to have conspired with her and the crew at Ballantine/Random House.

I will always remain grateful to Dan Jones of the *New York Times*, surely one of the finest gentlemen editors out there. None of this would have sprung to life without the paper's Modern Love venue and that pocketful of pixie dust Dan keeps at the ready, the stuff that's enabled many of us unknowns to fly. Thanks also to Alison Biggar of the *San Francisco Chronicle* for plucking this transitioning stay-at-home mom from the slush pile back in 2004.

So many folks in the trenches contributed their thoughts and expertise to *The Twisted Sisterhood*. I can't name you all but do wish to recognize Rosalind Wiseman and Elayne Savage, PhD, both of whom kindly answered my cold calls early on; you are busy folks, and I appreciate your gift of time. A heartfelt thanks to Jim Baack for his technical prowess and to Khun Pai for her crucial support on the Bangkok front. Holly Hayes Hanke and Maria Carson Breber gifted me with sage advice, laughter, and research assistance, often while power walking. (It is a swell thing indeed to have friends with great brains.) And what can I say about my amazing real-life sisters, Tricia and Stacy, who kept me on my toes with their brutally honest but constructive feedback? You guys are the best. Thanks, too, to the other ladies who supported this project from the start and checked in on me no matter where I happened to be living. You are too numerous to list, but certainly I owe a debt of gratitude to Teri Eaton, Celia Rogers, Beth Pennington, Jodi Blecker, Claudia Harrison, Cheryl Dyer Berg, Kara Baysinger, and Kelly Corrigan (for leading me to Andy, naturally). Mary Kay Lacey, I'd have lost it long ago were it not for your nurturing and guidance over the years. You are the consummate girlfriend.

I am woefully overdue in thanking two men who helped resuscitate and inspire me during some pretty dark moments relevant to this book, undoubtedly without even realizing it: Dr. Jeffrie G. Murphy at Arizona State, and Father James V. Schall at Georgetown, a man whose brutal but brilliant Socratic hazing helped rescue my twenty-year-old being from the abyss of self-doubt and lazy thinking. Educators and mentors, you absolutely make a difference—know this.

Lastly and mostly, I owe a huge thanks to my very cool dad and to my mother (for her fifty-four-day Rosary novenas, her spot-on insights about humankind, and for hitting up every woman she's ever known to take my survey); to my ever-supportive brothers, Jim and Mike; and to Steve and our kids for enduring my grumpy, cavelike existence for months. And months. Writing may be a mostly solitary endeavor, but it's impacted your lives profoundly and I thank you.

notes

INTRODUCTION

xi *women can scour my soul:* "The Duplicitous Female Maze," Feministe (December 2, 2007) (comment by Rebecca).

xiii *ran the piece in December 2007:* "My Sorority Pledge? I Swore Off Sisterhood," *New York Times* (December 2, 2007).

xvi *my friend Maria:* Maria Carson Breber proved the perfect person to consult with in formulating my survey. After securing her EdM from the Harvard Graduate School of Education, Maria conducted medical anthropological research and interviews with breast cancer patients at Harvard Medical School's Department of Social Medicine. She then spent three years as a general strategy consultant and market research practitioner for the Monitor company in Cambridge, Massachusetts, where she designed and implemented qualitative and quantitative research instruments, including complex surveys on an array of decision-making issues for strategic planning purposes. She's led research initiatives for Compaq and consulted on other research projects as well.

xvi *six-part, fifty-question survey:* The SurveyMonkey-hosted survey is now closed. A copy of it can be found, however, in the appendix.

xvi *females ages 15 to 86:* A snapshot of the respondent pool includes the following: ages 15–30 (18 percent), 31–40 (31 percent), 41–50 (33 percent), 51–60 (11 percent), 61–above (7 percent); Caucasian (84 percent); graduate degree/

PhD (37 percent), bachelor's degree (41 percent); married (66 percent); heterosexual (94 percent); no children (31 percent), one or more child (69 percent), one or more daughter (51 percent).

xxi *Even Michelle Obama has expressed concern:* "Mom First, Political Wife Second: Potential First Lady Balances Kids, Work & 2008 Campaign Trail," ABC News Online: Politics (January 24, 2008).

xxi *"evil, odious effects":* "Cyber Bully Posted Evil Death Threats," *Sun* (August 22, 2009) (reporting that "vile Keeley Houghton" was jailed for Internet bullying following a merciless campaign of website taunts against another teen, including a threat to "murder the bitch," becoming "the first person in Britain to be caged over such attacks").

CHAPTER 1: WE ARE *SO* WORTH IT

3 *a friendship quilt:* "The Comfort of Friends: A Circle of Women Sustains Her, Protecting Her Like a Quilt on a Cold Winter Night," *Los Angeles Times* (March 2, 1997).

5 *"In our constantly shifting lives":* Ibid.; see also Jeffrey Zaslow, *The Girls from Ames: A Story of Women and a Forty-Year Friendship* (New York: Gotham, 2009); Ann Patchett, *Truth and Beauty: A Friendship* (London and New York: Harper Perennial, 2005).

5 *"Nothin' like 'em, man":* "Gossip Girls," *Marie Claire* (March 2009) (interview with Jennifer Aniston, Ginnifer Goodwin, and Drew Barrymore); see also "Glam Girl Next Door," *Harper's Bazaar* (January 2010) (Kate Hudson explaining, "Let's be honest, I don't care how much you're in love with any man, you need to have your girlfriends to talk to. Without them, we're alone"); "I'm the Only Feminist There Is—The Others Are All out of Step/Saturday Interview with Fay Weldon," *Guardian* (August 22, 2009) ("We shelter children for a time; we live side by side with men; and that is all. We owe them nothing, and are owed nothing. I think we owe our friends more, especially our female friends").

7 *"just plain kibbitz":* "Book Review: *The Tending Instinct: How Nurturing Is Essential to Who We Are and How We Live*," *Human Nature Review* 3 (January 19, 2003), pp. 44–46 (reviewed by Judith Eve Lipton).

8 *socially nurturing brain:* See Shelley E. Taylor, *The Tending Instinct: How Nurturing Is Essential to Who We Are and How We Live* (New York: Holt, 2002), p. 39 (discussing our social, coordinating, and cooperative evolutionary past); see also Kathleen Vail, "How Girls Hurt," *American School Board Journal* 189, no. 8 (August 2002), pp. 14–18 (discussing biological predispositions in girls to value friendships).

8 *the very glue:* Deborah Tannen, *You're Wearing That? Understanding Mothers and Daughters in Conversation* (New York: Random House, 2006), p. 67.

8 *tweak Darwin's survival theory:* See Taylor, *Tending Instinct* (noting how many studies conclude that our stress levels go down when we're surrounded by supportive people); Louis Cozolino, *The Neuroscience of Human Relationships: Attachment and the Developing Social Brain* (New York: W. W. Norton & Company, 2006).

8 *fascinating research . . . while at UCLA:* Shelley E. Taylor, Laura Cousino Klein, et al., "Biobehavioral Responses to Stress in Females: Tend-and-Befriend, Not Fight-or-Flight," *Psychological Review* 107, no. 3 (2000), pp. 411–29.

9 *Oxytocin . . . is key:* See, for example, Taylor, *Tending Instinct;* "Hormone Oxytocin May Inhibit Social Phobia," *ScienceDaily* (July 23, 2008); "The Biology Behind the Milk of Human Kindness," *New York Times* (November 24, 2009); see also Susan Kuchinskas, *The Chemistry of Connection: How the Oxytocin Response Can Help You Find Trust, Intimacy, and Love* (Oakland, Calif.: New Harbinger Publications, 2009). Given oxytocin's promising propensities, I suspect we'll be seeing all sorts of wild pharmacological experiments on the horizon. According to at least one tech writer in the field, research wars are in fact already under way. See Kuchinskas's blog, www.hugthemonkey.com, devoted to oxytocin-related developments and how oxytocin can be used to harness greater happiness in humans.

9 *"dehumanize" ourselves:* See "Brain Trust," *Greater Good Magazine* 5, no. 2 (Fall 2008) (Michael Kosfeld discussing biology of trust and role of oxytocin).

9 *"undervalued resource":* "What Are Friends For? A Longer Life," *New York Times* (April 20, 2009); see also Barbara Moses, *Women Confidential: Midlife Women Explode the Myths of Having It All* (New York: Marlowe & Company, 2006), pp. 271–72 (explaining that positive female friendship and intimacy are not only good for us—they are crucial for health and ultimate survival); Sandy Sheehy, *Connecting: The Enduring Power of Female Friendship* (New York: William Morrow, 2000).

9 *"reap the benefits for generations":* See Taylor, *Tending Instinct.*

9 *"major indicator of happiness":* "The Power of Connection: Physical, Emotional and Spiritual Intimacy," Mayo Clinic Health Solutions: Special Report, Supplement to *Mayo Clinic Health Letter* (June 2008).

9 *six-year study:* Karen A. Ertel, M. Maria Glymour, and Lisa F. Berkman, "Effects of Social Integration on Preserving Memory Function in a Nationally Representative US Elderly Population," *American Journal of Public Health* 98, no. 7 (July 2008), pp. 1215–20 (senior researcher Lisa Berkman noting, "As our society ages and has more and more older people . . . it will be important to promote their engagement in social and community life to maintain their well-being"); see also "What Are Friends For?"

9 *nurses with breast cancer:* Candyce H. Kroenke, Laura D. Kubzansky, et al., "Social Networks, Social Support, and Survival After Breast Cancer Diagnosis," *Journal of Clinical Oncology* 24, no. 7 (March 1, 2006), pp. 1105–11.

10 *only a third of the women:* See also Nicholas A. Christakis and James H. Fowler, *Connected: The Surprising Power of Our Social Networks and How They Shape Our Lives* (New York: Little, Brown and Company, 2009), pp. 18, 20. Christakis and Fowler obtained similar results, noting that the "average American has just four close social contacts, with most having between two and six. Sadly, 12 percent of Americans listed no one with whom they could discuss important matters or spend free time." In fact, the authors say that "having an extra friend may create all kinds of benefits for your health, even if this other person doesn't actually do anything in particular for you"; see also "Is Happiness Catching?" *New York Times Magazine* (September 13, 2009).

10 *punishing toll on women's health:* See "When Friends Don't Keep You Healthy: A Study of Conflict in Older Women's Friendships" (study/paper by Robin Moreman, presented at 98th Annual Meeting of the American Sociological Association, Atlanta [August 16–19, 2003]).

10 *"Behind the curtain of sisterhood":* Luise Eichenbaum and Susie Orbach, *Between Women: Love, Envy, and Competition in Women's Friendships* (New York: Penguin Books, 1989), pp. 10–12.

CHAPTER 2: BREAKING THROUGH THE CONE OF SILENCE

11 *our "shadow side":* Phyllis Chesler, *Woman's Inhumanity to Woman* (New York: Thunder's Mouth Press/Nation Books, 2001).

11 *"the cheapest medicine":* See Taylor, *Tending Instinct.*

14 *constantly ask her to "do something":* Telephone conversation with Rosalind Wiseman (July 28, 2008); see also Wiseman, *Queen Bees and Wannabees: Helping Your Daughter Survive Cliques, Gossip, Boyfriends, and Other Realities of Adolescence* (New York: Crown, 2002).

14 *a new policy statement:* "Policy Statement—Role of the Pediatrician in Youth Violence Prevention," American Academy of Pediatrics (June 29, 2009), as printed in *Pediatrics* 124, no. 1 (July 2009), pp. 393–402.

14 *embroiled in litigation:* See, for example, "The Code of Miss Porter's," *Vanity Fair* (July 2009); "Trouble at Miss Porter's" thread on CollegeConfidential .com.

15 *the sisterhood's downside:* See "She's a Little Bit Country, A Little Bit Angry," *New York Times* (August 28, 2009) (noting how, at her concert, Taylor Swift "spoke and sang about being the girl left out, with no friends in junior high"); GOOP: Nourish the Inner Aspect, at "Be: Evil Tongue" (Paltrow's newsletter discussing frenemy who was "hell-bent" on taking her down); "Feuds: Kristen Stewart Was Too Cool for School," Celebuzz (discussing interview in which Stewart recalls being called a bitch and treated poorly by mean classmates); "Interview: Sienna Miller," *InStyle* (March 6, 2009); see also "Jennifer Garner: I Need to Find Balance," *Parade* (January 21, 2010) ("I will tell you what I

can't abide—and I think the Internet has really created a space for it—women criticizing other women and mothers criticizing other mothers. It just makes me crazy, whether it's between staying at home, going to work, how long you breast-feed, if you use formula. I feel like we should just assume everyone is doing the best they can. Women should take care of each other, not tear each other down").

15 *talking zeitgeist:* See the English Roses Collection at www.myenglishroses .net (Madonna's books); www.americangirloftoday.com/girloftheyear/2009 (Chrissa page).

17 *pick your poison:* See, for example, Anne Campbell, "Female Competition: Causes, Constraints, Content, and Contexts," *Journal of Sex Research* 41, no. 1 (February 2004).

18 *"My last best friend":* "Group Hug! The 5 Steps to Recovering from the 'Modern Love' That Will Make You Hate Women," Jezebel, December 4, 2007 (comment by "Senzaflash").

18 *excellent friends but terrible enemies:* Marion K. Underwood, *Social Aggression Among Girls* (New York: Guilford Press, 2003); see also Helen E. Ditzhazy and Ella M. Burton, "Bullying: A Perennial School Problem," *Delta Kappa Gamma Bulletin* 70, no. 1 (Fall 2003), pp. 43–48.

19 *"girls are social beings":* Chesler, *Woman's Inhumanity,* pp. 80–81.

22 *her own candid views:* "Hop on Pop (Culture): Article of the Week," Girlsgonechild.net (December 2, 2007).

22 *"tell a woman":* See, for example, "Can Gossip Be Good?" *Scientific American Mind* (October–November 2008), p. 31 (explaining that we pay closest attention to doings of same-sex competitors and that negative news about high-status potential rivals can be exploited as useful to us); see generally Jennifer Bosson, Amber Johnson, et al., "Interpersonal Chemistry Through Negativity: Bonding by Sharing Negative Attitudes About Others," *Personal Relationships* 13, no. 2 (May 2006), pp. 135–50; "Research Shows Negative Gossip Can Build Friendships, Release Tension," *USA Today* (September 18, 2006).

CHAPTER 3: INCIVILITY: HERE, THERE, SEEMINGLY EVERYWHERE

28 *this type of rant:* "The Self-Manufacture of Megan Fox," *New York Times Magazine* (November 11, 2009).

31 *office bullies are female:* See WorkplaceBullyingInstitute.org for this and a variety of other relevant studies, articles, and discussions related to woman-on-woman (WOW) bullying in the workplace.

31 *controversial article:* "Backlash: Women Bullying Women at Work," *New York Times* (May 10, 2009) (Mickey Meece reporting on the ramifications of intra-female work conflict).

33 *"Sisters or Saboteurs?":* Sarah Gibbard Cook, "When Sisters Turn into Sabo-

teurs," *Women in Higher Education* 17, no. 4 (April 2008), pp. 24–25 (Cook discusses Dr. Brock's speech, "Sisters or Saboteurs? When Sisterly Support Turns to Sabotage Against Women Leaders," delivered at the 2008 Women in Educational Leadership Conference, in Lincoln, Nebraska, promoted as follows: "Most women who aspire to leadership positions enjoy support and mentoring from other women. However, some women also experience sabotage from women that threatens their career goals. This presentation explores the dynamics of sabotage experienced by women in educational leadership positions").

33 *July 2009 study:* "Ulster Research Reveals High Level of Bullying in Midwifery," *University of Ulster News* (July 22, 2009). The study notes that more than half of 164 student midwives across the UK questioned for a survey said they'd been bullied at work, usually by their mentor or ward sister, although university lecturers and personal tutors were also identified; respondents reported lack of confidence, lack of self-esteem, and increased anxiety from excessive criticism, belittling their work, undervaluing their skills and efforts, and questioning their competency; see also "High Level of Bullying in Midwifery, Study Suggests," *ScienceDaily* (July 29, 2009).

33 *a four-article series:* "Bullying," *Midwifery Today*, no. 80 (Winter 2006); see also "Dying for the Cause," Birth International.com/articles (Carolyn Hastie detailing the midwifery community's bullying-related pressures that led to Wright's suicide).

33 *the sisterhood of all sisterhoods:* See Midwiferytoday.com/magazine.

35 *"cooperate in our own subordination":* Leora Tanenbaum, *Catfight: Rivalries Among Women—from Diets to Dating, from the Boardroom to the Delivery Room* (New York: Perennial, 2003), p. 25.

35 *American Bar Association survey:* "What Women Lawyers Really Think of Each Other: We Asked Who They'd Rather Work With—Men or Women. The Answers Were Surprising," *ABA Journal* (February 1, 2008) (detailing survey results of 4,449 female attorney respondents).

35 American Lawyer *magazine article:* Vivia Chen, "The End of Sisterhood," *American Lawyer* (May 1, 2009).

35 *study of U.S. workers:* Scott Schieman and Taralyn McMullen, "Relational Demography in the Workplace and Health: An Analysis of Gender and the Subordinate-Superordinate Role-Set," *Journal of Health and Social Behavior* 49, no. 3 (September 2008), pp. 286–300; "Boss' Gender Can Affect Workers' Stress," *LiveScience* (September 9, 2008).

38 *by age four or five:* See, for example, David A. Nelson, Clyde Clark Robinson, and Craig Hart, "Relational and Physical Aggression of Preschool-age Children: Peer Status Linkages Across Informants," *Early Education and Development* 16, no. 2 (April 2005), pp. 115–40 (noting that relational aggression

among girls such as exclusionary behavior and threatening to withdraw friendship may be associated with social prominence and begin by age four or five).

38 *"superior social intelligence":* Neil Marr and Tim Field, *Bullycide: Death at Playtime, an Exposé of Child Suicide Caused by Bullying* (Wantage, UK: Wessex Press, 2001).

39 *compromise her ability:* Audrey Osler, Cathy Street, et al., "Not a Problem? Girls and School Exclusion," National Children's Bureau (January 29, 2002).

39 *"Turning eighteen is not a magical age":* "Social Form of Bullying Linked to Depression, Anxiety in Adults," Medical News Today (April 23, 2008). The article also references Allison Dempsey, lead author of a 2008 study out of the University of Florida, who explains that "even though people are outside of high school, the memories of these experiences continue to be associated with depression and social anxiety." See *ScienceDaily* (August 4, 2008).

40 *why so many kids are floundering:* RacetoNowhere.com (2009); Madeline Levine, *The Price of Privilege: How Parental Pressure and Material Advantage Are Creating a Generation of Disconnected and Deeply Unhappy Kids* (New York: HarperCollins, 2006).

41 *YouTube glorification:* See, for example, "Suspects in Video Beating Could Get Life in Prison," CNN.com (April 11, 2008).

41 *half-time entertainment:* "Bring It On: Cheerleader Terrorized by Catfight Video Posted on Facebook," CBSnews.com (October 2, 2009).

41 *permanently handicapped:* "Child Beaten by Bullies," WICU12.com (April 4, 2008).

42 *one's name on a "slut list":* See "When the Cool Get Hazed," *New York Times* (September 26, 2009) (Tina Kelley discussing high school "slut lists" and increasingly explicit and sexual-based taunts among girls).

42 *being labeled a slut or a whore:* See, for example, Peggy Orenstein, *School Girls: Young Women, Self-Esteem, and the Confidence Gap* (New York: Doubleday, 1994); Leora Tanenbaum, *Slut! Growing Up Female with a Bad Reputation* (New York: Perennial, 2000). This calls to mind Tina Fey's much-cited admonition to girls in the film *Mean Girls:* "You have got to stop calling each other sluts and whores because you are going to make it okay for guys to call you sluts and whores."

43 *cyber bullying touched the lives:* See National Crime Prevention Council website's cyber bullying pages, www.ncpc.org/cyberbullying (noting that most kids say they believe cyber bullies do it because they think it's funny and that about 80 percent said they had no family rules about Internet usage or, if they did, found ways around them); "Cyberbullying," Pew Internet & American Life Project, at www.pewinternet.org (June 27, 2007).

43 *fifteen-year-old Phoebe:* See "The Untouchable Mean Girls," *Boston Globe* (Jan-

uary 24, 2010). The article details the torture that Phoebe Prince, who didn't "know her place," received at the hands of a group of "pretty, popular," and sporty girls, including relentless intimidation, being followed around, called a "slut," and having an energy drink thrown at her. One day after school, Phoebe walked into her bedroom closet, hung herself, and was found by her twelve-year-old sister. Showing zero remorse, the girls continued to make fun of her posthumously online and at school. The family buried Phoebe back in Ireland, apparently preferring to have "an ocean between her and the people who hounded her to the grave."

43 *made the mistake of reading her bad press:* Wendy Walsh, "Mom Commits Suicide, Felt 'Judged' by Peers," MomLogic (February 9, 2010).

44 *same kind of battle cry:* Ibid.

44 *fake MySpace account:* See, for example, "Jury Gets MySpace Hoax Suicide Case: Woman Who Taunted Teen Until She Killed Herself Faces 20 Years in Prison," CBSnews.com (November 24, 2008).

44 *posted a teenage girl's photo:* "Mo. Woman Charged with Cyberbullying Teen: Accused of Posting Girl's Photo, Personal Info on Craigslist for a Sexual Encounter," CBSnews.com (August 18, 2009).

44 *said enough's enough:* "Megan Meier Cyberbullying Prevention Act," 111th Congress (to amend title 18, United States Code, with respect to cyber bullying), 1st Session, H.R. 1966 (introduced April 2, 2009). After its introduction, the bill was referred to the House Committee on the Judiciary and, then, the Subcommittee on Crime, Terrorism, and Homeland Security. See, for example, "Cyberbullying Bill Gets Trounced During House Subcommittee Hearing," Infowars (October 3, 2009) (reprinted at GulagBlog.com).

45 *sentencing a teenage girl:* "Cyber Bully Posted Evil Death Threats."

48 *calls pure "evil":* "Wired to Connect/Dialogues on Social Intelligence: Knowing Our Emotions, Improving Our World," a conversation with Paul Ekman and Daniel Goleman/More Than Sound Productions (2007).

CHAPTER 4: THE POWER OF MEMORY AND OUR NOT-SO-SPOTLESS MINDS

55 *"The tragedy of the many ways":* Richard Holloway, *On Forgiveness, How Can We Forgive the Unforgiveable?* (Edinburgh, UK: Canongate, 2002), p. 12.

58 *finds these results unsurprising:* Conversation with Elayne Savage (August 20, 2008); see also Savage, *Don't Take It Personally! The Art of Dealing with Rejection* (Oakland, Calif.: New Harbinger Publications, 1997; Bloomington, Ind.: iUniverse, 2002).

58 *twirl them about in their minds:* Conversation with Elayne Savage; see also Moses, *Women Confidential*, pp. 271–72 (noting, in "Secrets of Sisterhood,"

that women often avoid confrontation with other women, which in turn causes them to stew, which in turn can lead to the ugly cycle of resentment, talking behind backs, and recruiting reinforcements); "Bullying Takes Twisted Turn for the Worse," *San Francisco Chronicle* (August 17, 2008).

58 *"heightened sense of vigilance"*: Cheryl Dellasega, *Mean Girls Grown Up: Adult Women Who Are Still Queen Bees, Middle Bees, and Afraid-to-Bees* (Hoboken, N.J.: John Wiley & Sons, 2005), p. 157.

58 *" 'I remember that moment' "*: "In Conversation with Cheryl Dellasega, PhD, Friends or Foes? Redefining Female Bonds," *Research Penn State: The Online Magazine of Scholarship and Creativity* (updated January 2005); see also Moses, *Women Confidential* (noting that virtually every woman has a story to tell of wounded friendship she can recount "blow by painful blow," even if it's a decades-old conflict).

58 *"Clearly, we never fully recover"*: Tanenbaum, *Slut!*; see "101 Secrets (and 9 Lives) of a Magazine Star," *New York Times* (June 29, 2008) (discussing the unlikely vulnerability of media powerhouse Bonnie Fuller, a woman who says she was "totally unprepared for the mean girls [she] encountered" in high school, remains a "surprisingly vulnerable" and raw target, and, in some sense, still has the "Heathers" after her and an "invisible kick-me sign" on her back).

60 *"Once a fat kid"*: "Kate Winslet Looks Ahead," *Harper's Bazaar* (August 2009), pp. 112–17.

60 *late in life:* See Margaret Atwood, *Cat's Eye* (New York: Doubleday, 1988).

61 *"who breaks a girl's heart"*: "At Home with Laura Lippman: When Friendship Fails You," *New York Times* (July 28, 2005).

62 *"Oh, that's what happens"*: See Young Shin Kim and Bennett Leventhal, "Bullying and Suicide: A Review," *International Journal of Adolescent Medicine and Health* 20, no. 2 (April–June 2008), pp. 133–54; "Bullying and Being Bullied Linked to Suicide in Children, Review of Studies Suggests," *ScienceDaily* (July 19, 2008).

63 *tragic manifestations:* Email conversation with Nicholas Carlisle (November 23, 2009); www.nobully.com; "Bullying Takes Twisted Turn for the Worse"; see also NoBully.com.

63 *groundbreaking project:* "Kidscape Survey: Long-Term Effects of Bullying" (November 1999) (Kidscape charity's retrospective survey of adults to discover if bullying affects people in later life, finding it indeed has a lingering legacy, with "dramatic, negative, knock-on" effects lasting throughout life); see also Dan Olweus, "Bullying/Victim Problems Among Schoolchildren," in D. J. Pepler and K. H. Rubin, eds., *The Development and Treatment of Childhood Aggression* (Hillsdale, N.J.: Lawrence Erlbaum, 1999).

63 *"drip-drip of torture"*: See Osler, Street, et al., "Not a Problem? Girls and School Exclusion" (Dr. Cathy Street explaining the toll relational aggression

takes on girls); "Mean Girls: Schoolgirls' Ways of Being Cruel to Each Other Are Now So Insidious and Sophisticated that Their Victims Can Feel the Devastating Effects Well into Adulthood," *Observer* (March 3, 2002).

64 *"emotional difficulties for life"*: Id.; see also Mark Dombeck, "The Long-Term Effects of Bullying," MentalHelp.net (July 24, 2007).

64 *"deserve to be isolated"*: Nicole Jaffe Weaver, Marina Skowronski, et al., "When Girls Become Bullies and Victims: Relational Aggression," *Communiqué* (newspaper of the National Association of School Psychologists) (March 2005).

64 *I could go on and on:* A major international study published in the *European Journal of Public Health* found that repeated, unwanted teasing by the more physically or socially powerful left permanent negative marks on young victims. Drawing on data from more than 120,000 students from twenty-eight countries, researchers found that bullied children were nearly twice as likely to struggle with loneliness and nervousness, exhaustion, sleep difficulties, a sense of helplessness, difficulty relating to people, and depression. An Amsterdam study of kids aged nine to thirteen found that depression and suicidal ideation were relatively common outcomes of bullying in both girls and boys, with stronger associations appearing for the more indirect types of aggression that girls favor, such as excluding, ignoring, isolating, and backbiting. Mona O'Moore, coordinator of the Anti-Bullying Centre at Trinity College Dublin, emphasizes that childhood bullying is conclusively linked with stress-related illnesses and suicide.

Other recent research links social bullying with loneliness, depression, and anxiety in adulthood. In February 2009, Dr. Jorge Srabstein, a highly regarded pediatric psychiatrist, bullying specialist, and medical director of a clinic that treats bullying-related health problems in Montgomery County, Maryland, gave compelling testimony to a state senate task force about the effects of bullying-related behaviors on children and adults. He explained the extreme costs to the state and to society as a whole and outlined "the urgent public need to address the issue":

> There is a growing recognition of the serious public health risks associated with bullying along the lifespan. Adolescents who are involved in bullying as victims and/or as bullies are at high risk of suffering frequent physical and emotional symptoms, including eating disorders, suicide attempts, injuries requiring hospital stay or surgery, abuse of over-the-counter medications, alcohol and drug abuse, daily smoking, runaway episodes, carrying weapons to school, serious absenteeism, and poor academic performance. Workers who are subjected to bullying at the workplace are more prone to be absent from work because

of sickness, and also suffer from cardiovascular disease, including hypertension, cerebrovascular disease, myocardial infarction, depression, and PTSD.

—Testimony of Jorge C. Srabstein, MD, Children's National Medical Center, Senate Bill 353, Task Force on Public Health Risks Linked to Bullying, Senate Education, Health, and Environmental Affairs Committee, Maryland General Assembly (February 18, 2009).

64 *multinational problem:* Richard Goldbloom, "Children's Inhumanity to Children," *Journal of Pediatrics* 144, no. 1 (January 2004), p. 3.

66 *"it's all about perception":* Leslie Morgan Steiner, "The Duplicitous Female Maze," *Washington Post* (December 17, 2007) (comment by "Meesh").

68 *women actually have stronger memories:* Louann Brizendine, *The Female Brain* (New York: Morgan Road Books, 2006).

68 *all memories are not created equal:* James McGaugh, *Memory and Emotion: The Making of Lasting Memories* (New York: Columbia University Press, 2006) (explaining how memories "come in many different forms and vary substantially in strength." Some, like what you ate for lunch, are brief, "while others can remain etched in our minds till the day we die").

69 *burning themselves "indelibly":* Joseph LeDoux, *The Emotional Brain: The Mysterious Underpinnings of Emotional Life* (New York: Simon & Schuster, 1996), p. 252. Dr. LeDoux writes, "Unconscious fear memories established through the amygdala appear to be indelibly burned into the brain. They are probably with us for life."

69 *"quick to learn":* "Drug May Help Dim Traumatic Memories," Scientists are testing a pill that, when taken after a bloody battle or a rape, may alter how the brain records the event, *Los Angeles Times* (February 5, 2006).

69 *a similar stress later on:* Cozolino, *Neuroscience of Human Relationships*, pp. 317–18.

CHAPTER 5: ONCE BITTEN, TWICE SHY

71 *simply paid too high a price:* Conversation with Elayne Savage; see also Phillip T. Slee, "Situational and Interpersonal Correlates of Anxiety Associated with Peer Victimisation," *Child Psychiatry and Human Development* 25, no. 2 (December 1994), pp. 97–107 (explaining that girls who'd been victimized by peers had subsequent fear of negative evaluations and tended to avoid social situations).

72 *"hasn't the heart to begin anew":* Chesler, *Woman's Inhumanity*, p. 81.

72 *scar tissue that remains:* Lyn Mikel Brown, *Girlfighting: Betrayal and Rejection Among Girls* (New York: New York University Press, 2003), pp. 187–88.

72 *"a sad number of women"*: Rachel Simmons, *Odd Girl Out: The Hidden Culture of Aggression in Girls* (New York: Harcourt Brace, 2002).

76 *profoundly underappreciated:* Telephone conversation with Roger Pitman (September 2008); see also "Spotless Mind? Scientists Working on a Pill: Doctors Test New Drug to Blunt Bad Memories," *San Diego Union Tribune* (January 15, 2006).

77 *"bloodthirsty predator"*: LeDoux, *Emotional Brain*.

77 maximized *life's advantages:* Cozolino, *Neuroscience of Human Relationships.*

77 *center on the old amygdala:* Ibid., pp. 247–48; see also Taylor, *Tending Instinct,* p. 48.

77 *otherwise composed scientists:* See TheAmygdaloids.com (rock band of NYU scientists who write and perform songs like "A Trace": "They say that time heals all pain / Time can't erase your place in my brain").

78 *"responded to a possible snake"*: LeDoux, *Emotional Brain;* ("If there's a chance that you'll be harmed, then you better attend to it. In other words, you better be afraid of it and be careful about what's going on"); Cozolino, *Neuroscience of Human Relationships,* pp. 245–46; see also Taylor, *Tending Instinct,* p. 48.

78 *"social situations are often survival encounters"*: LeDoux, *Emotional Brain,* pp. 176–77.

78 *the kids exercised less:* Eric A. Storch et al., "Peer Victimization, Psychosocial Adjustment, and Physical Activity in Overweight and At-Risk-for-Overweight Youth," *Journal of Pediatric Psychology* 32, no. 1 (January–February 2007), pp. 80–89; "Bullying Keeps Overweight Kids Off the Field," *ScienceDaily* (April 20, 2006).

79 *started working against us:* McGaugh, *Memory and Emotion.*

79 *"premature death in this country"*: See, for example, James J. Lynch, *A Cry Unheard: New Insights into the Medical Consequences of Loneliness* (Baltimore: Bancroft Press, 2000); "The Dangers of Loneliness," *Psychology Today* (July–August 2003).

79 *societal impact of isolation:* See John T. Cacioppo and William Patrick, *Loneliness: Human Nature and the Need for Social Connection* (New York: W. W. Norton & Company, 2008); "Loneliness Spreads Like a Virus," *LiveScience* (December 1, 2009); "Feeling Alone Together: How Loneliness Spreads," Time.com (December 1, 2009); "Female Suicides: Not If They Have Friends," Campus Crime, 14.2 (February 2004), p. 20.

80 *"evolved to connect deeply"*: "Mind Reviews: The Social Brain," *Scientific American Mind* (October–November 2008), p. 83 (review of Patrick Cacioppo's *Loneliness*).

85 *shared confidences often come back:* Underwood, *Social Aggression Among Girls.*

CHAPTER 6: TRIBES AND PACKS AND CLIQUES, OH MY!

88 *"My handful of great girlfriends"*: "Group Hug!" Jezebel (comment by "Blonde-girlz").

88 *catty and ugly dynamic*: "Duplicitous Female Maze," Feministe (comment by "Kelsey").

87 *manifestations of our "intense desire to connect"*: "Left Out in the Crowd," *Chicago Tribune* (January 19, 2005) (quoting Judith V. Jordan's perspective on cliques, inclusion, and rejection).

90 *focus is on excluding others*: "Left Out in the Crowd."

90 *"terrified of losing them"*: Atwood, *Cat's Eye*.

90 *one of life's greatest emotional disasters*: Kenneth A. Wesson, *"Where Is God in the Brain?* Emotions, Spiritual Connections, and the Brain," *Independent School Magazine* (Winter 2002); Anthony Stevens and John Price, *Evolutionary Psychiatry: A New Beginning*, 2nd rev. ed. (London: Routledge, 2001).

89 *same areas affected by physical pain*: Naomi Eisenberger et al., "Does Rejection Hurt? An fMRI Study of Social Exclusion," *Science* 302, no. 5643 (October 10, 2003), pp. 290–92.

89 *cause even greater lasting damage*: See NoBully.com.

97 *"Girlfriends can be so high maintenance"*: "Group Hug!" Jezebel (comment by "Hamburgerhotdog").

98 *"Sad but true"*: "Group Hug!" Jezebel (comment by "Habibi").

98 *she's self-conscious and uncomfortable*: Atwood, *Cat's Eye*.

98 *"GhaG—n. Acronym. Girl-hating Girl"*: Lexicon IX, DailyCandy.com.

98 *"man's woman" types*: Anna Quindlen.

99 *"women who don't go to their girlfriends"*: "Gossip Girls."

CHAPTER 7: REMNANTS OF DENIAL, DISTRACTION, DEPRESSION, AND WORSE

101 *whatever's distracted them*: See also Moses, *Women Confidential* (discussing how women obsess over female conflict but simply do whatever's necessary to move past it with their unresolved anger and hurt, believing they have closure but really do not).

102 *"world of girlfriendship upside down"*: Polly Drew, "It Takes Work, Time to Heal Sting of Lost Friendships," *Milwaukee Journal Sentinel* (November 12, 2005).

104 *first to point a finger*: Tanenbaum, *Slut!*, pp. 17–18, 20–21.

106 *forecast the likelihood*: See, for example, Chesler, *Woman's Inhumanity*; Simmons, *Odd Girl Out*; Cheryl Dellasega, *Surviving Ophelia: Mothers Share Their Wisdom in Navigating the Tumultuous Teenage Years* (New York: Ballantine Books, 2001); Brown, *Girlfighting*; see also Marcel F. van der Wal et al., "Psychosocial Health Among Young Victims and Offenders of Direct and Indirect

Bullying," *Pediatrics* 111, no. 6 (June 2003), pp. 1312–17; Maureen C. Kenny et al., "Peer Victimization in Schools: An International Perspective," *Journal of Social Sciences*, Special Issue no. 8:13–19, at chapter 2, "Female Bullying: Prevention and Counseling Interventions" (noting that beyond social and emotional fallout, harassed and bullied kids also suffer from poor academic performance, poor concentration, and absenteeism).

107 *"competitiveness of the female tribe":* Leslie Morgan Steiner, ed., *Mommy Wars: Stay-at-Home and Career Moms Face Off on Their Choices, Their Lives, Their Families* (New York: Random House, 2005).

CHAPTER 8: THE VICARIOUS STRUGGLES OF MOTHERS WITH DAUGHTERS

112 *lens of her own:* Simmons, *Odd Girl Out.*

114 *struggling vicariously themselves:* See Judith Warner, "My Daughters/My Self," *New York Times* (December 11, 2008); see also Judith Warner, "40 Is Not the New 12," *New York Times* (December 10, 2009); Judith Warner, "Helicopter Parenting Turns Deadly," *New York Times* (November 29, 2007) (all of which are Domestic Disturbances/Opinionator pieces viewable online at www.nytimes.com).

114 *perform the "double act":* Terri Apter and Ruthellen Josselson, *Best Friends: The Pleasures and Perils of Girls' and Women's Friendships* (New York: Three Rivers Press, 1998), pp. 9–10.

CHAPTER 9: GIVING THE BLAME GAME A REST

121 *"recognize ravening bitchery":* "Duplicitous Female Maze," Feministe (comment by "Alsojill").

122 *still don't quite feel qualified:* For a sense of how things look to those who have been studying these issues for far longer than I have, see Carol Gilligan, *In a Different Voice: Psychological Theory and Women's Development* (Cambridge, Mass.: Harvard University Press, 1982); Deborah Siegel, *Sisterhood Interrupted: From Radical Women to Grrls Gone Wild* (New York: Palgrave Macmillan, 2007); Gail Collins, *When Everything Changed: The Amazing Journey of American Women from 1960 to the Present* (New York: Little, Brown and Company, 2009); see also Betty Friedan, *The Feminine Mystique* (New York: W. W. Norton & Company, 1963).

124 *myopic male-dominance ideology:* See, for example, Peggy Reeves Sanday, *Women at the Center: Life in a Modern Matriarchy* (Ithaca, N.Y.: Cornell University Press, 2002) (lending thoughtful balance to male-dominant-society theory).

124 *men or women just acting that way:* "Duplicitous Female Maze," Feministe (comment by "Shayne").

125 *"Man, that doesn't do us any good"*: "Clinton Aides: Palin Treatment Sexist," (September 3, 2008).

125 *"[W]hen you use sexism"*: "Life of Her Party," *New York Times* (September 2, 2008).

127 *"note how far we've come"*: Sarah Seltzer, "Gail Collins' Whirlwind Tour Through Feminist History," RHRealityCheck (November 30, 2009). But see Amanda Fortini, "The Feminist Reawakening: Hillary Clinton and the Fourth Wave," *New York* magazine (April 21, 2008) (Fortini citing truly abominable examples of contemporary misogyny, particularly in politics and during Hillary Clinton's presidential candidacy).

127 *dismissiveness within feminist culture itself*: See, for example, Jessica Valenti, "The Sisterhood Split," *Nation* (March 24, 2008) (Valenti discussing infighting, generational tensions, and related bickering, particularly among women/feminists over Hillary Clinton's candidacy for president).

128 *running from the word* feminist: Jennifer Baumgardner and Amy Richards, *Manifesta: Young Women, Feminism, and the Future* (New York: Farrar, Straus and Giroux, 2000).

128 *"womanism" right here*: See Michael Gurian, *The Wonder of Girls: Understanding the Hidden Nature of Our Daughters* (New York: Atria Books, 2002), pp. 275–91 (discussing the term *womanism* as an alternative to *feminism*).

130 *frantic, neurotic quests*: See, for example, Judith Warner, *Perfect Madness: Motherhood in the Age of Anxiety* (New York: Riverhead Books, 2005); Allison Pearson, *I Don't Know How She Does It* (New York: Anchor Books, 2003); Lisa Belkin, *Life's Work: Confessions of an Unbalanced Mom* (New York: Simon & Schuster, 2002); Steiner, *Mommy Wars*; see also Cathi Hanauer, ed., *The Bitch in the House: 26 Women Tell the Truth About Sex, Solitude, Work, Motherhood, and Marriage* (New York: William Morrow, 2002); Domestic Disturbances, *New York Times* (Warner's former Opinionator blog on modern parenting).

130 *53 percent of the U.S. electorate in 2008*: See ThisNation.com: American Government & Politics Online.

131 *porn viewers are now female?*: "Why Millions of Women Are Using Porn and Erotica: Lisa Ling Reports," *The Oprah Show*, November 17, 2009; Nielsen Net Ratings/NetView 2003; "One in Three Porn Viewers Are Women," *Sydney Morning Herald* (May 26, 2007).

131 *quietly been taking over the porn industry's executive arm?*: "Women on Top: Female Execs Rise in Porn Biz: Some Say They're Trying to Instill Change While Others See Them as Traitors," msnbc.msn.com (December 3, 2008).

131 *formidable swing vote power*: See, for example, Joan Biskupic, *Sandra Day O'Connor: How the First Woman on the Supreme Court Became Its Most Influential Justice* (New York: Ecco, 2005).

131 *32 percent of the "top-tier administration jobs"*: "In the Loop/Al Kamen,"

Washington Post (December 4, 2009); "Tracking Obama's Appointments," washingtonpost.com/headcount.

131 *17 percent of congressional representation:* See Jennifer E. Manning and Colleen J. Shogun, "Women in the United States Congress 1917–2009, CRS Report for Congress, viewable online at www.Senate.gov/CRSReports (December 23, 2009).

134 *a "girl-poisoning" culture:* Mary Pipher, *Reviving Ophelia: Saving the Selves of Adolescent Girls* (New York: Ballantine Books, 1994).

135 *cavewomen were bickering:* "America's Anti-Gossip, Not Really About Mean Girls," E!Online: Ted Casablanca's the Awful Truth (September 12, 2008).

136 *grossed over $115 million:* "Bride Wars," Boxofficemojo.com (listing worldwide box office sales and related information).

136 *positive item on the singer Beyoncé:* See "America's Sweetheart: Beyoncé Sings Halo to a Special Little Girl at Her Concert," ShowHype.com (September 18, 2009).

138 *boxing our girls:* Deborah Solomon, "Questions for Susie Orbach: Her Beautiful Mind," *New York Times Magazine* (March 4, 2009) (discussing body hatred and impact of Western beauty standards on girls around the globe).

139 *readership of these publications is overwhelmingly female:* Each of these publications makes readership data public as part of its media kit, available online at NationalEnquirer.com, LifeandStylemag.com, StarMagazine.com, InTouch Weekly.com, People.com, UsMagazine.com.

140 *two of the better books:* Lyn Mikel Brown and Sharon Lamb, *Packaging Girlhood: Rescuing Our Daughters from Marketers' Schemes* (New York: St. Martin's Press, 2006); Diane E. Levin and Jean Kilbourne, *So Sexy So Soon: The New Sexualized Childhood and What Parents Can Do to Protect Their Kids* (New York: Ballantine Books, 2008).

140 *the miniprograms:* Target Women with Sarah Haskins, viewable online at www.current.com/target-women.

CHAPTER 10: MOTHERS, IT'S TIME TO ENGAGE!

149 *"social and political disconnections among women":* Brown, *Girlfighting*, pp. 180–81.

152 *"moms respond from the heart":* Cheryl Dellasega and Charisse Nixon, *Girl Wars: 12 Strategies That Will End Female Bullying* (New York: Simon & Schuster, 2003), pp. 87–93.

153 *"relational equivalent of math anxiety":* Brown, *Girlfighting*, p. 205.

153 *"not challenging bullying behavior":* Anti-Bullying Centre, Trinity College Dublin website, www.abc.tcd.ie (introduction by coordinator, Mona O'Moore).

154 *"a single act of passion":* Holloway, *On Forgiveness*, p. 63.

154 *bystanders are equally culpable:* "The Silent Majority: The Anti-Bullying Forces

Tried to Work with the Bullies and the Victims. Now They're Targeting the Bystanders," *Boston Globe* (July 18, 2009). Among his other antibullying efforts, Dr. Sege is working to help kids reinterpret the behavior of bullying "as weird" rather than something acceptable that can simply be ignored. Knowing the way kids' brains tend to work, I find this to be a brilliant approach; see also Laura Martocci, "Relational Aggression: The Social Destruction of Self Narratives" (paper presented at annual meeting of American Sociological Association, San Francisco, CA, August 14, 2004, reprinted at allacademic.com/meta/p109854_index.html), p. 3 (noting that "most kids will "go along with" this bullying, participating in, or implicitly sanctioning, the gossip, rumors, and cruelty du jour. In so doing, they "belong: or, at the very least, they avoid drawing attention to themselves. By avoiding notice, they [hopefully] avoid opening themselves up to ridicule and humiliation. This 'fitting in,' i.e., avoiding the critical gaze and scathing judgments of the peer group, becomes tantamount to acceptance and approval. And social acceptance, rather than academic achievement, is the yardstick used to measure success").

157 *thrilled to come across:* See www.kindcampaign.com (mission statement described as "a movement and documentary, based upon the powerful belief in KINDness, that brings awareness and healing to the negative and lasting effects of girl-against-girl 'crime' ").

157 *turned me on to a terrific group:* See SuEllen Hamkins and Renée Schultz, *The Mother-Daughter Project: How Mothers and Daughters Can Band Together, Beat the Odds, and Thrive Through Adolescence* (New York: Penguin, 2007); www.themother-daughterproject.com.

158 *that toughness and resiliency:* In her conference paper, "Relational Aggression: The Social Destruction of Self Narratives," sociology professor Laura Martocci explains how crucial it is to appreciate the emotional impact these behaviors can have, especially on kids. She illustrates how the very same incident of cruelty might influence, manifest, and be recalled in extremely variant ways for a given high schooler down the road:

> Thus the self-conscious, overweight girl in English class is aware of their sniggers. And her classmates' snide remarks regarding her girth and eating habits are not perceived to be slanderous lies made by a group of jealous girls, but rather taunts which (rightfully) disdain her entire being on the basis of her looks. When, as the svelte owner of an exercise spa, she recalls these incidents from high school, she perhaps recollects them as the galvanizing force behind her becoming the woman she is today. Or, as the pimply Wal-Mart employee and single mother of four, she perhaps remembers these incidents as painful emotional assaults, which drove her to seek solace in the arms of the first

boy who was willing to have a physical relationship with such an unattractive girl. Or perhaps, as NASA's top female scientist, she hardly remembers the petty remarks of girls who she dismissed as unable to see past the mall and the next keg party.

Id. at pp. 8–9.

158   *"We can strengthen girls"*: Pipher, *Reviving Ophelia*, p. 13.

CHAPTER 11: THE UPSIDE OF AGING?

165   *"spot the kinds of women"*: "Duplicitous Female Maze," Feministe (comment by "Racy T").
167   *"will lie there like an uncashed cheque"*: Holloway, *On Forgiveness*, p. 61.
168   *glories of Facebook forgiveness*: Rachel Cline, "Mean Girl: Exorcising the Past, with One Click, on Facebook," *More* (September 2009), pp. 110–17 (former "mean girl" Rachel Cline discussing lasting fallout of girlhood aggressions and ultimate virtues of Facebook forgiveness).
170   *"Trust is a tricky thing"*: See, for example, "How Can You Learn to Trust Again?" *Psychology Today* (March–April 2002).

CHAPTER 12: BETTING ON THE POWER OF FEMALES AND "SISTERHOOD"

174   *reconsidering notions of sisterhood*: See, for example, "When Discussing Rape, Notions of Sisterhood Dissipate," *Jewish Daily Forward*: The Sisterhood Blog: Where Jewish Women Converse (February 17, 2010) (Sarah Seltzer discussing British survey showing that women were more likely to blame female rape victims than men, and arguing for renewed consideration of old-school notions of sisterhood).
175   *"minimize the antagonisms"*: Tanenbaum, *Catfight*, pp. 23–24.
176   *face the world more effectively*: Christakis and Fowler, *Connected*, pp. 36, 134; see generally "Secrets of the Bonobo Sisterhood," *Ms.* magazine 15, no. 1 (Spring 2005), p. 44(6) (Amy Parish discussing the power of the bonobo sisterhood and noting that human women "are often characterized as petty, infighting and jealous . . . [b]ut in fact, when females get together, that gives them an incredible power base").
176   *"we lose everything"*: Christakis and Fowler, *Connected*, pp. 288, 303 (drawing on Thomas Hobbes's social contract theory and explaining that a disconnected life is "full of woe," calamity, and disorder).
178   *appointed a new White House Council*: See "President Obama Announces White House Council on Women and Girls," WhiteHouse.gov (March 11, 2009).
178   *Office of Global Women's Issues*: See "A New Gender Agenda, Interview with Secretary of State Hillary Rodham Clinton," *New York Times Magazine* (Au-

gust 23, 2009). It's worth noting that International Woman's Day, a day marked by Secretary Clinton's warm and vigorous commemoration, "doesn't get a great deal of attention within the United States, but many other countries honor it with a national holiday." Still, in 2007, government officials in Iran beat men and women for merely planning to celebrate the holiday. See "First Lady Marks International Women's Day with Hillary 'President' Joke," Yahoo! News (March 11, 2010).

178 *subcommittee on women's issues:* Press release, at http://Boxer.senate.gov (February 5, 2009); "Senator Boxer to Chair Foreign Relations Subcommittee on Global Women's Issues," PeaceWomen: Women's International League for Peace and Freedom (February 6, 2009).

178 *"A Woman's Nation Changes Everything":* See also " 'Girl Effect' Could Lift the Global Economy: Training and Supporting Young Women Can Transform Countries' Economic Development," Bloomberg BusinessWeek (April 8, 2009); www.girleffect.org.

178 *appreciate the tireless efforts:* "The Women's Crusade," *New York Times Magazine* (August 23, 2009); see also Nicholas D. Kristof and Sheryl WuDunn, *Half the Sky: Turning Oppression into Opportunity for Women Worldwide* (New York: Alfred A. Knopf, 2009).

178 *"poor black married woman in Somalia":* Tanenbaum, *Catfight*, p. 23.

180 *spread like disease:* See Christakis and Fowler, *Connected* (throughout).

182 *"smile and the world smiles with you":* Ibid., p. 33.

183 *Today's horoscope:* "Today's Horoscope by Holiday Mathis," *Washington Post* (December 8, 2009) (Cancer—June 22–July 22: "Plato said, 'Be kind, for everyone you meet is fighting a hard battle.' You will live this Platonic advice, giving people the benefit of the doubt whether they be coworkers, family, or strangers").

189 *Fill that undefined space:* See Martocci, "Relational Aggression" (arguing that girls must learn to rewrite personal narratives in a favorable light, not as loser, outcast, tramp, or whatever else peers have tried to reflect on them so that when rejected on one front, they have other fallbacks to assert themselves successfully); see also Kenny et al., "Peer Victimization in Schools" (explaining that girls rely heavily on peer feedback to form self-worth and tend to be more intimate and exclusive in friendship, thereby making them especially susceptible when problems arise with those peers).

appendix

WOMEN'S RELATIONSHIPS
SURVEY

1. INTRODUCTION

Hello. I am a writer and concerned mother of three girls researching female relationships for a book based on an article I wrote for the *New York Times* in December 2007. The book is being published by Ballantine/Random House sometime in the fall of 2010. The goal is to rally girls and women to come together and proactively promote a more unified, open, and supportive "sisterhood." One area of focus involves the feelings of discomfort, wariness, anxiety, awkwardness, intimidation, or even distrust we can feel in each other's company. We'll be examining how prior negative experiences (including the so-called mean-girl behaviors like gossip, betrayal, bullying, excluding, shaming, judging, and group cruelty) might impact our attitudes and social behaviors later in life.

If you are a woman interested in these issues for yourself, a daughter, and/or the greater society of women out there, would you please complete my confidential, SSL-encrypted (secure) survey? The study is completely anonymous, no identifying information will be used in the book, and I will not contact you unless you indicate an openness to further discussion. In other words, this is a great opportunity to explain how you are really feeling about women's relationships—the fabulous, the so-so, and the downright ugly. Be as brief or long winded as you like; the survey's commentary boxes are entirely optional. (Women are taking anywhere from five to forty-five minutes to finish, depending on how much they wished to share.)

To obtain a balanced perspective, we'd like to hear from women of all ages, backgrounds, and viewpoints. To that end, please consider forwarding the survey link to other women (friends, neighbors, your mother and other relatives, colleagues, book club pals).

If you have any questions or would like more information about my book, literary agent, or anything else, feel free to contact me via the form on www .kellyvalen.com. Thank you very much in advance for contributing to this important, awareness-raising project.

2. BACKGROUND INFORMATION

1. Your Age:
   _____ 15–19
   _____ 20–30
   _____ 31–40
   _____ 41–50
   _____ 51–60
   _____ 61–70
   _____ 71–80
   _____ 81 or above

2. Race/Ethnicity:
   _____ American Indian
   _____ Asian
   _____ Black
   _____ Hispanic
   _____ White/Caucasian
   _____ Biracial or multiracial
   _____ Other (please specify)

3. Where Do You Live?
   _____ Large city
   _____ Suburb
   _____ Town or small city
   _____ Rural area or mountains
   _____ Other (please specify)

4. Highest Level of Education Completed:
   _____ Elementary school
   _____ High school
   _____ Some college
   _____ Bachelor's degree

_____ Graduate degree/PhD
_____ Other (please specify)

5. Your Current Occupation or Status:

6. Marital Status:
_____ Unmarried/Single
_____ Unmarried/In committed relationship
_____ Married
_____ Divorced/Separated
_____ Widowed

7. Sexual Orientation:
_____ Heterosexual
_____ Lesbian
_____ Bisexual
_____ Transgendered
_____ Other (please specify)

8. Number of Siblings:
_____ 0
_____ 1
_____ 2
_____ 3
_____ 4 or more

9. Number of Sisters:
_____ 0
_____ 1
_____ 2
_____ 3
_____ 4 or more

10. Number of Children:
_____ 0
_____ 1
_____ 2
_____ 3
_____ 4 or more

11. Number of Daughters:

_____ 0

_____ 1

_____ 2

_____ 3

_____ 4 or more

3. YOUR FEMALE RELATIONSHIPS

1. Would you describe yourself as someone who generally feels comfortable around other women in social (i.e., nonprofessional) situations?

_____ Yes

_____ No

_____ It depends

In which types of situations do you find yourself feeling uncomfortable?

2. Do you currently enjoy what you consider "satisfying" and "fulfilling" friendships with other women?

_____ Yes

_____ No

Additional comments:

3. If yes to no. 2, do you feel your female friendships are "authentic," "intimate," and "reliable"?

_____ Yes

_____ Somewhat

_____ No

_____ Not applicable

Please explain:

4. If yes to no. 2, how many authentic, intimate, and reliable friendships with women do you feel you currently have?

_____ A few (1–3)

_____ Some (4–6)

_____ Several (7–10)

_____ Many (more than 10)

_____ Not applicable

5. If yes to no. 2, do you feel you can always be your "true self" with your female friends?

_____ Yes

_____ No

_____ It depends

Please explain:

6. For you personally, having authentic, intimate, and reliable friendships with women is:

_____ Extremely important

_____ Very important

_____ Important

_____ Somewhat important

_____ Not so important

Additional comments:

7. For you personally, feeling "accepted" and "liked" by other women is:

_____ Extremely important

_____ Very important

_____ Somewhat important

_____ Important

_____ Not so important

Please explain:

8. How often do you find yourself feeling uncomfortable, anxious, wary, awkward, cautious, intimidated, and/or distrustful around other women in social situations?

_____ Constantly or almost always

_____ Usually

_____ Often

_____ Sometimes

_____ Rarely

_____ Almost never

_____ Never

Additional comments:

9. If you responded positively to no. 8, do you think your feelings of discomfort, anxiety, etc. might relate to any past or prior experience(s) you've had with other females?

____ Yes

____ No

____ Not applicable

Additional comments:

10. Have you ever personally behaved in a manner that you would consider "mean," "manipulative," or "cruel" toward another female, whether such behavior was obvious, open, and overt, or more indirect, hidden, or subtle?

____ Yes

____ No

____ I don't know

Please explain the circumstances of your behavior:

11. If yes to no. 10, would you say that you eventually felt (or still feel) "bad," "remorseful," "regretful," or "guilty" about engaging in such negative behavior toward the other female(s)?

____ Yes, very much so

____ Yes

____ Yes, somewhat

____ No, not really

____ No

____ No, not at all

____ Not applicable

Why or why not?

12. If yes to no. 10, did you ever apologize, make amends, or otherwise try to repair or rectify the situation following your negative behavior toward the other female(s)?

____ Yes

____ No

____ Not applicable

Please explain what you did/what happened:

13. Have you ever personally felt "hurt" or "wounded" by what you would consider mean, manipulative, or cruel treatment by another female or group of females,

whether such treatment was obvious, open, and overt, or more indirect, hidden, or subtle?

_____ Yes

_____ No

Please describe the experience(s):

4. PERSONAL EXPERIENCES

1. In your lifetime, how many times would you estimate that you have personally felt hurt or wounded as a result of mean, manipulative, or cruel treatment by another female or group of females?

_____ A few times (1–5)

_____ A number of times (6–10)

_____ Many times (11–20)

_____ So many times I couldn't possibly count them

_____ Not sure

Additional comments:

2. Which of the following types of treatment or behaviors have you personally suffered or experienced at the hands of another female or group of females? (Check each one that has ever applied)

_____ Jealousy/Competition

_____ Criticism/Judgments

_____ Ridicule/Humiliation/Shaming

_____ Gossip/Spreading rumors/Talking behind back

_____ Lying/Deceitfulness

_____ Manipulation

_____ Group or clique cruelty

_____ Exclusion/Rejection/Shunning

_____ Avoiding

_____ Shifting alliances

_____ Revenge

_____ Bullying—indirect aggression

_____ Bullying—physical harm

_____ Betrayal/Disloyalty

_____ Other (please specify)

3. Would you say the experience(s) has impacted or affected the way you have viewed or related to other women since that time?

____ Yes

____ Somewhat

____ No

Please explain:

4. How much would you say the experience(s) has affected your attitudes and relationships with other women since that time?

____ Not really affected; I'm over it

____ Somewhat affected

____ Affected

____ Deeply, profoundly affected

Additional comments:

5. Would you describe your memories of such prior negative experiences as strong, vivid, and/or powerful?

____ Yes

____ No

If yes, please explain:

6. Do you feel that you have experienced any type of lasting distress, pain, trauma, or emotional scarring as a result of your prior negative experience(s) with females?

____ Yes

____ Possibly

____ No

Please explain:

7. Would you say that you currently hold a "grudge" or feelings of bitterness or anger toward any particular woman(en) or types of women as a result of your prior negative experience(s) with females?

____ Yes

____ Somewhat

____ No

Additional comments:

8. Which of the following have you ever personally felt or dealt with as a result of your prior negative experience(s) with females? (Check each one that has ever applied, even temporarily.)

____ Feelings of shame or worthlessness

____ Low self-esteem

____ Difficulty concentrating

____ Lack of motivation

____ Isolation/Loneliness

____ Depression

____ Feeling vulnerable or "exposed" around other women

____ Fear of having children

____ Fear of having a daughter

____ Worry about transferring own anxieties onto daughter

____ Reopening old wounds and memories through a daughter's relationship struggles

____ Feelings of anger or disgust toward other women

____ Eating disorders (anorexia, bulimia, etc.)

____ Alcohol or drug abuse/dependency

____ Suicidal thoughts or attempt(s)

____ Other (please specify)

9. How have you coped and/or managed your female relationships since your earlier negative experience(s)? (Check each one that has ever applied, even temporarily.)

____ Mistreated, intimidated, or bullied other females yourself

____ Do not easily trust or form close bonds with women

____ Generally withdraw from or avoid women

____ Avoid groups of women/Prefer one-on-one interaction

____ Avoid certain types of women

____ Keep female relationships simple, arm's length, and/or nonintimate

____ Generally feel more comfortable around men

____ Counseling with psychiatrist, psychologist, or other specialist

____ Distractions, compulsions, fantasies, and/or other behaviors to help forget or deny what happened

____ Motivated to succeed, achieve, or do "better" as a means of regaining control or getting "revenge"

____ None of the above

____ Other (please specify)

10. What, if anything, has proven helpful to you in coping with or managing your past negative experience(s) with females?

11. Have you ever felt the need to keep to yourself, hide, or otherwise suppress your anxieties, fears, difficulties, struggles, and/or true feelings about other women?
_____ Yes
_____ No
If yes, please explain why:

12. Do you find yourself wanting or wishing for authentic, intimate, and reliable female relationships despite your prior negative experience(s)?
_____ Yes
_____ Somewhat
_____ No
Please explain:

13. Have you been able to find or make satisfying friendships with women since the time of your prior negative experience(s)?
_____ Yes
_____ Somewhat
_____ No
What has enabled you to develop satisfying friendships?

5. OTHER WOMEN

1. Besides yourself, have you ever known another woman who often seemed uncomfortable, anxious, awkward, cautious, or distrustful around other women and/or seemed to avoid social situations with other women (for example, a friend, neighbor, acquaintance, mother, or other relative)?
_____ Yes
_____ No

2. If yes to no. 1, please explain your thoughts, feelings, and observations about this woman (or women) and her behavior, whether positive or negative:

3. If you have a daughter(s), how often have you felt concern about her female re-lationships and/or the ways in which she and other females treat and relate to one another?

    ____ Always, constantly

    ____ Pretty frequently

    ____ Sometimes

    ____ Rarely

    ____ Never

    ____ Not applicable; I don't have a daughter(s)

Please explain:

4. If you responded positively to no. 3, what specific concerns have you had about your daughter's female relationships? (Check all that apply.)

    ____ Jealousy/Competition

    ____ Criticism/Judgments

    ____ Ridicule/Humiliation/Shaming

    ____ Gossip/Spreading rumors/Talking behind back

    ____ Lying/Deceitfulness

    ____ Manipulation

    ____ Group or clique cruelty

    ____ Exclusion/Rejection/Shunning

    ____ Avoiding

    ____ Shifting alliances

    ____ Revenge

    ____ Bullying—indirect aggression

    ____ Bullying—physical harm

    ____ Betrayal/Disloyalty

    ____ Other (please specify)

5. If you responded positively to no. 3, has the level of concern you've had for your daughter's female relationships changed over time?

    ____ Yes

    ____ Somewhat

    ____ No

    ____ Not applicable (no concern)

If yes, please explain how and why your concern has changed:

6. If you answered yes to no. 3, are you aware of any incidents or times when your own daughter(s) engaged in mean, manipulative, or cruel behavior toward another female(s)?

_____ Yes

_____ No

Please explain the incident and your reaction/response to it, if any:

7. Would you describe your relationship with your mother or stepmother as "close" and/or "positive"?

_____ Yes

_____ Somewhat

_____ No

_____ Not applicable

Additional comments:

8. Do you feel your relationship with your mother and/or stepmother has influenced your relationships with other females?

_____ Yes

_____ Somewhat

_____ No

_____ Not applicable

Please explain:

6. GENERAL VIEWS ABOUT FEMALE RELATIONSHIPS

1. Do you feel that a culture of "mean" or negativity exists among females in our society, whether in plain view or hidden beneath the surface?

_____ Yes

_____ Somewhat

_____ No

Please explain:

2. If yes to no. 1, at what age(s) do you feel such "mean" behavior and/or negativity among females is a real and significant problem in our society? (Check all that apply.)

_____ Elementary school

_____ Middle school

_____ High school

____ College
____ Post-college adulthood
____ Not applicable
Additional comments:

3. If yes to no. 1, what do you feel might be causing or contributing to the mean behavior and/or negativity among females in our society?

4. If yes to no. 1, do you feel that a given female is personally responsible for her mean or negative behavior toward other females?
____ Yes
____ Somewhat
____ No
Why or why not?

5. If yes to no. 1, do you feel that a "male-dominant"/"sexist" society or related cultural influences are causing or contributing to the culture of mean and negativity among females?
____ Yes
____ Somewhat
____ No
____ Not sure
Please explain:

6. If yes to no. 1, how important do you feel a mother's behavior, example, and/or role modeling is in shaping, causing, or contributing to a daughter's mean or negative behavior toward other females?
____ Extremely important
____ Important
____ Somewhat important
____ Not all that important
____ Not important
____ Not sure
Additional comments:

7. If yes to no. 1, how important do you feel it is to find ways to improve the nature of female relationships in our society?

_____ Extremely important

_____ Important

_____ Somewhat important

_____ Not all that important

_____ Not important

_____ Not sure

8. If yes to no. 1, what do you believe would help improve female relationships in our society:

9. Do you believe female relationships generally get "better" (i.e., more authentic, stable, and/or reliable) with age?

_____ Yes

_____ Somewhat

_____ No

Why or why not?

10. "Women generally relate to one another openly, fairly, and honestly in our society."

_____ Strongly agree

_____ Agree

_____ Somewhat agree

_____ Disagree

_____ Somewhat disagree

_____ Strongly disagree

_____ Not sure

Please explain:

11. Books, movies, and television programs that discuss or portray mean, "catfighting," or competitive/aggressive behaviors among females (Check all that apply.)

_____ Pretty much accurately reflect what's going on among females

_____ Help raise awareness about an important problem

_____ Interest me as a concerned woman, parent, and/or human being

_____ Inappropriately stereotype and exploit female behavior

_____ Exaggerate the extent of the problem

_____ Perpetuate the problem/make it worse

_____ Annoy me; turn me off

Additional comments:

12. Please share any other comments or observations about your female relation-ships:

13. Are you open to further discussing the issues contained in this questionnaire for my upcoming book? If so, please include an email address and/or phone number. Again, all input will remain confidential—no personal or identifying information will be used in the book.

    _____ Yes:

    _____ Email and/or phone _____

    _____ No thanks

about the author

KELLY VALEN earned her JD from the University of California, Davis, where she was executive editor of the law review. A daughter, sister, wife, and mother of four (three of them daughters), she practiced law with a Chicago-based firm for more than a decade. Her writings have appeared in *The New York Times, Los Angeles Times, San Francisco Chronicle Magazine, Chicago Tribune, Baltimore Sun, Christian Science Monitor,* Minneapolis *Star Tribune,* and other publications.

about the type

The text of this book was set in Janson, a misnamed typeface designed in about 1690 by Nicholas Kis, a Hungarian in Amsterdam.
In 1919 the matrices became the property of the Stempel Foundry
in Frankfurt. It is an old-style book face of excellent clarity and
sharpness. Janson serifs are concave and splayed; the contrast between thick and thin strokes is marked.